Between Self and World
The Novels of Jane Austen

Also by James Thompson
Language in Wycherley's Plays

Between Self and World
The Novels of Jane Austen

James Thompson

THE PENNSYLVANIA STATE UNIVERSITY PRESS
University Park and London

To my grandmother,
Minna L. Dretzin,
from whom I learned the love of books

Library of Congress Cataloging-in-Publication Data

Thompson, James, 1951–
    Between self and world : the novels of Jane Austen /
James Thompson.
        p.   cm.
    Bibliography: p.
    Includes index.
    ISBN 0-271-00615-3
    1. Austen, Jane, 1775–1817—Criticism and interpreta-
tion.
I. Title.
PR4037.T48 1988
823'.7—dc19   87-17201
                                                                CIP

Contents

Acknowledgments

The greatest pleasure of writing a book on Jane Austen is that almost everyone who reads widely in English has read her novels and is more than willing to talk about them. In an age of alarming social fragmentation and professional specialization, in which it is often difficult to explain one's subject to a colleague in the same department, Austen's work provides a reassuring topic of common knowledge and common interest. When writing this book, I took full advantage of many others' interest in Austen's novels, from which this study has greatly profited. Scholars who have written on Jane Austen and the eighteenth-century novel from whose knowledge and conversation I have benefited include Katrin Burlin, Edward Copeland, Alistair Duckworth, John Dussinger, Charles Edge, Paul Hunter, Susan Morgan, John Richetti, Clifford Siskin, Patricia Meyer Spacks, Susan Staves, Albrecht Strauss, Alison Sulloway, Joel Weinsheimer, and Aubrey Williams. I must thank as well those who have read and commented on this manuscript at various stages, including Edward Copeland, Anne Hall, Patricia Meyer Spacks, Beverly Taylor, and especially Rob Chamberlain. Others, whose main interests often lie elsewhere, have helped to shape and to temper the ideas contained herein, through many conversations: Lennard Davis, Jeffrey Plank, Art Williams, and John Zomchick. Among my colleagues and friends at the University of North

Carolina at Chapel Hill, who have had to endure patiently the construction and reconstruction of this argument, step-by-step, I must thank Randy Hendrick, Linda Kauffman, Darryl Gless, and, most particularly, Ritchie Kendall and Anne Hall, whose endless patience and generosity over these matters approach sainthood. Despite the fact that this project was completed in the privacy of an enclosed office, I still aspire toward literary study and education as a collective enterprise.

Finally, on the practical rather than theoretical plane, I want to thank Sam, Benjamin, and Mary, with whom I have acquired what experience I have with love, intimacy, and marriage.

A loan of a Macintosh computer and a LaserWriter printer from Apple Computer happily made the production of the manuscript as effortless as is humanly possible. Three sections of this manuscript have appeared in other forms and versions: an earlier draft of chapter 1 in *Studies in Eighteenth-Century Culture* 13 (1986); a version of chapter 3 in the *Journal of English and Germanic Philology* 85 (1986); and a fragment of chapter 5 in *Postscript* 3 (1986).

Introduction:
Jane Austen and the
Language of Real Feeling

We have found the only true substance within ourselves:
that is why we have to place an unbridgeable chasm between cognition and action, between soul and created
structure, between self and world, why all substantiality
has to be dispersed in reflexivity on the far side of that
chasm; that is why our essence had to become a postulate
for ourselves and thus create a still deeper, still more
menacing abyss between us and our own selves.
—Georg Lukács[1]

The title of this introduction comes from a
passage in *Emma*. After Frank Churchill has
come to Highbury for the first time and gone away again, Emma reads his
letter, which is ostensibly addressed to Mrs. Weston but is plainly in-
tended for Emma as well:

> It was a long, well written letter, giving the particulars of his
> journey, and of his feelings, expressing all the affection, gratitude,
> and respect which was natural and honourable, and describing
> everything exterior and local that could be supposed attractive,
> with spirit and precision. No suspicious flourishes now of apology
> or concern; it was the language of real feelings towards Mrs.
> Weston. (E 265)[2]

The phrase "the language of real feelings" must strike any reader of this
novel as odd, since Frank Churchill is the last character we would
associate with real or sincere feelings. Rather, he is, to use Mr. Knightley's term, a manipulative "politician" (E 150), a master, not of genuine
emotion, but rather of civility and address. That Emma should take his
flattering letter of conventional pleasantries for genuine emotion is not
very surprising at this point in the novel, for the letter arrives shortly after

her conclusion that "*he* is undoubtedly very much in love" with Emma herself (E 265). And so her desire to find real feeling is entangled in her response to her own name in the letter supposedly addressed to another:

> *Miss Woodhouse* appeared more than once, and never without a something of pleasing connection, either a compliment to her taste, or a remembrance of what she had said; and in the very last time of its meeting her eye, unadorned as it was by any such broad wreath of gallantry, she yet could discern the effect of her influence and acknowledge the greatest compliment perhaps of all conveyed. (E 266)

A close reader, Emma can find the greatest compliment in the absence of her name. The highlighted passage refers to Harriet, but in her interpretation, so she thinks, of Churchill's complex code of admiration, real feelings are deciphered in the faintest trace. Readers of Jane Austen's *Emma*, presumably the last in line to look over this letter, will no doubt assume that Churchill's extravagant language of complimentary innuendo is but part of his disguise to divert attention from Jane Fairfax. In this letter, then, we seem to be as far removed as is possible from some original source of the language of real feelings.

Emma herself comes to understand something of the difficulty of using the language of real feelings when later in the novel she offers her carriage to Jane Fairfax, writing "in the most feeling language she could command" (E 390), only to be rebuffed. And finally in the proposal scene itself, such language goes astray once again when Emma sees "that what she had been saying relative to Harriet had been all taken [by Mr. Knightley] as the language of her own feelings" (E 430); that is, when Emma had interrupted him because she was afraid that he would reveal his love for Harriet: "'Oh! then, don't speak it, don't speak it,' she eagerly cried" (E 429). Shortly thereafter, when Emma and Mr. Knightley have come to their understanding, the narrator nonetheless concludes: "Seldom, very seldom, does complete truth belong to any human disclosure; seldom can it happen that something is not a little disguised, or a little mistaken; but where, as in this case, though the conduct is mistaken, the feelings are not, it may not be very material" (E 431). Though the examination of the language of feeling throughout *Emma* is gently ironic and comic, the implications are not: Austen's writing as a whole suggests that language and feeling are of two different orders, and what can be conveyed in language is rarely, if ever, real feelings. The subject of Jane Austen's fiction to a large degree is feelings, and so we are all left in the position of Emma, reading and rereading Frank Churchill's letter, searching for traces of feelings that were not there in the first place, or, worse, are fraudulent and deceptive. For readers of the novel, and of novels in general, Emma's interpretation of Churchill's letter projects a kind of narrative dread, suggesting the author's fear that her language will be entirely misconstrued, that it will be perceived as false, or as "novel slang," as Austen puts it in a letter (L 404), rather than as real, true, authentic, or genuine.[3]

Austen used the phrase "language of real feeling" once before, in *Mansfield Park*, in connection with the interpretation of another letter, but in a quite different sense. Here, Fanny Price in Portsmouth reads a letter from Lady Bertram that recounts Tom Bertram's illness:

> The sufferings which Lady Bertram did not see, had little power over her fancy; and she wrote very comfortably about agitation and anxiety, and poor invalids, till Tom was actually conveyed to Mansfield, and her own eyes had beheld his altered appearance. Then, a letter which she had been previously preparing for Fanny, was finished in a different style, in the language of real feeling and alarm; then, she wrote as she might have spoken. "He is just come, my dear Fanny, and is taken up stairs; and I am so shocked to see him, that I do not know what to do." (MP 427)

Austen does not credit Lady Bertram with the possession of particularly expressive powers or eloquence, but in this instance genuine emotion in the form of distress is conveyed in the actual process of breaking through the placid facade that makes up her accustomed language of unreal feeling. Lady Bertram, who is unused to distress, let alone to the labor of having to convey it to another, is capable of doing so only because she is unused to it, and her language thus momentarily becomes unexpectedly ordinary and therefore persuasive. As is the case in *Emma*, Austen does not suggest that there is no language of real feeling, but that feelings are exceedingly difficult to convey. This difficulty of expression holds for the best of circumstances, for the best of writers, and for the best of readers. In an entirely different reading situation, in a letter of Austen's to her favorite niece, Fanny Knight, we find an analogous desire to convey strong emotion and something of the same sense of dread, that the language will fail to convey the sincerity of the writer, that it fails to become, in the reading, genuine: "It is very, very gratifying to me to know you so intimately. You can hardly think what a pleasure it is to me, to have such thorough pictures of your Heart.—Oh! what a loss it will be when you are married" (L 478–79).

To explore more fully the implications of some of this dread, we should consider one more reading situation, for all of our examples so far involve one writer to one known reader. If Fanny Knight represents perhaps Austen's idea of the very best reader, that vast, unknown mass of buyers or renters and readers of novels, the anonymous reading public, must appear to Austen as the most treacherous and unpredictable audience—with them, there is always the possibility that even the language of real feeling may be mistaken for novel slang (or novel slang for the language of real feeling). The dangers of their misreading are explored in Austen's last work, *Sanditon,* where Sir Edward Denham is presented as the archetypal imbecile reader of novels, a voracious but indiscriminate consumer of the worst novels, but what is perhaps even more annoying, a consumer as well of the best novels, from commercial lending libraries:

> The novels which I approve are such as display Human Nature with Grandeur—such as shew her in the Sublimities of intense Feeling—such as exhibit the progress of strong Passion from the first Germ of incipient Susceptibility to the utmost Energies of Reason half-dethroned,—where we see the strong spark of Woman's Captivations elicit such Fire in the Soul of Man as leads him—(though at the risk of some Aberration from the strict line of Primitive Obligations)—to hazard all, dare all, atcheive all, to obtain her. (MW 403)

As the narrator bluntly summarizes at the end of this passage, "The truth was that Sir Edw: whom circumstances had confined very much to one spot had read more sentimental Novels than agreed with him" (MW 404). Novels, in short, may be purchased, read, and appropriated by the most foolish of readers.

How self-conscious was Jane Austen about these matters? We know from her letters how anxious she was to collect and preserve the responses of all of those in her immediate family and beyond who read her books, especially the opinions of those readers who were known to her but who did not know she was the author.[4] As an increasingly successful commercial author, Austen probably became ever more aware of and curious about her reading public and how they consumed her products. That she was delighted that the public bought her novels is clear, but how happy she was over the way her products were used is not so clear. Although home consumption is no doubt more or less a concern for all authors—see, for example, William Warner's suggestive exploration of this subject in Richardson and *Clarissa*—it must have been a peculiar irritant for novelists at the turn of the century.[5] Austen writes for a generation of readers trained on gothic novels and the novels of sensibility, readers whose expectations in fiction had been circumscribed by thirty years of novels crammed with both fine and excessive sentiment, in which that fine sentiment had been so drawn out, so mediated and repetitious, in short, so commercialized, that it is not surprising that a writer might worry about finding or creating or commanding the "language of real feeling." In *Sanditon*, Charlotte Heywood concludes that Sir Edward Denham has purchased his feelings from novels: "He seemed very sentimental, very full of some Feelings or other, & very much addicted to all the newest-fashioned hard words—had not a very clear Brain she presumed, & talked a good deal by rote" (MW 398). It is not simply that Austen is reluctant to cast her pearls before such swine. But more, her novels are about the careful discrimination of feeling, novels in which it takes a character such as Emma a year and four hundred pages of narrative to discover that Mr. Knightley should marry none but her, because she finally realizes that her respect and admiration and proprietary concern for him are also signs of love.

If Austen writes novels of feeling in a noticeably careful and even guarded fashion, we need to see that this guardedness is a historical phenomenon, not something that is peculiar to Austen's fiction or to her distanced or defensive nature, as Marvin Mudrick and, more recently, John Halperin have argued.[6] Rather, as Marilyn Butler has amply demonstrated, self-conscious care and precision in emotional matters are lessons taught by a great many novels of Austen's time.[7] Of these many novels from the 1790s, Austen's are the best remembered and perhaps even the best, but however appealing Austen's work is, and however skilled a writer she is, individual genius is not an adequate explanation of her work: Her subject and her language must also be understood in terms of larger social and historical forces. In this book, I argue that the expression of the language of real feeling in the late eighteenth century is historically determined, and by expression I mean not only the form of expression, that is, the view of language that is implied, but also feeling and the view of character that are implied. It is my object here to historicize Austen's language, as well as the feeling expressed in it, by examining emotion in Austen's fiction in the light of a wide range of historical circumstances, social and economic as well as literary.

In the last fifty years, criticism of Austen's novels, as Joel Weinsheimer has recently observed, has been remarkably traditional and conservative.[8] Unlike many earlier writers we read and study, Austen has been continually in print and continually read since 1811. Because Austen is part of the Great Tradition, we have never had to rediscover or recuperate her work, nor has there been any systematic reassessment of it. All the same, these novels have undergone a subtle but thorough transformation in their reading, in the ways they are appropriated, and in the needs they are asked to satisfy. To put this another way, the major difficulty we have with Austen is that her novels are simply too familiar: Her work is not supposed to present problems for us because we understand it so thoroughly. But far too often, what has passed for criticism of Austen's fiction is really appreciation, one form or another of explaining how well she writes. If we approach Austen's novels with the aim of showing how good they are, there is little chance that we will ever begin to understand them, because we begin by sharing their assumptions. As an example of such nostalgic criticism, Fredric Jameson examines Wayne Booth's celebration of Austen's narrative: In the *Rhetoric of Fiction*, Booth holds up the narrator of *Emma* as a model of human perfection, but Jameson observes of such celebration:

> The fact is that the implied or reliable narrator described by Booth is possible only in a situation of relative class homogeneity, and indeed reflects a basic community of values shared by a fairly restricted class of readers: and such a situation is not brought back into the world by fiat. . . . Thus the ultimate value of Booth's work is that of the conservative position in general: useful as diagnosis, and as a means of disengaging everything that is problematical in the existing state of things, its practical recommendations turn out to be nothing but regression and sterile nostalgia for the past.[9]

Michael McKeon argues in his study of Dryden's political poetry that no criticism can proceed adequately until it stands outside the unexamined, unrecognized, a priori assumptions within which the work was first conceived.[10] We will never see Austen's work clearly if we accept her fiction as right or correct or natural: Rather, we need to see it as explicitly time-bound and historical, not the product of right or truth or nature or even a powerful morality. The task of criticism here is not to celebrate Austen's vision, however brilliant that vision may be, but rather to estrange her novels so that we can read them anew, or, at the very least, recognize their differences from our own world rather than actively seek to minimize or deny that difference.

In a recent study, *Jane Austen and the Drama of Woman*, LeRoy W. Smith observes, "By virtually unanimous agreement Austen is a social novelist, focusing on the interaction of individuals and groups within a clearly defined community and hoping to reconcile the demands of self and society."[11] This is an unexceptional statement, one that it is difficult to disagree with, and as such it is typical of our unexamined consensus about

Austen's novels. Austen's narrators do, in point of fact, spend a good deal of time and emphasis asserting moral virtue and social responsibility. Having agreed to this reasonable proposition, Austen scholars then fail to go on to observe that, although social values are celebrated, at the same time characters are represented or envisioned in opposite terms—of separateness, privacy, intimacy, and interiority.[12] Examination of the language of real feeling (and therefore the disjunction between public, social language and private, interior feeling) reveals a central contradiction at the heart of Austen's fiction, between the gentry's nostalgic code of paternalism, their rhetoric of social obligation, on the one hand, and on the other a remarkable representation of the solipsistic experience of interiority and a concurrent celebration of the individual subject.[13]

This argument for a contradiction between the interiority and intimacy of the courtship plot and the moral of social responsibility runs counter to more traditional readings. More conventionally, in her studies of the political context of literature at the turn of the nineteenth century, Marilyn Butler aligns Jane Austen with other conservative writers or anti-Jacobins, who include such reactionaries as Jane West:

> Like other conservative moralists, Mrs. West denigrates the individual's reliance on himself. She shows for example how dangerous it is to trust private intuition or passion in forming judgements of others. Far better in her view to go to the external evidence. . . . The same discovery—that objective evidence should be preferred to private intuition—is made by a succession of Jane Austen heroines, Catherine Morland, Marianne Dashwood, Elizabeth Bennet, Emma Woodhouse. And if feeling is an unreliable aid in choosing a husband, it is equally wayward as a general guide to conduct. Instead of the doctrine of cultivation of self, Mrs. West [and Austen too, by association] recommends humble, selfless service of others.[14]

In other words, the heroine must examine, study, and know her suitor rather than trust to her own feelings or, worse, give in to her (or his) passion. Butler attributes this rejection of feeling to a consciously moral, if not explicitly political, identification with the conservative, anti-Jacobin cause in a generation of novelists, such as Austen, who "consciously rejected emotional experience as a proper field of interest."[15] The sides line up as follows: Along the right side is the anti-Jacobin Austen, a "conservative Christian moralist of the 1790's," who, following Edmund Burke, celebrates the greater claims of society over the individual; along the left side are the radical Jacobins, supporters of the French Revolution and followers of Thomas Paine and William Godwin, who celebrate the rights of man over a repressive society.[16] This conservative/radical dichotomy boils down to an objective/subjective opposition, with Austen on the former side: "The tendency of her fiction is to rebuke individual self-assertion. . . . [and so it is] inclined on the contrary to idealize 'feminine' traits in female characters, such as humility, contentment with a domestic role, and absence of sexuality."[17] The problem with this implicitly political and explicitly moral explanation of the proper method of courtship is that, although it fits Jane Austen's Elizabeth Bennet and Maria Edgeworth's Belinda Portman, the same formula fits far too many earlier works and characters, from Angelica in Congreve's *Love for Love* or Millamant in *The Way of the World*; and on through Fielding's Sophia Western, Richardson's Harriet Byron, and Burney's Evelina, Cecilia, and Camilla; along with countless other pre-1790 eighteenth-century heroines from fiction and drama, each of whom is counseled to accept a proposal of marriage only with extreme caution and prudence, and not on the basis of evanescent and easily mistaken passion, lest she throw herself away on a Sir John Brute or a Lovelace. Thus, to ascribe the advice of prudence in courtship to the politically repressive atmosphere of the 1790s will not do. Nor will it do to divide culture and politics in this period into clear and nonintersecting halves: On the contrary, conservative Austen, as much as moderate Edgeworth or radical Godwin and Bage, enacts in her novels the dominant bourgeois ideology of a thoroughly individualistic society. Austen's implicit references to politics may be as conservative as Butler suggests, and her novels may be as explicitly moral as Butler suggests, but Austen's representation of character cannot be attributed wholly to a conscious moral design: Rather, her representation of character enacts bourgeois ideology of the individual subject within a high capitalist, consumer society, an ideology that conservative, radical, and moderate novelists alike embody at the turn of the nineteenth century.

Rather than simply divide England into Jacobin and anti-Jacobin camps, Raymond Williams offers a more complicated and contradictory but I think more accurate view of Austen's society:

> no single, settled society, it is an active, complicated, sharply speculative process. It is indeed that most difficult world to describe, in English social history: an acquisitive, high bourgeois society at the point of its most evident interlocking with an agrarian capitalism that is itself mediated by inherited titles and by the making of family names. Into the long and complicated inter-

action of landed and trading capital, the process that Cobbett observed—the arrival of "the nabobs, negro-drivers, admirals, generals" and so on—is directly inserted, and is even taken for granted. The social confusions and contradictions of this complicated process are then the true source of many of the problems of human conduct and valuation, which the personal actions dramatize. An openly acquisitive society, which is concerned also with the transmission of wealth, is trying to judge itself at once by an inherited code and by the morality of improvement.[18]

Austen embodies this backward-looking "inherited code" of noblesse oblige and social obligation in estate management and genealogical as well as social continuity in figures such as Darcy and Knightley, but also in the more rigidly moral heroines such as Elinor and Fanny, with their dependence upon and vigorous approbation of traditional social form and obedience to external authority. More mobile figures such as Captain Wentworth, however, bespeak a "morality of improvement," which, in Wentworth's accumulation of personal fortune, is pictured as something quite different from the voracious acquisition of the likes of John Dashwood, and so in *Persuasion*, as many have noted, Austen is far less certain and insistent about the value of traditional, fixed social hierarchy. And with someone such as Emma ("whom no one but myself will much like"), Austen is decidedly ambivalent, at once rebuking and celebrating Emma's wayward but nonetheless attractive individualism.

Following Butler, David Monaghan makes a similar case for a socially conservative Austen: "Jane Austen's . . . thesis [is] that the fate of society depends on the ability of the landed classes to live up to their ideal of concern for others, and on the willingness of the other groups to accept this ideal."[19] No one would argue that Austen is unconcerned with social or moral responsibility. Nevertheless, traditionally moral and social readings of Austen's novels fail to account for how individualized and privatized they have become, how much more fragmented and incoherent the society imaged in *Persuasion* is compared with that of *Sense and Sensibility*. In *Emma*, the heroine must endure the burden and encumbrance of community, with little of its reward. Several commentators observe how much Anne Elliot is alienated from her society, that in fact there is little sense of traditional community in *Persuasion*.[20] Austen's novels pass from objective to subjective, becoming increasingly private, personal, and domestic, or, as Julia Brown puts it, they pass from a "tradition-directed to an inner-directed society."[21] With *Pride and Prejudice*, the old saws have it that Elizabeth represents the private or personal or subjective view of things, whereas Darcy represents the public or social or objective view of things, and that Darcy's view ultimately dominates. But Elizabeth's view is not repudiated, for the narrative narrows down to her increasingly subjective perspective, and it is this view that prevails at the end. Darcy's patriarchal and feudal perspective is never really shown, except by inference through his housekeeper at Pemberley. However noisily introduced, the public or social or objective side of Darcy is confined to the political lesson of Pemberley and its spokesperson, the housekeeper, and as such it remains but a trace, a vestige of the old social order, embedded within the personal story of Elizabeth.

My point here is not that the novels become more bourgeois, but rather that by the time of *Persuasion*, and even more obviously in the grossly fragmented, uprooted, commercialized, and exploitative world of *Sanditon*, there is much less of a gap or contradiction between the implicit (or unconscious) ideological dimensions of character and social relations on the one hand, and the explicit (or conscious) moral and social dimensions of the novels on the other hand. That is to say, the fragmentation and subjectivity of the seaside resort in *Sanditon* or Bath and the estate in *Persuasion* are produced by an ideology of the individual subject and interiority that runs from Elinor in *Sense and Sensibility* through Charlotte and Clara in *Sanditon*.

Thus, I would like to argue that this central relation between self and society (to return to the traditional terms of Austen criticism) is not, as Smith would have it, a universal or eternal or natural opposition, nor, as Butler would have it, is this dynamic determined solely by the political struggles of the 1790s. Rather—and this is my central argument—the problematic status of the individual subject in Austen's six novels is a particular one that is determined by large-scale historical developments of eighteenth-century Europe, that is, the development of the "antinomies of bourgeois thought: subject/object; freedom/necessity; individual/society; form/content."[22] To use the terms of classic, nineteenth-century German sociology, the transition from *Gemeinschaft* to *Gesellschaft* or from genuine human community to a legally defined and impersonal society is a demonstrably and specifically historical matter and should be analyzed as such.[23] To that end, the work of Georg Lukács, the first great theorist of the novel, is indispensable. That is to say, to analyze the problematic of the individual subject and her narrative at this historical juncture, we need to turn to Lukács. Paul de Man summarizes Lukács's program in *The Theory of the Novel*: "The emergence of the novel as the major modern genre is seen as the result of a change in the structure of human consciousness; the development of the novel reflects modifications in man's way of defining himself in relation to all categories of existence."[24] The novel according to Lukács is determined by the characteristic dualisms of modern society, for "the hero of the novel . . . is the product of estrangement from the outside world."[25] The novel develops in an age in which the subject expects but can no longer find adequate definition within larger social structures, and so she experiences a disturbing disjunction between her individual nature and the larger expectation of social order or meaning: "The novel is the epic of an age in which the extensive totality of life is no longer directly given, in which the immanence of meaning in life has become a problem, yet which still thinks in terms of totality."[26] In his study of Lukács and his theory of the novel, J. M. Bernstein sums up this dynamic: "the novel is necessarily an interpretation as well as repetition of reality"; that is, "for Lukács the novel is a dialectic of form-giving and mimesis, a dialectic of interpretation and representation. These two aspects or moments of the novel correspond to the Kantian worlds of freedom and causality, ought and is; the dialectic of the novel is the attempt to write the world as it is in terms of how it ought to be."[27]

In effect, Bernstein "completes" *The Theory of the Novel* in the light of Lukács's later masterwork, *History and Class Consciousness*, by demonstrating that the central premise of *The Theory of the Novel* is "that the dualisms which permeate the bourgeois world are the result of the reification and rationalization of the social world caused by commodity production."[28] The form of the novel embodies the alienation or objectification inevitable under capitalism: "the antinomic relation between subject and structure, between form-giving subjectivity with its premised freedom and reified structural complexes which leave no room for freedom or (authentic) subjectivity. . . . the dualisms which permeate the bourgeois world are the result of the reification and rationalization of the social world caused by commodity production."[29] As Lukács puts it, the central dualism is experienced as a fundamental disjunction between the individual feeling subject and the inexplicable objective world:

> man in capitalist society confronts a reality "made" by himself (as a class) which appears to him to be a natural phenomenon alien to himself; he is wholly at the mercy of its "laws," his activity is confined to the exploitation of the inexorable fulfillment of certain individual laws for his own (egoistic) interests. But even while "acting" he remains, in the nature of the case, the object and not the subject of events. The field of his activity thus becomes wholly internalized: it consists on the one hand of the awareness of the laws which he uses and, on the other, of his awareness of his inner reactions to the course taken by events.[30]

Under a fully developed market capitalism and its consequent "fetish of the commodity," exchange value comes to dominate over use value, and so products and their producers become dissociated from both intrinsic and traditional values. Exchange value in precapitalist modes of production had been "episodic," but under capitalism, commodity has become "the universal structuring principle."[31] As the principal event of exchange, wage labor is rationalized or quantified, while, through industrial mechanization and specialization, the worker is separated or alienated from the overall process of production: "We can see a continuous trend towards greater rationalization, the progressive elimination of the qualitative, human and individual attributes of the worker."[32] In this way, she is alienated from the product of labor, as well as from the means of production: "the personality can do no more than look on helplessly while its own existence is reduced to an isolated particle and fed into an alien system."[33] Thus, not just the behemoth factory, or, what is closer to Austen's own experience, the improvements of agrarian capitalism, but the whole mechanized and rationalized system of production comes to seem separate, external, preexisting, self-sufficient, and "natural." It is this universal, distanced, externalized world of commodity relations that produces the sense of objectification of the external world; in this objectified world, each individual is stripped of any genuine sense of community or participation in social relations and is left instead with a contemplative stance toward the world, a stance that in a precapitalist society may have been the characteristic and privilege of the leisure class but under capital becomes universal.

The correlative to objectification and the contemplative stance is the heightened interiority or subjectivity of individualism, or, as Bernstein writes, "the world where freedom is exiled into subjectivity."[34] Here is Lukács's explanation of the "fetish of the commodity":

> a man's own activity, his own labour becomes something objective and independent of him, something that controls him by virtue of an autonomy alien to man. There is both an objective and a subjective side to this phenomenon. *Objectively* a world of objects and relations between things springs into being (the world of commodities and their movements on the market). The laws governing these objects are indeed gradually discovered by man, but even so they confront him as invisible forces that generate their own power. The individual can use his knowledge of these laws to his own advantage, but he is not able to modify the process by his own activity. *Subjectively*—where the market economy has been fully developed—a man's activity becomes estranged from

himself, it turns into a commodity which, subject to the non-human objectivity of the natural laws of society, must go its own way independently of man just like any consumer article.[35]

The ideological consequences of the objectification of social relations under capital are effectively summarized by Bernstein:

> It is not difficult to see in this description of a causally determined world resulting from human activity, and a "world" of freedom exiled into interiority a metaphysical statement of the Marxist theory that in the historically conditioned exercise of our freedom and rationality we have created the "alienating" world of capital which leaves no objective, social space where our freedom and reason may express itself. . . . Freedom and value must hence retreat into subjectivity.[36]

In short, the mystification of commodity centers on the ways in which social relations, between capitalist and laborer, or, it might be argued, between husband and wife, assume "the fantastic form of a relation between things."[37]

It may be objected that this radical subjectivity is just what Austen so vigorously writes against, but nevertheless her novels engender or reproduce just this sense of subjectivity, even while they appear to celebrate the gentry's code of nostalgic paternalism. Her novels re-create the essential ideological contradiction between the rhetoric of social obligation and the solipsistic experience of individuality and interiority, for, inevitably, "true authenticity" is only found within, experienced as interiority: As Lukács puts it in his "Reification" essay, "Ideologically, we see the same contradiction in the fact that the bourgeoisie endowed the individual with an unprecedented importance, but at the same time that same individuality was annihilated by the economic conditions to which it was subjected, by the reification created by commodity production."[38]

Despite Austen's self-conscious political, moral, and religious conservatism, and despite her class identification with the gentry, and their sentiments of noblesse oblige, the way in which Austen's heroine defines herself in relation to all categories of existence is inevitably determined by the alienating effects of capital, under which social relations and practices are externalized and objectified and from which, consequently, the individual is alienated. Elizabeth Bennet and Emma Woodhouse, Austen's most obviously subjective, interiorized characters, embody that characteristic stance of distance that Marvin Mudrick attributes to Jane Austen's personality, but that for Lukács typifies the essence of modern subjectivity: "We have found the only true substance within ourselves: that is why we have to place an unbridgeable chasm between cognition and action, between soul and created structure, between self and world."[39]

What have such apparently distant matters to do with our understanding of Jane Austen's novels? After all, Emma Woodhouse, heiress to £35,000 and a modest paternal estate, is not an exploited or alienated factory laborer, nor was her creator. But Lukács's argument is not confined to one class, but rather it embraces all categories of experience under capitalism. Objectification, Lukács insists, is not so much a kind of deceptive mythology or a false consciousness as it is consciousness itself: Under capital, "economic factors are not concealed 'behind' consciousness but are present *in* consciousness itself (albeit unconsciously or repressed)."[40] Furthermore, the nature of commodity production and exchange is not something Austen is unfamiliar with (Mary Crawford quotes that "true London maxim, that every thing is to be got with money" [MP 58]), nor, as we shall see, is she unfamiliar with the transformative effects of agrarian capitalism and the morality of improvement, though it is true that such matters have traditionally received scant attention in her fiction. The conditions of objectification—of isolation, fragmentation, and atomization—are represented by Austen in mystified and confusing or contradictory fashion, but still these conditions are seen as a real human problem.[41] As Lukács remarks in an interview, "the art of any time—and this is the essential thing—relates the immediate problems of its age to the general development of mankind and links them with it, a connection which may of course be quite hidden from the writer himself."[42] In *The Historical Novel,* Lukács praises Austen's contemporary Sir Walter Scott for his sense of "historical necessity": "it is a complex interaction of concrete historical circumstances in their process of transformation, in their interaction with concrete human beings."[43] In examining Austen's representation of the objectification of social relations, we are observing a similar instance of historical necessity, though her chosen realm is self-consciously not large-scale political history, as in *Waverley,* but rather domestic, private experience. Nevertheless, domestic, private experience is as much subject to the determinations of history as national politics, and so we should look for the same interaction of concrete historical circumstances and concrete individuals in Austen's novels as we do in Scott's.

In order to historicize the fictional representation of private experience, we can begin by exploring the sense of disparity between subject and object, between internal feeling and external event. In Austen's novels this disjunction is most evident in the interrelation between feeling and expression or character and language, what may be termed the ideology of the language of real feeling. Our first order of business, therefore, is an examination of Austen's conception of language, and in particular what Austen suggests cannot be said, her narrative dread: Her heroines are regularly described by the narrator as experiencing emotions which cannot be clothed in words.[44] This phrase is not casual or formulaic, but rather a part of a consistent effort in the novels to indicate what they cannot name, an area of experience and emotion that lies outside language. To explore what lies within and without language, this study is organized into two halves, the first of which traces the transformation of a central semantic metaphor, the language-as-clothing metaphor, which undergoes substantial change during the eighteenth century. Austen's use of the language-as-clothing metaphor is quite close to Wordsworth's, and, further, I argue that her conception of, or theory of, language, as well as her use, is essentially Romantic. Unlike earlier eighteenth-century conceptions of language, this Romantic or Wordsworthian notion of language acknowledges limits past which language cannot go, insisting that thought and feeling are infinite, but language is finite. Austen's use of clothing is the subject of the first three chapters: literal clothing, the clothing of emotion, and language as clothing. The first chapter concerns her portrayal of material dress in the novels; the second examines the emotions characteristic of her marriage proposal scenes as compared with such scenes from earlier eighteenth-century novels; and the third deals directly with the transformation of the metaphor of language clothing thought in words. The second half consists of three chapters that examine Austen's conception and portrayal of character, her representation of marriage, and, finally, her celebration of intimacy. In other words, the two halves of this study are made up of a description of a Romantic ideology that Austen shares and, second, an analysis or critique of that ideology.[45]

In Austen's language and in her descriptive technique, we can discern a recurrent pattern in which the fundamental elements of her fictional world, material things as well as ideal sentiments, are indicated but not described—they are briefly exposed and then withdrawn from view again. The "inner life" of characters in general is both presented and protected by a pattern of privacy. Austen's representational technique, her form of narrative, then, needs to be related to the social history of privacy. And, when this relation is combined with the later discussions of changing concepts of language, of character, and of marriage, we will be able to trace the development of some modern notions of individuality, interiority, intimacy, and romance. It is not just that the novel is the best record of these changes concerning the fundamental conception of the relationship between the individual subject and others around her—that is, ideology—but rather it is the unique cultural work of the novel to mediate what we think we are.[46] If "ideology represents the imaginary relationship of individuals to their real conditions of existence," in Louis Althusser's famous phrase, the novel is both the expression of and site for the development of that imaginary relationship.[47] In literary history, Austen's work has come to be valued as a significant moment in the technological development of fictional representation; what I want to do here is to locate these developments within social and economic history. To put this another way, what I am particularly interested in tracing in this book is the novel as a record of the interrelation between exterior and interior events, between economic, political, and social changes and their private or domestic consequences. That is to say, I am interested in the relation between history and the individual subject, and, moreover, the ways in which we have come to think in terms of just this sort of opposition. If "history is what hurts," as Fredric Jameson puts it,[48] in Austen's novels, and indeed throughout the nineteenth-century novel, love is what soothes, for private or domestic romance comes to function as the ideological negation of history, a refuge into a "natural" and "timeless" world of privacy and intimacy. Intimacy functions to efface the ideological contradiction between social responsibility and private withdrawal, for intimacy serves as the private "solution" to alienation and the objectification of social relations—romance and reification are two sides to the same coin or two sides of an ideological contradiction. Austen's achievement is to integrate the privatization of human relations into the appropriate vehicle, the courtship narrative or domestic love story.

Again, it is my argument that Austen's notions of private experience and public performance are neither natural nor eternal but peculiar to this period and that these notions are best understood in Lukács's terms of the objectification of social relations under capital. Lukács's Marxist analysis brings to the study of Austen a totalizing explanation. As commentators have observed regularly for several decades now, formerly the study of Austen was stunted by her gender and her domestic subject, limitations that were conveniently condensed in Austen's own trivializing remark "on the little bit (two Inches wide) of Ivory on which I work with so fine a Brush" (L 469). Contemporary Austen scholars make substantially greater claims for her work and worth: In Janet Todd's words, "Jane Austen is the first indubitably great woman writer in English."[49]

But despite such great claims, since 1970 work on Austen has given in to the specialization and fragmentation evident everywhere in literary studies.[50] Whatever its other weaknesses, the Hegelian wing of Marxism, and Lukács remains its most powerful theorist, aspires to totalizing explanation—in his defense of Lukács, Jameson quotes "Hegel's great dictum, 'the true is the whole.'"[51] It is of course crucial to understand and allow for the political topicality and historical specificity of Lukács's argument, and, furthermore, because of his precarious situations in exile, he is often difficult to pin down, especially when revising and reevaluating his own work from the past. Nonetheless, his is the most expansive, and I believe the most compelling, explanation of social changes in response to the advent of market capitalism and commodity exchange.[52] That his model underwent various modifications and changes in vocabulary over time in no way undermines its or his insight. As will be clear later, in using Lukács's theory here, I am also heavily indebted to the work of his most able contemporary proponent, Fredric Jameson. In short, this study is based primarily on Lukács's Marxist theory and its contemporary revision in Jameson on the one hand, and balanced on the other hand with the historical analysis of Raymond Williams and E. P. Thompson and the sense of eighteenth-century culture that they have so painstakingly recovered and reconstructed.

This theoretical alliance will allow us to place and to understand Austen within the largest historical framework, within the frame advocated by Jameson: Interpretation

> of a particular text must take place within three concentric frameworks, which mark a widening out of the sense of the social ground of a text through the notions, first, of a political history, in the narrow sense of punctual event and a chroniclelike sequence of happenings in time; then of society, in the now already less diachronic and time-bound sense of a constitutive tension and struggle between social classes; and, ultimately, of history now conceived in its vastest sense of the sequence of modes of production and the succession and destiny of the various human social formations.[53]

Furthermore, if traditional Austen criticism is governed by a moral vision that celebrates her dialectic of self and society, Lukács and Jameson are able to situate historically this very dialectic: "Marxism subsumes other interpretive modes or systems; . . . the limits of the latter can always be overcome, and their more positive findings retained, by a radical historicizing of their mental operations, such that not only the content of the analysis, but the very method itself, along with the analyst, then comes to be reckoned into the 'text' or phenomenon to be explained."[54]

From the work of social and family historians such as Lawrence Stone, we have begun to see the degree to which Austen's fiction embodies late-eighteenth-century views of courtship and marriage: No longer primarily financial transactions or transfers of property, arranged by parents for the benefit of large kinship systems, marriage for Austen's class was coming to be idealized as an individual compact of love and affection. Feminist criticism has particularly invigorated Austen studies by enabling us to see that Austen's novels are situated at the beginning of the formation of this view of courtship and marriage, a view from which we are only now, two hundred years later, beginning to extricate ourselves.[55] Austen's appeal, in large part, lies in the fact that her novels are among the first in English to codify the values of love and affection in marriage, marriage envisioned as private intimacy, set against the threat of loneliness and solipsism. It is the task of dialectical analysis to correlate Austen's moment in history with our own, the two of which are situated on opposite ends of a distinct and definable era that celebrates individual emotion. As a consequence of two decades of feminist revision, we are finally in a position to begin to make visible the ideology of this period that lies between Austen and ourselves.

1
Clothing

We are still faced with an abyss; a gulf yawns before us; on the other side are the working classes. The writer of perfect judgement and taste, like Jane Austen, does no more than glance across the gulf.

—Virginia Woolf, *Essays*[1]

In a letter to Cassandra written during a visit to London in 1813, Jane Austen sent her sister a little fantasy about the heroines of *Pride and Prejudice*:

> Henry & I went to the Exhibition in Spring Gardens. It was not thought a good collection, but I was very well pleased—particularly (pray tell Fanny) with a small portrait of Mrs. Bingley, excessively like her. I went in hopes of seeing one of her Sister, but there was no Mrs. Darcy;—perhaps however, I may find her in the Great Exhibition which we shall go to if we have time. . . . Mrs. Bingley's is exactly herself, size, shaped face, features & sweetness; there never was a greater likeness. She is dressed in a white gown with green ornaments, which convinces me of what I had always supposed, that green was a favorite colour with her. I dare say Mrs. D. will be in Yellow. (L 309–10)[2]

That none of these details of appearance, taste, and dress appears in *Pride and Prejudice* proper supports what R. W. Chapman observed of Austen long ago: "Miss Austen knows all the details, and gives us very few of them."[3] We need to inquire why Austen would have envisioned these details if she was not going to disclose them in her novel. In the novel in question, we are never told what the two characters wear, let alone their favorite colors. Despite her reputation for realism and exactly rendered detail, Austen's novels give us very few specifics of clothing, even though her letters are filled with just such details. Again, Austen must have assumed that her own interest in dress had no place in fiction. One reader complains that her letters "deal wearisomely with details of dress."[4] We may weary easily of such details because we are accustomed to read Austen, and novels in general, by moving from objects to values, interpreting the objects portrayed as a foundation upon which to construct elaborate social and ethical systems. On the one hand, novels are supposed to satisfy our insatiable appetite for the material detail of everyday life, and, on the other hand, such detail is supposed to serve the greater purpose of meaningful structure. That is to say, the novel is said to offer a (relatively) random or ordinary sample of material existence, as a representation of life, yet that representation is also an interpretation of life, an ordering of these data into an apprehensible or sensible whole.[5] In short, novels must be familiar and novel at the same time, for they must present ordinary life in extraordinary form: the inherent disorder of detail must be made meaningful.

The formation of odd detail into a meaningful whole is an idealizing move, and this movement from material to ideal obscures the real pressures of material life, pressures that qualify, if not undercut, the more obvious morals exemplified in Austen's novels. Careful focus on the material details of Austen's fiction shows the relation between objects and the moral structures in which they are embedded. Yet the material and the moral always remain separable, for Austen relies on private or personal moral explanation for social ills. Problems of unequal distribution of wealth in these novels are inevitably subsumed under morality, transforming material conditions into ideal relations. As the most personal of possessions, clothing is a subject eminently suited to this investigation. Examination of how Austen clothes her characters should provide some insight into how she constructs her fiction, and the ways in which she instructs her readers to imagine her characters. If nothing else, examination of her use of clothing and other objects undermines the traditional lesson that an interest in clothing is vain and frivolous, for Austen inevitably calls this familiar homily into question by suggesting the many social and economic demands on women.

We may begin by observing that articles of clothing are rarely mentioned in Austen's fiction and then not gratuitously. Even the most casual reference can be said to help set the scene, as when Catherine Morland's haste to get dressed is overcome by her curiosity about an old chest: "At length, however, having slipped one arm into her gown, her toilette seemed so nearly finished, that the impatience of her curiosity might safely be indulged" (NA 164). More commonly, specific items of dress are mentioned that others may comment on them, as with Elizabeth Bennet's "dirty stockings," which provoke various and telling reactions at Netherfield (PP 36). Similarly, we discover what Willoughby wears when we are told that Marianne "soon found out that of all manly dresses a shooting-jacket was the most becoming" (SS 43). This specific item of clothing exposes Marianne's thinly veiled attraction to Willough-by's person, and further, a shooting-jacket, with its association of youth and sport, contrasts favorably with Colonel Brandon's flannel waistcoat, with its associations of age and infirmity (SS 38). Particular stockings, jackets, and waistcoats, then, are brought to our attention in order to reveal attitudes and assumptions of the characters; like physical objects in general, as Joel Weinsheimer notes, they are included "primarily for the purpose of characterization."[6] As with all sign systems, clothing has no inherent, but only relative, value: That is, Austen contrasts one character's dress with another's and in this way denies any significance to shooting-jackets per se.

Beyond this obliquely metonymic function, clothing tends to fade into the vague description of "fashionable" or "elegant," and we are told almost nothing of what these terms signify. When elegance intrudes on our notice, it tends to slip into overelegance and vulgarity, and fashion into precipitous, irrational change, as in *Sanditon,* where Mr. Parker calls to his wife: "Look my dear Mary—Look at William Heeley's windows.—Blue Shoes & nankin Boots!—Who wd have expected such a sight at a Shoemaker's in old Sanditon!—This is new within the Month. There was no blue Shoe when we passed this way a month ago.—Glorious indeed!—Well, I think I *have* done something in my Day" (MW 383). Whenever Austen narrates so particular an interest in dress as this, it is to arouse our suspicions, for those characters who think so much of small matters are inclined to think improperly of great matters. In *Northanger Abbey,* Mrs. Allen is presented as a kindly, but thoughtless woman whose major concern is clothing: "Dress was her passion. She had a most harmless delight in being fine" (NA 20). Excessive concern with appearance, we are shown, precludes further thought; when asked about the impropriety of driving about with single men, Mrs. Allen is distracted by surface matters: "Open carriages are nasty things. A clean gown is not five minutes wear in them. You are splashed getting in and getting out; and the wind takes your hair and your bonnet in every direction. I hate an open carriage myself" (NA 104). Austen's works are full of such empty-headed characters as typified by Miss Stanley in the early fragment "Catherine": "All her Ideas were towards the Elegance of her appearance, the fashion of her dress, and the Admiration she wished them to excite. She professed a love of Books without Reading, was Lively without Wit, and generally good humoured without Merit" (MW 198). Judgment of such interests as these ranges in Austen's works from harmless frivolity to emptiness and even to meanness. In *Persuasion*, for example, the Miss Musgroves would seem to exemplify average intelligence and goodness, for they are well-tempered and friendly; but compared with Anne Elliot, Austen's most perfect heroine, they appear to squander their advantages:

> the only two grown up, excepting Charles, were Henrietta and Louisa, young ladies of nineteen and twenty, who had brought from a school at Exeter all the usual stock of accomplishments, and were now, like thousands of other young ladies, living to be fashionable, happy, and merry. Their dress had every advantage, their faces were rather pretty, their spirits extremely good, their manners unembarrassed and pleasant; they were of consequence at home and favorites abroad. Anne always contemplated them as some of the happiest creatures of her acquaintance; but still, saved as we all are by some comfortable feeling of superiority from wishing for the possibility of exchange, she would have not given up her own more elegant and cultivated mind for all their enjoyments. (P 40–41)

Excessive interest in clothing can suggest not only frivolity but vulgarity, as is the case in *Sense and Sensibility* with the eldest Miss Steele, the most foolish character in all of Austen:

> Nothing escaped *her* minute observation and general curiosity; she saw every thing, and asked every thing; was never easy till she knew the price of every part of Marianne's dress; could have guessed the number of her gowns altogether with better judgment than Marianne herself, and was not without hopes of finding out before they parted, how much her washing cost per week, and how much she had every year to spend upon herself. The impertinence of these kind of scrutinies, moreover, was generally concluded with a compliment, which though meant as its douceur, was considered by Marianne as the greatest impertinence of all; for after undergoing an examination into the value and make of her gown, the colour of her shoes, and the arrangement of her hair, she was almost sure of being told that upon "her word she

looked vastly smart, and she dared say would make a great many conquests." (SS 249)[7]

The connection between a devotion to clothing and small-mindedness is constantly stressed with Mrs. Elton, Austen's supreme vulgarian, whose "studied elegance" (E 321) gives elegance a bad name. Of an evening's gathering at Hartfield, the reader overhears Mrs. Elton eliciting admiration for her gown from Jane Fairfax:

How do you like it?—Selina's choice—handsome, I think, but I do not know whether it is not over-trimmed; I have the greatest dislike of the idea of being over-trimmed—quite a horror of finery. I must put on a few ornaments *now*, because it is expected of me. A bride, you know, must appear like a bride, but my natural taste is all for simplicity; a simple style of dress is so infinitely preferable to finery. But I am quite in the minority, I believe; few people seem to value simplicity of dress,—shew and finery are every thing. I have some notion of putting such a trimming as this to my white and silver poplin. Do you think it will look well? (E 302)

Such a passage functions like Mrs. Elton's references to her brother-in-law's carriage, the much admired barouche-landeau, wherein Mrs. Elton exposes a mind misdirected toward the wrong things, in fact, toward things, as opposed to ideas of right and duty. Though this statement must be carefully qualified, in her fiction Austen condemns excessive love of things, whether gowns or carriages or houses or estates, and often this condemnation is indicated by the placement of details of clothing next to invaluable intangibles. Wedding clothes, for example, are often juxtaposed with the idea of marriage. In the last sentence of *Emma*, Austen exhibits Mrs. Elton's concern only with externals, with the thinnest veil of appearance, as opposed to any lasting value of friendship, union, or community:

Mrs. Elton, from the particulars detailed by her husband, thought it all extremely shabby, and very inferior to her own.—"Very little white satin, very few lace veils; a most pitiful business!—Selina would stare when she heard of it."—But, in spite of these deficiencies, the wishes, the hopes, the confidence, the predictions of the small band of true friends who witnessed the ceremony, were fully answered in the perfect happiness of the union. (E 484)

In *Pride and Prejudice*, too, Mrs. Bennet's obsession with wedding clothes suggests a mind closed to all but possession and the appearance of it. Because Lydia has eloped, her father refuses to pay for the clothes, and Mrs. Bennet is horrified: "to refuse his daughter a privilege, without which her marriage would scarcely seem valid. . . . She was more alive to the disgrace, which the want of new clothes must reflect on her daughter's nuptials, than to any sense of shame at her eloping and living with Wickham, a fortnight before they took place" (PP 310–11). Lydia similarly condemns herself with reference to clothing: "And there was my aunt, all of the time I was dressing, preaching and talking away just as if she was reading a sermon. However, I did not hear above one word in ten, for I was thinking, you may suppose, of my dear Wickham. I longed to know whether he would be married in his blue coat" (PP 319).

In short, Austen would seem to employ her characters' interest in clothing to illustrate their concern with the surface of things, with lives wasted on the acquisition of objects rather than on the acquisition of ideas and values, a judgment that the narrator of *Northanger Abbey* moralizes upon at some length:

> What gown and what head-dress she would wear on the occasion became her chief concern. She cannot be justified in it. Dress is at all times a frivolous distinction, and excessive solicitude about it often destroys its own aim. Catherine knew all this very well; her great aunt had read her a lecture on the subject only the Christmas before; and yet she lay awake ten minutes on Wednesday night debating between her spotted and her tamboured muslin, and nothing but the shortness of the time prevented her buying a new one for the evening. This would have been an error in judgment, great though not uncommon, from which one of the other sex rather than her own, a brother rather than a great aunt might have warned her, for man only can be aware of the insensibility of man towards a new gown. It would be mortifying to the feelings of many ladies, could they be made to understand how little the heart of man is affected by what is costly or new in their attire; how little it is biassed by the texture of their muslin, and how unsusceptible of peculiar tenderness towards the spotted, the sprigged, the mull or the jackonet. Woman is fine for her own satisfaction alone. No man will admire her the more, no woman will like her the better for it. Neatness and fashion are enough for the former, and a something of shabbiness or impropriety will be most endearing to the latter.—But not one of these grave reflections troubled the tranquillity of Catherine. (NA 73–74)

Austen often uses concern for clothing to suggest this sort of frivolity. All the same, this particular passage is one of the most pretentious in all of *Northanger Abbey*, and, were it not for the slight snarl in "shabbiness and impropriety," it might sound suspiciously like the high-toned moral essayists that Austen mocks throughout the novel. And further, with respect to the situation at hand, this advice is patently false, for Henry Tilney, the object of Catherine's solicitude, is quite attentive to dress, and indeed he sees and understands the difference between the spotted and the sprigged.[8] If "excessive solicitude" is condemned, solicitude is not; although Austen may hold excessive personal vanity up for ridicule, at the same time she presents careful, attractive dress, not as a self-satisfying frivolity so much as a necessary courtesy, if not a prudent or shrewd business investment.[9] To the Miss Beauforts, two lodgers at the seaside resort in *Sanditon*, expensive dress is construed as a kind of packaging for the product they are promoting: "they were very accomplished & very Ignorant, their time being divided between such pursuits as might attract admiration, and those Labours & Expedients of dexterous Ingenuity, by which they could dress in a stile much beyond what they *ought* to have afforded; they were some of the very first in every change of fashion—& the object of all, was to captivate some Man of much better fortune than their own" (MW 421). They dress expensively in hopes of achieving the good fortune of *Mansfield Park*'s Lady Bertram, whose own uncle "allowed her to be at least three thousand pounds short of any equitable claim to" a match with Sir Thomas (MP 3; throughout *Mansfield Park*, Lady Bertram and her sister Mrs. Norris make very explicit the equation between beauty and the material wealth it brings; see pp. 31 and 332). For a woman in Austen's lifetime (and, of course, beyond), an attractive appearance is her most valuable and marketable asset, a resource to be carefully husbanded. Maria Edgeworth makes the connection between dress and marriage explicit in *Belinda*: "nothing to my mind can be more miserable than the situation of a poor girl, who, after spending not only the interest, but the solid capital of her small fortune in dress, and frivolous extravagance, fails in her matrimonial expectations."[10] The consequences of Marianne's neglect of her appearance are most clearly and cruelly put by John Dashwood, her avaricious half-brother, in this conversation with Elinor:

> I am sorry for that [Marianne's illness]. At her time of life, any thing of an illness destroys the bloom for ever! Her's has been a very short one! She was as handsome a girl last September, as any I ever saw; and as likely to attract the men. There was something in her style of beauty, to please them particularly. I remember

Fanny used to say that she would marry sooner and better than you did; not but what she is exceedingly fond of *you*, but so it happened to strike her. She will be mistaken, however. I question whether Marianne *now*, will marry a man worth more than five or six hundred a-year, at the utmost, and I am very much deceived if *you* do not do better. (SS 227)

John Dashwood's direct calculations of Marianne and Elinor's prospects (their exchange value in marriage) may seem quite removed from Mrs. Allen's foolish but harmless devotion to her dress, and yet the principle at work in both cases is the same, and that is a principle of economic competition in a sexual marketplace. When Mrs. Allen meets an old acquaintance, she sits "consoling herself, however, with the discovery, which her keen eye soon made, that the lace of Mrs. Thorpe's pelisse was not half so handsome as that on her own," and later, "Mrs. Allen was now quite happy—quite satisfied with Bath. She had found some acquaintance, had been so lucky too as to find in them the family of a most worthy old friend; and, as the completion of good fortune, had found these friends by no means so expensively dressed as herself" (NA 32 and 36). Mrs. Allen and Mrs. Elton no longer need to dress so as to attract a mate, but they still intend their dress to display their social and economic status. Then as now, a woman's evening attire could be very expensive, and the purpose of wearing expensive clothes is to show that one can afford them.[11] The Miss Beauforts of *Sanditon* dress more expensively than they "ought" because they wish to advertise more wealth than they have, again "to captivate some Man of much better fortune than their own" (MW 421). Like Indian brides who wear their wealth in gold, such young women wear their wealth in muslin, lace, and pearls.

If characters wear their wealth, then we ought to be able to read the signs of personal economy in the details of their dress, and, in fact, the novels employ an elaborate and consistent dress code that announces various social and economic facts. The principal object of the code is to ensure that one dresses appropriately to one's station, where station is usually defined in monetary as well as class terms. One commonly voiced complaint about the vast increase in the influence of the fashion industry in England at this time was aimed at its leveling tendency, for middle-class women copied the styles of their betters, and so on, up and down the social scale.[12] Mr. Collins officiously spells out Elizabeth's place at Rosings:

Do not make yourself uneasy, my dear cousin, about your apparel. Lady Catherine is far from requiring that elegance of dress in us, which becomes herself and daughter. I would advise you merely to put on whatever of your clothes is superior to the rest, there is no occasion for any thing more. Lady Catherine will not think the worse of you for being simply dressed. She likes to have the distinction of rank preserved. (PP 160–61)

There is, of course, always more or less of an inconsistency between strictly monetary and strictly social or class status in Austen. But more than most other indications of status, dress exemplifies a realm in which station is defined almost exclusively by money, by what one can afford, rather than what is ideally appropriate to one's rank. Other details are encoded into clothing; for example, in *Mansfield Park*, Mary Crawford and Thomas Bertram discuss at length how dress is employed to signify whether a girl is "in or out" (MP 49 and 51), that is to say, whether she is nubile. Social distinction is also directly related to the splendor and variety of one's dress. When Fanny Price returns to Portsmouth, the local girls complain that she has no real claim to gentility because she does not wear "fine pelisses" (MP 395), and when Fanny first came to Mansfield Park at age ten, her cousins "could not but hold her cheap on finding that she had but two sashes. . . . and the maid-servants sneered at her clothes" (MP 14). In the juvenilia, one impoverished character is insulted by Lady Greville, a prototype of Lady Catherine, for dressing above her station:

> Why could you not have worn your old striped one [gown]? It is not my way to find fault with people because they are poor, for I always think that they are more to be despised & pitied than blamed for it, especially if they cannot help it, but at the same time I must say that in my opinion your old striped Gown would have been quite fine enough for its wearer—for to tell the truth (I always speak my mind) I am very much afraid that one half of the people in the room will not know whether you have a Gown on or not—but I suppose you intend to make your fortune tonight. (MW 156)

The economy of dress is something that Jane Austen is constantly conscious of, though it is much more obvious in her letters than in her novels: "Mrs. Powlett was at once expensively & nakedly dress'd; we have had the satisfaction of estimating her Lace & her Muslin; and she said too little to afford us much other amusement" (L 105). Austen's letters are full of details of her own and others' clothing, though the details are often of price rather than of appearance. She can fill up pages describing sundry purchases of fabric and ribbon, swelling the report with the price of everything (see, for example, the letter of 18 April 1811, L 268–69). Aside from an occasional discussion of legacies, financial details in the letters generally surround clothing, cloth, and trimming, with the price per yard of muslin being the single most repeated item of news.[13] Austen's interest in clothing tends to be motivated by money more than vanity, amusement, or aesthetic concerns, because, judging from the letters, clothing was her largest expense. For a woman in her station, unmarried and dependent, it was certainly the most basic expense: in "Catherine," a poor relation is described as being "Dependant even for her Cloathes on the bounty of others" (MW 205–6).

One aspect of clothing peculiar to the last thirty years of the eighteenth century that is difficult for us to catch solely from reading her novels and letters is the degree to which clothing had become fashionable and fashion itself competitive, and the consequent burden this competition placed on young women, particularly those of modest means. In a study of the eighteenth-century English revolution in consumer spending and the development of emulative spending or conspicuous consumption, Neil McKendrick demonstrates how fashion, especially in clothing, became a powerful and lucrative industry in this period, as never before.[14] As clothing becomes fashionable and commercialized, it becomes commodified; that is, dress is transformed into an object dominated not by any essential (aesthetic or functional) qualities, or use value, but rather by exchange value, and the exchange value of clothing was of course determined by its evanescent association with the prevailing fashion. Where the emphasis on fashion may earlier have been the sole province of the wealthy, and even of the very wealthy, only among the urban and courtier classes, it was now held up as an acceptable if not an expected model of conduct for middle-class women, particularly those who expected to profit from fashionable dress by acquiring a husband. The ways in which London fashions had come to dominate dress in the provinces were commonly mentioned in literature, such as in Oliver Goldsmith's *She Stoops to Conquer*, where Kate Hardcastle wears a homely, country housekeeper's dress in the evening to please her father, but during the day she is allowed to wear a more fashionable gown to impress her London lover.[15] And despite their provincial location, the Hardcastles' familiarity with the fashions comes directly from London by way of the monthly magazines. Mrs. Hardcastle, aspiring to the heights of town elegance, claims to have all from the mail: "I take care to know every *tête-à-tête* from the *Scandalous Magazine*, and have all the fashions, as they come out, in a letter from the two Miss Rickets of Crooked Lane." So too, Mrs. Hardcastle says of her hair, "I protest, I dressed it myself from a print in the *Ladies' Memorandum-book* for the last year" (II, i, 625–35).[16]

Austen also acknowledges the dominance of London fashions when she shows how style travels from the capital to the provinces, that is, from Mrs. Gardiner to Mrs. Bennet: "I am very glad to hear what you tell us, of long sleeves" (PP 140; see also 222; Austen herself uses much the same language in describing fashion to her sister: "I learnt from Mrs. Tickars's young lady, to my high amusement, that the stays now are not made to force the bosom up at all; *that* was a very unbecoming, unnatural fashion. I was really glad to hear that they are not to be so much off the shoulders as they were," L 322). In her own letters, Austen notes the increasing rate of change in fashion:

> I am amused by the present style of female dress; the coloured petticoats with braces over the white Spencers and enormous Bonnets upon the full stretch, are quite entertaining. It seems to me a more marked *change* than one has lately seen.—Long sleeves appear universal, even as *Dress*, the Waists short, and as far as I have been able to judge, the Bosom covered.—I was at a little party last night at Mrs Latouche's, where dress is a good deal attended to, and these are my observations from it.—Petticoats short, and generally, tho' not always, flounced.—The broad-straps belonging to the Gown or Boddice, which cross the front of the Waist, over white, have a very pretty effect I think. (L 507; Austen can be much more particular than this general summary would suggest; see, for example, the very detailed description of a jacket, L 125).

Rapid change of fashion must have been especially burdensome for the marginally well-to-do, like the young women of *Sanditon*, who wished to appear by their clothing to belong to a financial class to which they had no real claim. McKendrick concludes that by 1800, an annual transformation of fashions had been institutionalized for all but the poor and laboring classes:

> By the 1770s contemporary observers found the pace of change so accelerated that they regarded fashions as annual, and amongst the super-fashionable as monthly. As the pace of fashionable change stepped up, not everyone could keep up. The costume museums of eighteenth-century dress are very revealing as to the skillful feminine subterfuges that were employed . . . to keep up with the short-lived modes of the eighteenth century. Not even the fashionable could always afford to buy new clothes when the whirligig of fashion was spinning as rapidly as it did in the reign of

George III, and the rest of society had to make constant use of the needle and their own ingenuity. But however ingenious the changes they devised, the evidence of increased spending suggests that the eighteenth-century fashion manipulators made them buy more than ever before.[17]

Austen's letters and novels are filled with evidence of this subterfuge and this increased pressure to maintain appearances. For the young women in the novels, clothing is presented as the most important area of financial autonomy, and so interest in clothing for these women is, in a sense, professional. As Sandra Gilbert and Susan Gubar point out, it is an interest to which Catherine Morland has been carefully socialized:[18] "At fifteen, appearances were mending; she began to curl her hair and long for balls; her complexion improved, her features were softened by plumpness and colour, her eyes gained more animation, and her figure more consequence. Her love of dirt gave way to an inclination for finery, and she grew clean as she grew smart" (NA 14–15). There may be no self-conscious pun in "smart," but still, Catherine has been directed to the proper feminine interests, which Austen delineates in *Persuasion*: "The Mr. Musgroves had their own game to guard, and to destroy; their own horses, dogs, and newspapers to engage them; the females were fully occupied in all the other common subjects of house-keeping, neighbours, dress, dancing, and music" (P 42–43).

Most readers of her novels would probably agree that Austen takes a dim view of both of these sets of pursuits, but similar statements from the letters are much more difficult to interpret; of a woman just met, Austen writes, "We shall not have two Ideas in common. She is young, pretty, chattering, & thinking cheifly (I presume) of Dress, Company, & Admiration" (L 419).[19] For all the air of condescension here, at the age of thirty-nine, Austen knows full well that these are subjects that young ladies are directed and encouraged to think about: for women they amount to professional concerns, as in this summary of Mrs. Bennet's occupation: "The business of her life was to get her daughters married" (PP 5). That this business of "Dress, Company, and Admiration" is trivializing and limiting for Austen may be inferred from a single sentence to her sister: "I have read the Corsair, mended my petticoat, & have nothing else to do.— Getting out is impossible" (L 379). This sentence from the letters seems worlds away from the narrator's moralizing on Catherine's desire for a new ball gown in *Northanger Abbey*, and so it is necessary to ask how they may be related. How much sense of regret is mixed in with these feelings of enclosure or confinement ("getting out is impossible") is an un-answerable question, but even so, what application or connection such regret may have to the novels can only be speculative and tangential. Still, Austen's interest in clothing in her letters and her character's interest in clothing in her novels need to be brought together not so much because one explains or clarifies the other but because they are parallel. In Austen's life and fiction, clothing is seen as inherently interesting and revealing, and interest in clothing is seen as demeaning but necessary, or rather, demeaning because it is necessary.

If this qualified view of clothing in Austen is accurate, then we have descended a great way from the high moral tone with which we began, where concern for dress was vain and frivolous, for in the world that Austen creates, characters are not able to be above such concerns. That such high-mindedness is not possible undercuts the obvious moral, as so often happens to obvious morals in Austen's fiction.[20] Austen manages to qualify both high-mindedness and practicality, in the same way that her heroines marry for love but not without concern for income. Novels that begin with realistic and accurate details of income end with fairy-tale marriages, a dualism that can be seen in the dress and appearance of the heroines. All of them are conventionally attractive, and their good looks are instrumental in attracting husbands, as Darcy is drawn to Elizabeth's "fine eyes" (PP 27). And yet, despite personal beauty, they are not supposed to turn it to advantage, for in that case they would appear too similar to fortune hunters such as Isabella or Lucy Steele. Rather, the heroines must be like Emma or Jane Bennet, beautiful but somehow unconscious of their beauty.[21] Thus Austen shows how important female beauty is, but her heroines are not allowed to use theirs. The beauty is present but not present; that is, it is initially described in vague, generalized terms, but thereafter not called attention to, except incidentally by potential suitors, by others, but not by the central figure, the possessor of the beauty.

The importance of good looks is poignantly underscored by the example of Charlotte Lucas, to whom Austen lends a good deal of sympathy:[22]

> Without thinking highly either of men or of matrimony, marriage had always been her object; it was the only honourable provision for well-educated young women of small fortune, and however uncertain of giving happiness, must be their pleasantest preservative from want. This preservative she had now obtained; and at the age of twenty-seven, without having ever been handsome, she felt all the good luck of it. (PP 122–23)

Stranded in the world without fortune or beauty, Charlotte Lucas is presented as lucky to have secured the idiot Collins. Austen will leave her heroines without fortune, but not without the personal beauty to repair that want.

Austen has it both ways: That is, she can make us fully aware of the economic threats to her heroines and yet free them to happy and reasonably wealthy marriages. As Lukács observes, the novel is commonly poised between these two points, the submission to necessity in the external world and the promise of freedom within the individual self, the dialectic of what is and what ought to be. In one sense, Austen's opposition obviously follows the pattern of comedy, which works by overcoming threats. Austen's references to estates and incomes do not, however, follow this straightforward comedic pattern, for her use of economic details is not regular. Her novels present a half-realistic or half-mercenary view of the world, one from which economic concerns are never long absent, but still their absence can be suffered. The narrative begins with rich and specific detailing of estates and income, in this way locating the characters on a firm economic base and in a specific social class, the country gentry and pseudogentry. However, once under way, Austen turns from financial matters, only to return in detail at the close of the story, when, having safely married, her heroine wants a new estate to secure her. *Sense and Sensibility* follows this pattern very closely, opening with a full account of the paternal estate at Norland, and closing with the annual financial report of Elinor's new home, the Delaford parsonage. The novels then are not consistently attentive to economic detail; this inconsistency explains why commentators alternatively say that Austen is and is not a realist.[23] In part, we can observe that Austen does not need to describe or explain her characters' financial affairs fully because she can assume the reader's familiarity with their particular class and with society as a whole; by briefly indicating her characters' habits of acquisition, she can locate them within the larger social and economic structure. Most often she performs this location by detailing characters' income, and as Alistair Duckworth has pointed out, these figures of capital and income are very accurate.[24] Yet beyond these details Austen rarely goes: She does not follow up with descriptions of person, home, clothing, or possessions. Norman Page quite accurately observes that "the material solidity and circumstantiality of this world is something that she has relatively little interest in rendering."[25] In a letter to a niece who was trying to write a novel, Austen advises her to minimize physical description in her fiction: "You describe a sweet place, but your descriptions are often more minute than will be liked. You give too many particulars of right hand & left" (L 401).

Clothing, beauty, details of personal appearance and possession are all elements that Austen employs with a great deal of restraint and even with a certain degree of reluctance. Ian Watt's praise of Austen's "realism of presentation" notwithstanding, when compared with the detail and specificity of earlier novelists, Austen's representation to objects is lacking in substantiality; Elizabeth's or Emma's dress is left general and vague, unlike the minute description of Crusoe's furs, Moll's bolts of cloth, Pamela's aprons or the itemization of clothing received from her late lady, Humphrey Clinker's britches, Werther's blue frock coat and yellow waistcoat, and the numberless veils and habits of Radcliffe and Lewis.[26] After her, Jane Eyre's wedding clothes or Catherine's change of clothing from Wuthering Heights to the Grange are items of dress invested with considerable significance that extends beyond their first appearance in the narrative. Austen's details of clothing never acquire such extensive significance, not even Fanny Price's amber cross, the most obviously symbolic item of dress in all of her novels. Whatever metaphoric or symbolic value that is attached to this cross is exploited for a single chapter and then dropped; its significance is local and finite, and we never hear of it again.

Things in Austen's fiction, particularly items of dress, serve their purpose and are then dismissed. That purpose is not, as in later nineteenth-century novels, to enable us to visualize the characters in their setting and so to represent life whole. When Austen describes a setting, such as Pemberley or Sotherton, like Pope's, it is a landscape moralized, not visualized. As Weinsheimer observes, the details of Mrs. Elton's dress are provided so that we may see her ostentation, not so that we may see her.[27] Objects and possessions do not define and circumscribe Emma Woodhouse with anything like the exactitude or specificity that they describe Emma Bovary. Austen may stand at the precipice of nineteenth-century realism, but she is not of it: the epic "totality of objects," that perfect synthesis of idealism and materialism or social system and individual object that Lukács so praises in Tolstoy, is just what Jane Austen does not present in her novels.[28]

On the contrary, the uncommon object in Austen's fiction is usually introduced by way of or suspended within a system of morality. Consider the Portsmouth section of *Mansfield Park,* which is, for a number of reasons, uncharacteristically physical.[29] This part of the fictional world is described so minutely, with all its darkness, noise, and filth, dust floating in the air, in the milk, and in the tea, quite obviously because such things and such filth do not intrude on Fanny's consciousness when at Mansfield Park. As we observed of the signs of dress, clothing has no inherent, but only comparative, value: Mansfield is quiet and clean, for the Bertrams can afford to employ a sufficient number of servants to make and serve tea; at the Park no family member has to concern him- or herself with sewing shirts and uniforms. But in Portsmouth, in a passage reminiscent of Smollett, the very dirt on the walls reveals carelessness and sloth, exposing labor not performed:

> sun-shine appeared to her a totally different thing in a town and in the country. Here, its power was only a glare, a stifling, sickly glare, serving but to bring forward stains and dirt that might otherwise have slept. There was neither health nor gaiety in sunshine in a town. She sat in a blaze of oppressive heat, in a cloud of moving dust; and her eyes could only wander from the walls marked by her father's head, to the table cut and knotched by her brothers, where stood the tea-board never thoroughly cleaned, the cups and saucers wiped in streaks, the milk a mixture of motes floating in thin blue, and the bread and butter growing every minute more greasy than even Rebecca's hands had first produced it. (MP 439)

The very materiality of the world itself, its light and surfaces and solidity, is represented here as oppressive.

The most prominent object in this section of the novel is the silver penknife over which Fanny's younger sisters Susan and Betsey squabble. In Fanny's hands, the knife is employed as an object lesson for Susan: A well-bred lady would never fight over a mere possession. The new knife serves as a reminder of familial tranquility, not an object of contention, or even, moreover, of use. Further, the purchase of the second knife is introduced as an example or an emblem of Fanny's newfound and newly asserted financial autonomy. In any number of ways, the physical object here dissolves into a moral. In this particular instance, the material penknife is perfectly integrated with the ideal moral, but still the knife remains a singular, isolated object, brought out into the narrative glare, as it were, to illustrate a particular lesson. Lukács might point out that in the effort to employ this single object as representative, no horizontal connection is drawn to the rest of the material world from which it is presumed to have been drawn, from knife maker, knife seller, or even knife user (we never see either of the sisters using the knife, only quarreling over it). This sort of connectedness is exactly what Austen does not embody in her fiction, because for her fictional objects serve an antithetical purpose; she can and does "synthesize" the material and the ideal, but her technique is to do so in consciously isolated instances. Thus the presentation of objects in Austen's fiction is consistent with the ideology of her class, which, as Terry Eagleton suggests, is marked by the very absence of materiality: "For without the exclusion of the real as it is known to historical materialism, there could be for Austen nothing of the ethical discourse, rhetoric of character, ritual of relationship or ceremony of convention which she presents—nothing, in short, of those elements for which we find her fiction 'valuable.' "[30]

Any specific material object tends to stick out like a sore thumb in *Mansfield Park*. After the trip to Sotherton, everyone takes note of the spoils that Mrs. Norris carries away with her, the cheese and pheasant's eggs: "Maria was just disconcerted enough to say directly, 'I think *you* have done pretty well yourself, ma'am. Your lap seems full of good things, and here is a basket of something between us, which has been knocking my elbow unmercifully' " (MP 105). Once again, our attention is not directed to the thing itself, but rather the objects are there to attract attention to Mrs. Norris's "spunging," as Maria puts it (MP 106). She runs off with the material for the theatrical curtain for the same reason: "Mrs. Norris contrived to remove one article from his [Sir Thomas's] sight that might have distressed him. The curtain over which she had presided with such talent and such success, went off with her to her cottage, where she happened to be particularly in want of green baize" (MP 195). Here the object does not serve so much as a "symbol" of Mrs. Norris's greed, as it functions within a larger, social and moral vision of her relationship to the estate itself, for her appropriation is set in conjunction with others' use of estate property. In a conversation with Edmund that has wide-ranging implications concerning everyone's, but particularly Fanny's, relation to and dependence upon the paternal estate, Mrs. Norris attempts to solidify her position on the estate by accusing another, more expendable dependent of improper appropriation:

> I *am* of some use I hope in preventing waste and making the most of things. There should always be one steady head to superintend so many young ones. I forgot to tell Tom of something that happened to me this very day.—I had been looking about me in the poultry yard, and was just coming out, when who should I see but Dick Jackson making up to the servant's hall door with two bits of deal board in his hand, bringing them to father, you may be sure; mother had chanced to send him of a message to father, and then father had bid him bring up them two bits of board for he could not no how do without them. I knew what all this meant, for the servants' dinner bell was ringing at the very moment over our heads, and I hate such encroaching people, (the Jacksons are very encroaching, I have always said so,—just the sort of people to get all they can), I said to the boy directly—(a great lubberly fellow of ten years old you know, who ought to be ashamed of

himself,) *I'll* take those boards to your father, Dick; so get you home again as fast as you can.—The boy looked very silly and turned away without offering a word, for I believe I might speak pretty sharp; and I dare say it will cure him of coming marauding about the house for one while,—I hate such greediness—so good as your father is to the family, employing the man all the year round! (MP 141–42)

The boy's father presumably is the Christopher Jackson mentioned as the estate's carpenter who builds the stage (MP 127) of which Sir Thomas says, it "does my friend Christopher Jackson credit" (MP 184). These bits of deal board, along with the green baize, are plainly subordinated to the larger issue of property and ownership, stewardship, and finally one's place at Mansfield Park. Once again, though, the objects that started off Mrs. Norris's digression, the two bits of deal board, get lost in the shuffle. In a similar manner, all material objects in Austen's fiction are introduced in order to be effaced, presented so that their significance may be denied or overshadowed by the more important lesson. The larger issues of authority, subordination, and dependence rise up to divert attention from the deliberately trivial objects that set this train of thought, example, and morality in motion. Fanny's place at Mansfield and her relationship to the Bertram family are under question from the very beginning of the novel. Mrs. Norris maintains a hierarchy in which she defines herself as proper family, and Fanny as a poor relation, a marginal hanger-on. She obviously does not extend the umbrella of "family" to cover workmen and servants, retainers and dependents on the estate, even though Sir Thomas can refer to Christopher Jackson as a friend. Yet the juxtaposition of her appropriation of the green baize and young Jackson's possession of the bits of deal board suggests the overall leveling of categories (despite Mrs. Norris's obvious resentment): They are all dependents on the estate and therefore on the owner, Sir Thomas, lord of the manor.[31]

The way in which Austen dissolves things into morality is perhaps most clearly demonstrated by its ironic inversion, the reverse process at work at the very beginning of *Sense and Sensibility*. Here, the deathbed promise of fraternal vigilance and guardianship, that is to say, familial relationship and social obligation, are in a matter of a few short steps reduced to a relationship of things, of petty objects, as John Dashwood and his wife pare the promised obligation of care for his mother and half sisters down to "helping them to move their things, and sending them presents of fish and game, and so forth, whenever they are in season" (SS 12). This is Austen's most blatant case where the social relations among individuals assume "the fantastic form of a relation between things," where the transfer of objects (game only in season, when it is plentiful and therefore the John Dashwoods have more than they can themselves use) takes the place of social relationships.[32] Indeed it is in *Sense and Sensibility* where objects have a tendency to assume the most fantastical forms that draw attention to their being "out of place." Compare, for example, what would appear to be a normative purchase of ribbons by Harriet in *Emma* with the purchase of a custom toothpick case by Robert Ferrars, an obvious emblem of tasteless luxury and waste:[33]

> He was giving orders for a toothpick-case for himself, and till its size, shape, and ornaments were determined, all of which, after examining and debating for a quarter of an hour over every toothpick-case in the shop, were finally arranged by his own inventive fancy, he had no leisure to bestow any other attention on the two ladies. . . . At last the affair was decided. The ivory, the gold, and the pearls, all received their appointment, and the gentleman having named the day on which his existence could not be continued without the possession of the toothpick-case, drew on his gloves with leisurely care, and bestowing another glance on the Miss Dashwoods, but such a one as seemed rather to demand than express admiration, walked off with an happy air of real conceit and affected indifference. (SS 220 and 221)

This toothpick case serves as an ostentatious example of emulative spending, a product that has no imaginable function beyond the lavish display of wealth. To be sure, the case is an object handcrafted by an artisan and so is still far removed from the industrially mass-produced objects of the mid-nineteenth century through the present-day society of consumption. During this early stage of incipient commodification, Austen recognizes and represents not so much the fetishized nature of commodities, that "fantastic form of a relation between things," as the encroachment of exchange over use value, again, of that "true London maxim, that every thing is to be got with money" (MP 58). The purchase of the toothpick case seems to function as a parody of the useless object, as houses or estates often do in Austen. Just as the case is overlaid with jewels in order to transform something of (at last minimal) use into something current or fashionable, so the fashion for landscape gardening is supposed to transform the supposedly timeless hereditary estate into something current; Robert Ferrars tells Elinor in *Sense and Sensibility*, "I advise every body who is going to build, to build a cottage" (SS 251), because cottages are now fashionable. In *Mansfield Park*, Henry Crawford bemoans the fact that he has already greedily "used up" the potential improvements on the estate he has inherited, and so he desires to share in others' improvements. Thornton Lacy, in particular, gets much attention in the desire to transform a home or a place of shelter and comfort into a display of social prestige and exchange value.[34]

In Austen's only other shopping scene (other than *Sanditon*), Harriet's small purchase of muslin and ribbon at Ford's is, in contrast, presented as relatively utilitarian (E 235). As was claimed previously, in her fiction Austen condemns excessive love of things, whether gowns or carriages, and her condemnation is expressed by placing material objects next to invaluable intangibles. In *Emma,* the Fords, along with the Perrys and even the Misses Bates, represent a notion of the community of Highbury:

> At this moment they were approaching Ford's, and he [Churchill] hastily exclaimed, "Ha! this must be the very shop that every body attends every day of their lives, as my father informs me. He comes to Highbury himself, he says, six days out of seven, and has always business at Ford's. If it be not inconvenient to you, pray let us go in, that I may prove myself to belong to the place, to be a true citizen of Highbury. I must buy something at Ford's. It will be taking out my freedom.—I dare say they sell gloves."
>
> "Oh! yes, gloves and every thing. I do admire your patriotism. You will be adored in Highbury. You were very popular before you came, because you were Mr. Weston's son—but lay out half-a-guinea at Ford's, and your popularity will stand upon your own virtues." (E 199–200)

Though they both make light of the centrality of Ford's, all the while they acknowledge that to buy at Ford's draws one into the very heart of and makes one a part of the community. At the same time, the passage may also serve to undermine the notion that community can be defined by purchases at the central store; in the more idealized passages of community, we are shown Mr. Knightley or Emma supplying the Bates with various forms of produce, apples grown on his farm, pork from Hartfield. Even further, Austen may imply that the store has come to serve as the town's central institution, gradually replacing the function which the church ought to serve in a more ideal community.

This discussion is not designed to reduce Austen's novels to the simple expression of haut bourgeois ideology in the first decade of nineteenth-century England; indeed, we might say that it is the very clarity or sharpness with which Austen embodies this ideology in her fiction that reveals the complexities and contradictions between morality and the real material world.[35] No reader can miss the way she dissociates the genteel rhetoric of being "above sordid material possessions" from the actual practice of voracious acquisition. The first chapter of *Sense and Sensibility* makes crystal clear her condemnation of John Dashwood's rapacious greed, property acquired by impoverishing others. Yet it condemns without questioning in any way the fundamental principle of the accumulation of land and capital or the present distribution of wealth. Whatever problems Austen sees are individual ones, confined to the private or personal sphere, for they are seen as moral rather than as political or social problems. Even in *Mansfield Park*, where Austen comes closest to examining class relations, social problems are finally attributed to Sir Thomas's errors in judgment, and not to a corrupt or repressive patriarchy. In his discussion of Austen's social vision, Raymond Williams concludes that her culture "is not seen flatteringly," for her object is to present an "uncompromising morality which is in the end separable from its social basis."[36] In essence, Williams goes on to explain this separation between morality and social reality by arguing that Austen does not, cannot see social problems in terms of class conflict: "All her discrimination is, understandably, internal and exclusive. She is concerned with the conduct of people who, in the complications of improvement, are repeatedly trying to make themselves into a class. But where only one class is seen, no classes are seen."[37] Another way to state this distinction is to say that Austen's morality is ideological, for it serves as a form of justification or defense of her class, but it does not consciously serve as a form of exclusion, containing or repressing an opposing class. As Fredric Jameson writes: "It is an often-taught and often forgotten lesson that ideology is designed to promote the human dignity and clear conscience of a given class at the same time that it discredits their adversaries; indeed, these two operations are one and the same, and as a cultural or intellectual object ideology may be defined as just such a reversible structure, a complex of ideas which appears either systematic or functional depending on the side from which it is approached."[38] In this light, *Mansfield Park* represents Austen's clearest expression of class conflict; for her, the upper-middle class or gentry is systematically defended by rejecting, on the one side, the vulgar or undeserving lower classes, as seen in the Portsmouth episodes, as well as rejecting, or at least correcting, the decadent upper class on the other, as in the treatment of Mansfield itself or, more obviously, fast and loose London aristocracy.

Because the laboring classes rarely enter into this picture except as docile servants, there is no need to exclude them from the park or to represent them as a contained class.[39] But despite the narrow section of society displayed in Austen's fiction, the language of class difference was becoming ever more audible during her lifetime. In *Origins of Modern English Society,* Harold Perkin insists that "it was the first five years of peace, between Waterloo and the Queen's trial, that the vertical antagonisms and horizontal solidarities of class came for the first time, clearly, unmistakably, and irrevocably, to supplant the vertical connections and horizontal rivalries of dependency and interest."[40] Additionally, E. P. Thompson describes Austen's writing years as the crystallization of a horizontal class consciousness of laborers; perhaps in response to signs of this growing class solidarity, Austen envisions her society in more traditionally vertical and integrated terms, with an ideal, paternal lord of the manor, a Knightley or a Darcy, or perhaps a chastened and revitalized Sir Thomas who oversees and cares for them all.[41] And yet we don't see much of the estate and its obligations, only the lord and his prospective bride, such that if the emergence of the language of class is repressed or denied in these novels, the old paternal order is envisioned, paradoxically enough, in the privatized ideology of the new class structure, in a bourgeois vision of the single family rather than in terms of a whole class's obligation. These contradictions between a conservative or nostalgic aristocratic vision and a more progressive bourgeois vision become less troublesome from a more distant historical perspective. Resisting the language of the new class-conscious society, Austen conspicuously employs the language of the old, classless, familial, and paternal structures. However, the very society that she envisions in this old language is itself bourgeois, romantic, and privatized; membership in it is based on goodness and morality, not on aristocratic bloodlines, genealogical continuity, or ownership of land. As a clergyman's daughter, sister of a banker, and novelist, Austen falls betwixt and between. As pseudo-gentry, or professional apologist, ideologue for the gentry, Austen celebrates the gentry, while chastising the decadent aristocracy.[42] Austen is at once identified with the pseudo-gentry and, through her brother Edward, with the very wealthy, and she evidently is envious and nervous about that relation; thus, Austen is at once affiliated with the middle classes that will eventually devour the gentry and the aristocracy both, while they are blind to the threat of class consciousness and class conflict from below.[43] (These confusing and contradictory states can only be resolved through multiple or widening historical perspectives, that is, by correlation of Austen and her class(es) in the years between 1815 and 1820, in the twenty years on either side, and the hundred years on either side.)[44]

One barely visible dimension of this class conflict in Austen's novels can be seen in her choice of male protagonists, each of whom, more or less, represents an infusion of capital into the financially ailing rural squirarchy. In fact, the plot of all Austen's novels involves a transfusion of capital into the failing minor gentry; the difference between early and late is that in the early novels, her infusions come from above, from the higher gentry. In the early novels culminating in *Pride and Prejudice,* the heroine marries a man from a higher social and financial station. Darcy, in this view, is a conservative savior, coming to rescue the Bennet family out of the old social past and old social order, that is, from above. (But this conservative figure is equally identified with Pemberley as with ground-rent, the £10,000 a year that make him such a good catch; even in the early novels the conservative association of worth with inherited, titular land appears as both obtrusive and vestigial.) By the time of *Persuasion,* however, the male protagonist comes from an entirely different class, or at least his fortune comes from an entirely different source, not from the inherited estate. Captain Wentworth has acquired his personal fortune by way of prize money; his source of money has been mythologized, through patriotic service, into an acceptable form of accumulation, not through vulgar trade (as was the case with Bingley). Nevertheless, it is only in her last novel that Austen is able to accept the possibility of an influx of capital from below.[45]

We have seen in Austen's presentation of clothing and material objects in general that obvious moral implications are consistently qualified, if not actively undercut, by practical economic and social considerations. Though her stories begin and end with details of income, Austen's procedure is to pass quickly from finance to feelings in the same way that she passes from things to morality. The bulk of her narrative does not focus on the physical details of domestic life so much as it traces intangible feelings, relationships, and change, in short, inner, emotional life. Austen initiates each novel with accurate reports of income and then withholds subsequent details of possession, dress, and appearance in part because her most valued characters are those who, she wants to suggest, cannot be defined solely by their income, class, and habits of acquisition. Nevertheless, the same ideological tension or contradiction between high morality and practical economics, between physical objects and the idealism that would repress them or dissolve them into lessons of conduct, runs through Austen's central subject, courtship and marriage, as well. Marriage in Austen's fiction serves as a practical and even necessary means of survival as well as an idealized locus of emotional fulfillment. Just as financial hardship is never denied in an Austen novel, even while her narrative technique presents the things of necessity only to deny or minimize them, so it is with marriage, for marriage is graphically shown to exist in the realm of economic necessity, and yet the heroines are able to escape or transcend the chains of necessity. Though beauty and wealth are plainly shown to be very important in this fictive world, the heroines' use of wealth is as circumscribed as their use of beauty. More practically acquisitive characters are presented as typical, whereas heroines are presented, economically at least, as anomalous, for they all retain the right to refuse wealthy suitors. Elizabeth at Pemberley, for example, is charmed by the splendor, wealth, and power of the estate, but Austen does everything possible to suggest that Elizabeth must finally base her decision on her need for Darcy. That is to say, even the landed estate of Pemberley, like all of Austen's objects and possessions both great and small, is introduced in order to be repudiated, for Elizabeth must be shown to have chosen Darcy for himself, not for his income or his estate. Within the novels, Austen never questions the value of love any more than she examines private property, wage labor, or capitalism, or any connection between capitalism and romantic love—the latter is the a priori assumption on which the fiction is built. Love is presented as an ideal concern for selfless conduct that will humble the proudest Darcy or Elizabeth, Emma or Knightley, that is, as something fundamentally private, that serves finally as an escape from the world of necessity and its threat of poverty. In Austen's novels, and indeed throughout the nineteenth-century novel, private or domestic romance comes to function as the ideological negation of History, a refuge into a "natural" and "timeless" world of privacy and intimacy. It is through this separation of a private sphere of emotion and a public sphere of money that Austen can resolve the generic differences or tensions between her initial material realism and her concluding romantic comedy. Mary Poovey formulates this tension very well:

> Austen legitimizes romance by making it seem the corrective—not the origin or the product—of individualism. By such narrative magic, Austen is able to defuse the thematic conflict between sense and sensibility—or reason and feeling, or realism and romance—that troubled her earlier works. What is more, by forcing her reader to participate in creating the moral order that governs the novel's conclusion, Austen is able to make this aesthetic "solution" seem, at least momentarily, both natural and right.[46]

We are finally in a position to address the issue with which we began this chapter, the way in which Austen materializes or objectifies her fictive world. It should be clear by now that she clothes her characters in the same way that she fills this world with physical objects: by way of a kind of narrative prestidigitation or ideological slight of hand, writing about clothes only to efface them. Just as with the other things of this world, however necessary they may be, clothes are inevitably shown to substitute for or to distract from something more important. The "Blue Shoes & Nankin Boots" that so impress Mr. Parker in *Sanditon* highlight for the reader the folly of his speculation in real estate, his empty ventures in novelty. Mrs. Elton's pearls and Mrs. Allen's fine gowns function in the same way, calling attention to something more important that is missing, like the dirt on the wall in Portsmouth. At the heart of Austen's descriptive technique lies this central ideological contradiction—that is, the social contradiction that it is the function of ideology to solve or to mask. This technique of contradiction, offering with one hand, withdrawing with the other, or more precisely, revealing a world of commodity while distancing it with moral ideas, at once announces and denies the presence of economic determinism. In short, Austen has created a gestalt picture of a text that from one side appears idealist, and from the other side appears materialist. In this way, then, Austen's characters do and do not live in the material world; they can and cannot rise above it, for Austen insists upon as much as she obscures the cold world of economic necessity. At least in part we may relate this paradox to the dialectic that Lukács finds in the novel, which is at once a representation and an interpretation of the world, simultaneously "is" and "ought." In this respect, Austen's fiction differs from more ordinary satiric formulae, in which lesser characters, who are flawed by greed and acquisitiveness, serve to distinguish the few who are elevated, the socially worthy, morally good, and emotionally loving (which in Austen amount to the same thing). For though her narratives work increasingly to isolate her heroines from the rude world of necessity, Austen never severs their connection with it; rather, their private marriages do not escape that larger, crueler world from which we have been shown they are lucky to have found protection. The oppositions between material and ideal, objects and morals, things and feelings, correspond to the opposition between the external world of necessity and the private, interior world of freedom, and marriage comes to function as a domesticated version of the plot to wrest a highly individualized freedom from the realm of necessity.

2
Proposals of Marriage

Our minds shine not through the body, but are wrapt up
here in a dark covering of uncrystalized flesh and blood;
so that if we would come to the specifick characters of
them, we must go some other way to work.
　　　　　　　　　　　　—Laurence Sterne, *Tristram Shandy*[1]

Jane Austen's novels are about courtship and
marriage, rather than the adventures more
common to male protagonists, as in *The Life and Adventures of Joseph
Andrews* or *The Life and Opinions of Tristram Shandy*. Her plots trace
emotional change, particularly falling in love, and the moment of crisis
toward which the story builds is an internal moment of recognition, a
"comic anagnorisis," to use Robert Heilman's phrase, a moment of
insight epitomized in Elizabeth Bennet's "Till this moment, I never knew
myself" (PP 208).[2] But despite the fact that Austen's particular subject is
intricate emotional change, the range of emotion portrayed in Austen's
novels is still highly circumscribed. In *Sense and Sensibility*, for example,
Elinor Dashwood's response to the knowledge that Edward Ferrars is
finally free to marry her represents an iron control over the public display
of emotions:

> Elinor could sit it no longer. She almost ran out of the room, and
> as soon as the door was closed, burst into tears of joy, which at
> first she thought would never cease. Edward, who had till then
> looked any where, rather than at her, saw her hurry away, and
> perhaps saw—or even heard, her emotion; for immediately after-

wards he fell into a reverie, which no remarks, no inquiries, no affectionate address of Mrs. Dashwood could penetrate. (SS 360)

This passage, and particularly the phrase "almost ran," has been cited to demonstrate the restraint that Elinor, and her author, recommend as appropriate behavior in times of crisis.[3] Firm control over feeling is just what such readers as Charlotte Brontë find most repulsive in Austen, for so Brontë complains in her famous letter to W. S. Williams:

> the Passions are perfectly unknown to her [Austen]; she rejects even a speaking acquaintance with that stormy Sisterhood; even to the Feelings she vouchsafes no more than an occasional graceful but distant recognition; too frequent converse with them would ruffle the smooth elegance of her progress. Her business is not half so much with the human heart as with the human eyes, mouth, hands and feet; what sees keenly, speaks aptly, moves flexibly, it suits her to study, but what throbs fast and full, though hidden, what the blood rushes through, what is the unseen seat of Life and the sentient target of death—*this* Miss Austen ignores; she no more, with her mind's eye, beholds the heart of her race than each man, with bodily vision sees the heart in his heaving breast.[4]

Elinor's almost running provokes this sort of complaint—that Austen portrays feeling not passion, surface not depth.[5] A "distant recognition" characterizes what the reader sees of the interaction between Elinor and Edward, for after partial disclosure of emotion, both characters are withdrawn from scrutiny, into another room and into a daze, which no one can penetrate.[6] Charlotte Brontë implies that the feeling and passion are there, but they remain locked within Austen's creations, hidden from our view. The impression of depth, however, is one that Austen has carefully developed. Though the narrator does not fully describe emotion, that emotion is not negated; rather, it is explicitly hidden. Elinor's tears of joy are indicated, though they are not displayed in public or described in detail. Mixing visual metaphors of display with spatial metaphors of surface and depth, Brontë suggests, on the one hand, that Austen cannot see beneath the surface of her own creations, and, on the other, that what cannot be seen does not exist. Elinor's sister Marianne is given to the same judgment; at their reconciliation, Marianne suggests that Elinor's emotion can be so easily controlled because it is so slight. Marianne further accuses Elinor of substituting "resolution" and "self-command" for feelings, as if the presence of self-command asserts the absence of strong emotion: "You do not suppose that I have ever felt much" is Elinor's response (SS 263). This basic distinction between feeling emotion and displaying it is central to Austen's narrative method, for she will indicate emotion, but she will not display it directly; it is reflected through free indirect discourse, filtered through and mixed with or covered by a narrative voice rather than given directly in dialogue. Elinor's running from the room emblematizes a narrative strategy that turns on withdrawal from the public or social scene into privacy.

This technique of withdrawal or deferral is one of the principal ways by which Austen convinces us of the trueness of her sentiment, by its pointed absence, which is supposed to mark the presence of emotion too strong to show. Her sentiment, it is suggested, is so real, so genuine, it is too fragile to be exposed to public view. The false article can be conveyed fully to the reader, but the genuine article must stay at home, in the heart. Unlike Fielding or Richardson or Burney, who claim that they have told us all, Austen creates the suggestion of depth, that there is more here than meets the eye, just below the exposed surface. Readers are forced to supply their own understanding of what resides inside, beneath the skin. This reliance on imaginative supplement is of course at the heart of all reading experience, but Austen exploits it more than her predecessors, for it is foreign to the chumminess of Fielding's or Sterne's narrator or the intimacy of Richardson's. Austen's habit of exteriorizing the narrative at moments of emotional crisis has the effect of privileging the interior, for what is truly important resides within, even if it cannot be clothed in words. On the one hand, Austen's ability to exteriorize, to move outside her characters, is dependent upon her perfection of a narrative that exploits the technique of free indirect discourse, which results in that happy synthesis of Fielding's realism of assessment with Richardson's realism of presentation. On the other hand, beyond mere technical innovation, this narrative form is determined by the need to represent the inside and the outside of the individual character, representing the antithesis between the feeling individual and the objectified social world.

Such a narrative strategy embodies the increased emphasis on privacy as a social value. Social and architectural historians of the period point to the changing layout of country houses, which, more than ever before, placed a premium on private space, isolated closets for meditation or reading. When bedrooms became connected by halls and corridors, private sleeping quarters were no longer open spaces through which others had to pass. In any number of ways, privacy was coming to be regarded as a desirable privilege of withdrawal, against more traditional insistence on the social or familial, that is, public spaces, public behavior, and public values. In her fiction, Austen can be seen developing a method of narration that both accommodates and respects the new private values and spaces.[7] Additionally, privacy must be understood as well in terms of the ideological privileging of individual autonomy, in that individual character is both valuable and private, exposed and hidden at the same time, showing surface features, while promising depth and complexity.

Once again, our task is to historicize these particular techniques for the representation of feeling and character. We do not want to treat Austen's characters as people and her narratives as reality, by suggesting that she is getting closer to what is real, or that she is more accurate than her predecessors. We have a tendency to turn such narratological and historical issues into psychological ones: Are these characters true to life; can they be approached with depth psychology? Rather we need to see that both the desire and the technology for representing the ordinary subject are, as Michael McKeon has recently shown in great detail, complex historical phenomena.[8] Again, Austen's particular ways of representing feeling must be grounded in history, not seen as technological progress or as a way station toward contemporary individualism. Analogously, as Fredric Jameson argues of a similar narratological revolution in the nineteenth century, Henry James's codification of a depersonalized narrative "is a genuinely historical act . . . [and] part and parcel of a whole ideology."[9]

Austen's emphasis on withdrawal and privacy differs from earlier fiction. Compared with *A Sentimental Journey, The Man of Feeling, The Fool of Quality, The Mysteries of Udolpho,* or with later fiction such as *Wuthering Heights* and *Jane Eyre,* Austen's expression of emotion is much more restrained. Austen never lingers over emotion, in the way that Harley in *The Man of Feeling* is shown to encourage his tears or that our horror is encouraged in Monk Lewis's underground cells of the abbey. To understand fully Austen's choice not to describe emotion, it is necessary to establish first which emotions these restrictions apply to; discussions of Austen's reticence to display emotion rarely if ever distinguish which emotions can and cannot be anatomized. As we shall see, anger, resentment, and humiliation are more commonly and more easily displayed in these novels than are affection and love. Second, the narrative techniques that divert or withdraw the reader's attention from the direct description of strong emotion want examination. We shall trace the scenes of marriage proposals, for these often contain as well as defer dramatic emotional display.[10] Almost all of the novels contain more than one proposal, implicitly contrasting the emotions of failed proposals—anger, resentment, or ridicule—with the affection of successful proposals. Further, comparison of Austen's construction of proposal scenes with the practice of a number of previous novelists will show what Austen has chosen to do. Austen's refusal to write of passion may stem from personal reticence, either because of inexperience or some sense of social decorum, though such motives of reserve are difficult to document. A literary reaction to the excesses of sentimental and gothic fiction, on the other hand, is easier to see, for so much of Austen's early writing parodies such excess. If gothic and sentimental novels fail in their attempt to express grand human passion, Austen suggests that that is because these are areas of human experience that lie outside language. As the narrator of *Mansfield Park* puts it, "there were emotions of tenderness that could not be clothed in words" (MP 369–70).

This survey of representational techniques, when combined with discussions of changing expectations of language (examined in chapter 3), developing concepts of character (chapter 4), and transformations of the institution of marriage (chapter 5), will finally enable us to see clearly the development of emotion. Survey of these diverse social changes is a way of showing some modern emotions coming into being, tracing their gradual appearance in recognizable form. Austen is at the precipice of modernity; it is not so much that she is instrumental, but that the novel itself is, and hers serve as particularly revealing documents in the creation of modern notions of individuality, interiority, intimacy, and romance.

Parallelism of proposal scenes is a technique that Austen always uses. The most familiar example contrasts Darcy rejected and Darcy accepted, but these are only two of five proposals in *Pride and Prejudice*. Austen juxtaposes foolish and intelligent suitors as well as indifferent and affectionate suitors, as in *Northanger Abbey*'s John Thorpe and Henry Tilney or *Emma*'s Mr. Elton and Mr. Knightley. To some degree, doubling is a conventional and necessary part of the suspense found in courtship plots; Sophia faces a kind of choice of Hercules between Blifil and Tom Jones, as does Clarissa between Soames and Lovelace. None of Austen's choices is quite so threatening, though she can increase the stakes: The projected plan for *The Watsons* calls for the impoverished Emma Watson to refuse the rich Lord Osborn's offer of marriage in favor of that of his more modest clergyman. The abundance of proposal scenes suggests that this is a kind of "novel topos," a fixed formula used by writer after writer, and even to our day, proposals are still highly ritualized.[11] As such, there is little room for variation, since we know how such scenes are going to conclude. The conventional nature of these scenes may help explain why each novel's first, failed proposal is always more detailed and more elaborate than the second proposal: by the end, we know pretty much what to expect. Even so, the courtship plots in Austen are plainly constructed around proposal scenes, as the points that long stretches of the novel lead up to and away from. However familiar such scenes are, the courtship plot of *Pride and Prejudice* makes Darcy's second and successful proposal of marriage to Elizabeth the climax of the novel.

Though the courtships of the two sisters are always implicitly compared, *Sense and Sensibility* has only one genuine proposal scene. Edward's proposal is so compressed that nothing but the result is reported:[12]

> How soon he had walked himself into the proper resolution, however, how soon an opportunity of exercising it occurred, in what manner he expressed himself, and how he was received, need not be particularly told. This only need by said;—that when they all sat down to table at four o'clock, about three hours after his arrival, he had secured his lady, engaged her mother's consent, and was not only in the rapturous profession of the lover, but in the reality of reason and truth, one of the happiest of men. (SS 361)

The event that the reader has been waiting for takes place in a narrative hiatus, as Austen assertively refuses to gratify the reader's curiosity. "The reality of reason and truth" is distinctly different from "the rapturous profession of the lover," and rather than attempt the latter, the narrator will only give us the former. This refusal does not transform love into a rational event or discourse, but it asserts that they are of two different orders, and so rapturous profession of love cannot be encompassed in rational discourse. In the novel at hand, this is a sentiment we would expect from Marianne, and, in fact, "Marianne could speak *her* happiness only by tears" (SS 363), with gesture, not with words. The narrator admits of similar difficulty conveying Elinor's feelings:

> But Elinor—How are *her* feelings to be described? . . . she was oppressed, she was overcome by her own felicity;—and happily disposed as is the human mind to be easily familiarized with any change for the better, it required several hours to give sedateness to her spirits, or any degree of tranquillity to her heart. (SS 363)

Colonel Brandon's proposal to Marianne is only rendered by means of a rhetorical question: "with a conviction of his fond attachment to herself, which at last, though long after it was observable to everybody else—burst on her—what could she do?" (SS 378). Just as Sterne refuses to describe the Widow Wadman, Austen seems to suggest that the reader's imagination will succeed where narration or description cannot.[13]

Sterne's *Tristram Shandy* originated in parody of novelistic conventions, as did Austen's first finished novel, *Northanger Abbey*, and in different ways both parody the novel's claim to realism. Sentimental and gothic fictions attempt to render two extremes of emotion, tenderness and pity on the one hand, and horror and disgust on the other. By the time of *Northanger Abbey*, Austen suggests, thirty years of such novels and such novel reading have rendered the language bankrupt for emotion. Austen writes to her sister of a forgotten novel by Miss Owenside, "If the warmth of her Language could affect the Body it might be worth reading in this weather" (L 251), as if her extravagant language is incapable of touching the mind. Katrin Burlin argues that in *Northanger Abbey* Austen indicates that it is better not to attempt to describe emotion at all than to resort to the bathetic language of a second-rate gothic novel:

> For Jane Austen, language is not the appropriate medium for the expression of strong emotion. She *distrusts* the language of emotion: in making the expression of feeling too facile, it dissipates its strength and encourages insincerity and hypocrisy. Language is a corrupt mirror for feeling: it distorts emotion by reflecting it as either grotesquely overblown or excessively shallow.[14]

At every point in this novel, the overly emotional and overly pathetic language of the gothic is ridiculed, and, as we might expect, its proposal scene is narrated in a distant summary, not as the emotional climax that her readers have been awaiting for two hundred and fifty pages: "She was assured of his affection; and that heart in return was solicited, which, perhaps, they pretty equally knew was already entirely his own. . . . a new circumstance in romance, I acknowledge, and dreadfully derogatory of an heroine's dignity" (NA 243).

Northanger Abbey is the most overtly satiric of the six novels and its narrator the most ironic, the most willing to undercut readers' expectations about poetic justice, concluding morals, and displays of emotion. Because of these elements, and perhaps also because Austen is most unsure of her narrative control here, this narrator is difficult to interpret at times. Of Catherine, notably, the narrator's attitude seems to waver between ironic condescension and affection.[15] But even with her simplest heroine, Austen will only describe her emotion from the outside, from her mother's point of view, and not from within: "Catherine, meanwhile,—the anxious, agitated, happy, feverish Catherine,—said not a word; but her glowing cheek and brightened eye made her mother trust that this good-natured visit would at least set her heart at ease for a time" (NA 242). We assume that we can see further than her obtuse mother, that we can penetrate within, imaginatively extending or explicating the emotion that the character is presumed to feel, but however confident we are that we understand what this brightened eye signifies, Austen will not describe it. After the proposal, she is shown, "wrapt in the contemplation of her own unutterable happiness" (NA 243). The reader can see her outside, her feverish look, but even for naive, inexperienced, and silly Catherine, emotion is "unutterable." It is possible that "unutterable" is somewhat ironic here, suggesting inarticulateness as much as ineffability, but if the narrator seems to laugh, it is more likely at the reader's expense than at the heroine's, at the reader's expectations of novels, rather than at Catherine's inability to live up to the romantic hopes of readers trained on Charlotte Smith.

Pride and Prejudice is the first of the novels to utilize the technique of contrasting proposal scenes to full advantage, with five such scenes. All of these scenes are implicitly offered up for comparison, as they contrast with and qualify one another, leading up to the final, dramatic, and characteristically abbreviated proposal of Darcy to Elizabeth. In effect, this set of perspectives on one event not only reveals the possibilities, but it also defines by negation what a proper proposal ought to be, indicating what emotions this scene ought to involve. This process revolves around Elizabeth, whose emotional development is clarified in being proposed to so often, as she passes through Collins's cold and unemotional offer; Darcy's first offer of pride, anger, and resentment; to his final offer, which is tendered with the appropriate affection. In particular, the early proposals reveal the bankruptcy of the language of strong emotion. Collins proposes to Elizabeth in the language of sensibility that Austen ridicules at length in her early parody, *Love and Freindship*. Out of the mouth of a cold and emotionless character comes the speech of a rapturous lover: In his most practiced voice, Collins carefully expresses his fear of running away with his feelings. After he explains himself at his usual length, he concludes: "And now nothing remains for me but to assure you in the most animated language of the violence of my affection" (PP 106—the following sentence moves directly on to Elizabeth's marriage portion of £1,000 at 4 percent interest).

"Violence of affection" is a phrase singled out for particular attention in *Pride and Prejudice*, for it is the phrase Mrs. Gardiner objects to in Elizabeth's description of Bingley and Jane:

> "He was violently in love with [her] only a few days before."
> "But that expression of 'violently in love' is so hackneyed, so doubtful, so indefinite, that it gives me very little idea. It is so often

applied to feelings which arise from an half-hour's acquaintance, as to a real, strong attachment. Pray, how *violent was* Mr. Bingley's love?"

"I never saw a more promising inclination. He was growing quite inattentive to other people, and wholly engrossed by her." (PP 140–41)

Mrs. Gardiner objects to Elizabeth's expression in very much the same way that Austen herself objects to a hackneyed phrase for the protagonist in her niece Anna's novel manuscript: "I wish you would not let him plunge into a 'vortex of Dissipation.' I do not object to the Thing, but I cannot bear the expression;—it is such thorough novel slang—and so old, that I dare say Adam met with it in the first novel he opened" (L 404). "Violence of affection" is also "novel slang," an expression so hackneyed that it no longer signifies the "Thing." Though Elizabeth attempts to parry her aunt's objection with playful irony, she has been caught using the same language as Collins, and both of them, Elizabeth as well as Collins, speak with the conventions of fiction.

The contrast of conventional with spontaneous or natural experience is clearly at work in the marriage of convenience arranged between Charlotte Lucas and Collins. Here both parties carefully observe the established rituals and the proper language, though plainly any "violence of affection" here is verbal, not actual. This scene is quite brief, for all of Collins's pomposity has been displayed before this point:

> In as short a time as Mr. Collins's long speeches would allow, every thing was settled between them to the satisfaction of both; and as they entered the house, he earnestly entreated her to name the day that was to make him the happiest of men; and though such a solicitation must be waved for the present, the lady felt no inclination to trifle with his happiness. (PP 121–22)

If one sympathizes with Charlotte Lucas, his clichés about "the happiest of men" must seem grotesque when applied to a marriage of convenience: "Mr. Collins to be sure was neither sensible nor agreeable; his society was irksome, and his attachment to her must be imaginary. But still he would be her husband"; these rather chilling "reflections were in general satisfactory" for Charlotte (PP 122). To describe this arrangement with the language of sensibility exaggerates the gap between feeling and expression. Both of Collins's proposals form a fine contrast to the real violence of emotion that attends Darcy's proposal to Elizabeth at Huntsford.

Pride and Prejudice's first two proposal scenes are emotionless, but this one is violent, as is apparent from Darcy's first words: " 'In vain have I struggled. It will not do. My feelings will not be repressed. You must allow me to tell you how ardently I admire and love you.' Elizabeth's astonishment was beyond expression" (PP 189). Elizabeth soon finds words, however, making this by far Austen's longest proposal scene, filling a full chapter in contrast to the single sentence in *Sense and Sensibility*. That Elizabeth does find expression for her emotions here indicates that anger, resentment, and humiliation can be expressed or described in full, and it is respect, affection, and love that cannot. So too in the next two novels, the proposals that are angrily refused, Elton's and Crawford's, will be described much more fully than the subsequent proposals that are accepted. Plainly Austen finds it far easier to portray anger than affection. In this present scene, Elizabeth is described with such words as *sorry, resentment, anger, exasperate, distained, indignation, dreadful*, and *angry*; Darcy is described with *surprise, anger, indignation, contemptuously, ashamed, astonishment, incredulity*, and *mortification* (PP 189–93). Both characters are carefully described passing through a great range of emotion. Further, the scene is constructed, not in indirect discourse or free indirect discourse, as are the accepted proposals, but in direct dialogue, making this one of Austen's best, most complete dramatic vignettes, with movement, gesture, facial expression, and timing, all of the details that Austen does not give the next time Darcy proposes:

> Mr. Darcy, who was leaning against the mantle-piece with his eyes fixed on her face, seemed to catch her words with no less resentment than surprise. His complexion became pale with anger, and the disturbance of his mind was visible in every feature. He was struggling for the appearance of composure, and would not open his lips, till he believed himself to have attained it. The pause was to Elizabeth's feelings dreadful. (PP 190)

A similar range of emotion is described, dissected, and lingered over through all of its phases in Elizabeth's subsequent reaction to Darcy's letter. And again the contours of emotional change are minutely described during Elizabeth's meditation over Darcy's portrait and later after her reading of Mrs. Gardiner's letter describing Lydia's marriage. Darrel Mansell has pointed out that all of Austen's heroines receive crucial information through letters, less, one suspects, for grammatological reasons than because the device allows the recipient to respond in private.[16] Even after the heroines have been proposed to, they customarily withdraw into private to examine and absorb what they have just experienced. As is the case with Elinor Dashwood, when Austen's heroines experience powerful emotion, they withdraw into privacy. Austen will not even provide them with a confidant to speak with: Elizabeth's feelings for Darcy are communicated to Jane only after she and Darcy come to an understanding. If these two are not shown declaring their feelings to one another, they do not share these feelings with anyone else either.

Such reticence reflects conventions of courtship that indicate that display of emotion is imprudent.[17] In courtesy literature of the period women are directed to remain passive and are prohibited from showing affection until it has been offered in turn. Austen certainly does not recommend imprudent or premature display of affection, Marianne Dashwood's openness with Willoughby being the obvious case in point. In contrast, Austen recommends slow, painstaking development of a mature, complex emotional attachment, and in the vocabulary she uses to describe this development, she rigorously refuses to call *regard* or *esteem* or *affection love* until it becomes so, even though Marianne Dashwood is offended by Elinor's word *esteem* to describe her feeling for Edward (SS 21).[18] This verbal restraint can be very effective, as when, to return to *Pride and Prejudice*, Elizabeth declares to her father, for the very first time in the novel: " ' I do, I do like him,' she replied, with tears in her eyes, 'I love him' " (PP 376). This statement is just what Austen very rarely lets her heroine say and never directly to the hero. Here Elizabeth is allowed to say to her father what the reader is allowed only to imagine she says to Darcy, for their second proposal scene is far shorter than their first. Once again, as soon as he asks, the narrator intrudes, the narrative is thrown into indirect discourse, and Elizabeth's response is hidden:

> "If your feelings are still what they were last April, tell me so at once. *My* affections and wishes are unchanged, but one word from you will silence me on this subject for ever."
> Elizabeth feeling all the more than common awkwardness and anxiety of his situation, now forced herself to speak; and immediately, though not very fluently, gave him to understand, that her sentiments had undergone so material a change, since the period to which he alluded, as to make her receive with gratitude and pleasure, his present assurances. The happiness which this reply produced, was such as he had probably never felt before; and he expressed himself on the occasion as sensibly and as warmly as a man violently in love can be supposed to do. Had Elizabeth been able to encounter his eye, she might have seen how well the expression of heart-felt delight, diffused over his face, became

him; but, though she could not look, she could listen, and what he told her of feelings, which, in proving of what importance she was to him, made his affection every moment more valuable. (PP 366)

The success of this paragraph can be attributed, at least in part, to Austen's characteristic abbreviation. Although Darcy's proposal serves as the climax of the courtship plot, the event itself can take so little space because it has been prepared for so well. Again, we know what to expect from proposals by this time because we have witnessed so many of them, and a gently ironic reminder of previous failure appears in the phrase, "as sensibly and as warmly as a man violently in love can be supposed to do." In the transformation of emotion through which these two are supposed to have passed, Austen here suggests that for the first time "violently in love" is an accurate description. This phrase serves as a kind of shorthand for the emotions that have previously been absent but are now present. It should also be noted that Austen observes a practical economy of description: To dwell further on this scene risks boring the reader. Austen's success lies in her ability to convey what appears to be genuine emotion, while not allowing its expression to become cloying; so Elizabeth's awkwardness is set alongside her happiness, just as the "violence" of Darcy is gently mocked. Beyond these practical considerations, the difficulty of speech has been given larger proportions here than in earlier scenes, as the event takes place on the edge of silence: "one word from you will silence me on this subject forever." This threat is designed to make all the more dramatic Elizabeth's imperative to speak, but it also serves to highlight the difficulty that lies in making public private, concealed feelings, in expressing emotion. And the narrator indicates that even in such a crisis, the expression is not very fluent, for Darcy as well as for Elizabeth. The truest "expression" of his love is said to be seen on his face, not deciphered from his words.[19] The educated and experienced Darcy finds happiness as "unutterable" as it is for naive Catherine Morland, suggesting that the expression of strong emotion is not something to be taught or learned. Rather, it is as impossible for them as for the narrator, and perhaps even for Austen herself. Austen suggests that this extreme happiness exists, that it can be felt, and that it can be shown to register on the face, but that it cannot be successfully translated into words: In this way, the narrator's refusal to describe the scene mirrors the inadequacy of language within the scene.

Inability to make oneself understood is also apparent in the failed proposal scenes. Here, after all, Darcy does get his message across, and Elizabeth is able to answer. With unsuccessful proposals, however, language is likely to fail because one or more of the participants fails to comprehend the subject of discourse, emotion itself. In *Northanger Abbey*, for instance, John Thorpe manages to propose to Catherine without her ever understanding what he is about. Elizabeth is considerably more frustrated by her inability to make Collins understand her refusal:

> "Really, Mr. Collins," cried Elizabeth with some warmth, "you puzzle me exceedingly. If what I have hitherto said can appear to you in the form of encouragement, I know not how to express my refusal in such a way as may convince you of its being one."
>
> "You must give me leave to flatter myself, my dear cousin, that your refusal of my addresses is merely words of course." (PP 108)

Elizabeth and Collins are unable to communicate because at bottom there is no correspondence between their ideas of marriage. This is not the case with Elizabeth and Darcy, who, we are given reason to believe, come to agree on the subject, but even so, their agreement is difficult to acknowledge and to utter. Elizabeth, in fact, finds it easier to speak with Collins, as she rejects him: "to accept them [your proposals] is absolutely impossible. My feelings in every respect forbid it. Can I speak plainer? Do not consider me now as an elegant female intending to plague you, but as a rational creature speaking the truth from her heart" (PP 109). Elizabeth cannot convey her emotions to Collins because he understands too little, and she cannot convey her emotions to Darcy because he understands too much. This same situation is repeated in *Mansfield Park*, when Fanny Price is caught between Henry Crawford and Edmund Bertram, unable to speak to the former because he cannot understand and to the latter because he can.

Though *Pride and Prejudice* and *Mansfield Park* seem quite dissimilar, their proposal scenes are quite alike. Fanny Price pursued by Crawford is a repetition of Elizabeth pursued by Collins, though Fanny is made more dependent and vulnerable, and so the episode is less comic. *Mansfield Park* is Austen's only novel that seriously threatens to marry off the heroine to the wrong man, and, in this, its oppressive atmosphere comes closest to the early volumes of *Clarissa*, in which Soames preys upon Clarissa. Fanny Price also has the least social and economic status of Austen's heroines, and as a result, she is the most subject to persuasion, having, as a dependent female, to agree and to obey. For this reason, the chapters narrating Crawford's proposals convey an oppressive sense of male authoritarian figures bearing down: "She did not know what to do, or what to think. There was wretchedness in the idea of its being serious; there was perplexity and agitation every way. . . . She was more silent than ever" (MP 304). Fanny appears paralyzed in every way: Not only can she not make herself understood; for several chapters she even has trouble understanding what is happening. She has as much trouble believing Crawford serious, as Collins has with Elizabeth; Fanny "considered it all as nonsense, as mere trifling and gallantry, which meant only to deceive for the hour" (MP 301). If she does not know Crawford's mind, it is suggested that the situation is so bewildering that she does not know her own mind: "She was feeling, thinking, trembling, about every-thing;—agitated, happy, miserable, infinitely obliged, absolutely angry. It was all beyond belief" (MP 302). These pages describe Fanny's frustrating attempt to interpret her situation: "Fanny, meanwhile, speaking only when she could not help it, was very earnestly trying to understand what Mr. and Miss Crawford were at. There was every thing in the world *against* their being serious, but his words and manner" (MP 305). At times of emotional crisis, words are of little help, and the most extreme breakdown of language can be seen in Fanny's letter to Mary Crawford, an inarticulate expression of frustration and confusion:

> I am very much obliged to you, my dear Miss Crawford, for your kind congratulations, as far as they relate to my dearest William. The rest of your note I know means nothing; but I am so unequal to any thing of the sort, that I hope you will excuse my begging you to take no further notice. I have seen too much of Mr. Crawford not to understand his manners; if he understood me as well, he would, I dare say, behave differently. I do not know what I write, but it would be a great favour of you never to mention the subject again. With thanks for the honour of your note. (MP 307)

This whole section of *Mansfield Park* extends the frustrations of Eliza-beth's short interview with Collins over several chapters of broken dis-course and failed communication. In her inarticulateness, Fanny is most like the naive and inexperienced Catherine Morland, but unlike the narrator of *Northanger Abbey*, the narrator of *Mansfield Park* sees most often from within Fanny, giving the reader an often painful sense of disjunction between the internal, private, emotional world of feeling and the external, public, social world of action:

> Fanny knew her own meaning, but was no judge of her own man-ner. Her manner was incurably gentle, and she was not aware how much it concealed the sternness of her purpose. Her diffidence, gratitude, and softness, made every expression of indifference seem almost an effort of self-denial; seem at least, to be giving nearly as much pain to herself as to him. . . . The effect of the whole

was a manner so pitying and agitated, and words intermingled with her refusal so expressive of obligation and concern, that to a temper of vanity and hope like Crawford's, the truth, or at least the strength of her indifference, might well be questionable. (MP 327 and 328)

Fanny Price is the least autonomous of Austen's heroines: prohibited from any action beyond refusal, here, as with Clarissa, even her right to refuse is denied. Austen, in effect, equates autonomy and language, for Fanny cannot exert her will until she develops a voice to speak it, a process that begins in Portsmouth with Fanny's interaction with Susan and then is completed upon her return to Mansfield Park. But even as Fanny comes to assert her opinion and her advice, she never speaks of her affections; they can only be fleetingly overseen from without.

Except for Fanny's and Edmund's conversation about Mary Crawford, however, no one but the narrator speaks in the last section of the novel, which contains the marriage proposal. In the last chapter, the narrator withdraws to a distant judgmental view, distributing rewards and punishments in a Providential manner. Worthy characters are raised to eminence, and the unworthy are banished from the Park. Such a sequence of judgment prohibits close description of Edmund and Fanny's developing intimacy and marriage. In this respect, the union is treated much like that of Colonel Brandon and Marianne in *Sense and Sensibility*: It is almost dismissed as inevitable, part of the narrative closure, merely another reward. This is also no simple history to narrate, for it would not do to dismiss abruptly Edmund's attraction to Mary Crawford, a threat that much of the novel tries to make convincing. Fanny and Edmund's marriage may be inevitable, yet Austen attempts to make it seem hard won.[20] These last few pages follow Edmund, for it is he who must take the initiative, and Fanny's feelings toward him have been revealed long ago. The reader is told what happens to Edmund but is pointedly refused entry into Fanny's state of mind:

His happiness in knowing himself to have been so long the beloved of such a heart, must have been great enough to warrant any strength of language in which he could clothe it to her or to himself; it must have been a delightful happiness! But there was happiness elsewhere which no description can reach. Let no one presume to give the feelings of a young woman on the receiving the assurance of that affection of which she has scarcely allowed herself to entertain a hope. (MP 471)

It is a commonplace that Austen never described a scene between two men supposedly because she could never witness one, and yet here the male character's state of mind concerning love and marriage is given, however briefly, and the female character's feelings are explicitly said to be beyond description. His happiness warrants any strength of language; hers is beyond any strength of language. This juxtaposition of possibilities suggests quantitative as well as qualitative differences: His emotion stretches the capacity to narrate, whereas hers is so fine that it is beyond that capacity, as if Austen's fiction has brought us to the limits of her language and our imagination. Such happiness can be felt, but not told, for to tell it would only be to offer a crude simulacrum. Hereafter, the last two pages of narrative withdraw to distant ground again; the marriage is seen and evaluated by parental authority, Sir Thomas Bertram. We are told that "their home was the home of affection and comfort" (MP 473)—few sentences could say less. The sentence that precedes this one is particularly enigmatic: "With so much true merit and true love, and no want of fortune or friends, the happiness of the married cousins must appear as secure as earthly happiness can be" (MP 473). Their domestic felicity is qualified not just by the religious warning of earthly transience, but also by the qualification "must appear." At the very least, the two characters have been transformed into a private family, and accordingly have been withdrawn from scrutiny.

The weighty tone of Providential judgment and religious warning is absent from Austen's next novel, and in tone and character as well, *Mansfield Park* and *Emma* seem very different. Yet in a number of ways, Emma is not really so far removed from Fanny Price. If Fanny appears isolated in a world of "transcendental homelessness," as Lukács puts it, so too is Emma, though it takes Emma much longer to recognize her abandonment.[21] Like Austen's previous heroines, Emma must endure false proposals and work toward a true one. Whereas Elizabeth endures Collins's emotionless proposal and an angry, humiliating proposal from Darcy before his proper offer, Emma merely varies the order, passing first through an angry proposal from Mr. Elton and an imaginary, emotionless proposal from Frank Churchill before she can accept Mr. Knightley. Elton's proposal is a more complex version of Collins's, selfish, mercenary, and comic, characterized by misunderstanding and resentment. As before, this is the novel's most fully narrated proposal scene, filling four pages of dialogue and description. Emma is mortified, almost at a loss for words: "It would be impossible to say what Emma felt, on hearing this— which of all her unpleasant sensations was uppermost. She was too completely overpowered to be immediately able to reply: and two moments of silence being ample encouragement for Mr. Elton's sanguine state of mind, he tried to take her hand again" (E 131). Emma's unpleasant reflections are not too debilitating, lasting only two moments, and she has herself back under control again in a page. All of these obstructions are typical: Collins, Crawford, and Elton have the power to annoy, but not really to hurt.

It is instead Frank Churchill's absent proposal that is the most interesting variation on the pattern. With considerable encouragement from Churchill himself, Emma has come to fancy that Churchill is in love with her, and, when he parts, she expects a proposal or at least a declaration of love:

> He looked at her, as if wanting to read her thoughts. She hardly knew what to say. It seemed like the forerunner of something absolutely serious, which she did not wish. . . . He stopt again, rose again, and seemed quite embarrassed.—He was more in love with her than Emma had supposed; and who can say how it might have ended, if her father had not made his appearance? (E 260–61)

She is quite willing to believe him "violently in love," though she has more difficulty interpreting her own feelings on the subject:

> "I certainly must [be in love]," said she. "This sensation of listlessness, weariness, stupidity, this disinclination to sit down and employ myself, this feeling of every thing's being dull and insipid about the house!—I must be in love; I should be the oddest creature in the world if I were not—for a few weeks at least." (E 262)

Powerful emotion is so alien to Emma's experience that she is able to interpret as love the mere nervousness, anticipation, or anxiety that this event generates. Emma condemns Jane Fairfax because "her composure was odious" (E 263), though of course Emma herself contentedly comes to admit that her attachment to Churchill is imaginary. It is just this contentedness or control that Emma must lose; as Knightley says, with only slight malevolence: "I should like to see Emma in love, and in some doubt of a return; it would do her good" (E 41). The process of loss begins at Box Hill, where Emma's self-control is finally ruptured. Box Hill is the first time in the novel that any character's emotional distress is exposed. For the first time, Emma is out of control, unable to displace her humiliation, and she cries for the first time:

> He had misinterpreted the feelings which had kept her face avert-
> ed, and her tongue motionless. They were combined only of anger
> against herself, mortification, and deep concern. She had not been
> able to speak; and, on entering the carriage, sunk back for a
> moment overcome. . . . She was vexed beyond what could have
> been expressed—almost beyond what she could conceal. Never
> had she felt so agitated, mortified, grieved, at any circumstance in
> her life. She was most forcibly struck. The truth of his representa-
> tion there was no denying. She felt it at her heart. How could she
> have been so brutal, so cruel to Miss Bates! (E 375–76)

The obvious repetition of key terms here recalls their earlier use: the
momentary embarrassment with Mr. Elton that Emma then called "humiliation" and "mortification," as well as the perturbation of spirits
occasioned by Churchill's departure. In comparison, this humiliation is
presented as genuine, if only because Emma is several times said to be
unable to speak, something that has never happened before. In the midst
of her crisis with Mr. Elton, Emma was never reduced to silence: "Emma
then felt it indispensable to wish him a good night" (E 132). Nor was
Emma without words in dealing with Churchill: "Forcing herself to
speak, therefore, in the hope of putting it [his proposal] by, she calmly"
spoke (E 261). But at Box Hill, extreme emotion is accompanied with
loss of words, a withdrawal into silence and privacy: "she was vexed
beyond what could have been expressed—almost beyond what she
could conceal" (E 376). That characteristic "almost" recalls *Sense and
Sensibility*, where Elinor "almost ran out of the room" (SS 360). Like
Elinor's, Emma's emotion is expressed through tears, not words: "Emma
felt the tears running down her cheeks almost all the way home, without
being at any trouble to check them, extraordinary as they were" (E 376).

This momentary lapse in control begins to reveal to Emma that her
apparent maturity and autonomy have been illusory. Mistress, or so she
thought, of herself, her household, and her village, in fact, she is fully
dependent upon paternal authority. The Box Hill episode exposes a
whole cluster of truths that Emma has kept hidden from herself. In these
respects, *Emma* is Austen's most linear novel, proceeding directly toward
the heroine's moment of anagnorisis, when knowledge of self is revealed
as knowledge of feeling:

> She saw, that in persuading herself, in fancying, in acting to the
> contrary, she had been entirely under a delusion, totally ignorant
> of her own heart. . . . This was the conclusion of the first series of

reflection. This was the knowledge of herself, on the first question of inquiry, which she reached; and without being long in reaching it.—She was most sorrowfully indignant; ashamed of every sensation but the one revealed to her—her affection for Mr. Knightley. (E 412)

Emma is Austen's most fallible heroine, and so, along with Catherine Morland and Elizabeth Bennet, she must be brought down before she can be rewarded. In *Emma,* humiliation prepares for a brilliant proposal scene, for here, more clearly than anywhere else, Austen asserts that love is predicated on a recognition of personal inadequacy. Before she can realize her need for another, Emma must accept the fact that she is not self-sufficient. Paradoxically then, as in countless later romantic novels, the heroine faces a sense of failure or inadequacy just prior to the climactic proposal. Such emphasis on failure may be predicated on conventions of suspense, as at the end of the *Mysteries of Udolpho,* say, but more important, it underscores the heroine's desire, her need for the other. Such conventions help to explain the strong sense of fulfillment apparent in *Emma*'s proposal scene. Compared with other such scenes in Austen, this one is unusually long and unusually expansive, with a wide panorama of place, time, mood, and weather. Austen's proposals usually take place out-of-doors, away from familial supervision, and this one is a most emphatically exterior scene, removed from the claustrophobic interiors of her father's hypochondria, outside in Mr. Knightley's English sunshine.

Mr. Knightley explains himself at some length, though how Emma responds is, as usual, not revealed: "She spoke then, on being so entreated.—What did she say?—Just what she ought, of course. A lady always does.—She said enough to show there need not be despair—and to invite him to say more himself" (E 431). This reticence is as close as Austen gets to narrative coyness, though here it seems in part motivated by Emma's own reticence, for she has much to conceal: "Seldom, very seldom, does complete truth belong to any human disclosure; seldom can it happen that something is not a little disguised, or a little mistaken" (E 431). Complete disclosure certainly does not belong to Austen's proposal scenes. The narrator continues: "but where, as in this case, though the conduct is mistaken, the feelings are not, it may not be very material.—Mr. Knightley could not impute to Emma a more relenting heart than she possessed, or a heart more disposed to accept of his" (E 431–32). Gaps in disclosure, like differences between act and intention, are acknowledged but minimized. Narrator and reader are willing to grant

Emma a little leeway, for her intentions are good. Yet in *Emma* the lingering problem of how to dispose of Harriet has the effect of deferring complete disclosure past the close of the story.

Though Emma's ability to tell the complete truth is said to be doubtful, there are no such doubts about Austen's next heroine, Anne Elliot of *Persuasion*. Austen's published works alternate between fallible and infallible heroines, and the difference between Emma Woodhouse and Anne Elliot seems immense. In this case, the difference is as real as it is apparent, for Anne Elliot is a very different sort of heroine, and different from all of the previous ones, not just Emma. Anne Elliot is older, more mature, more reflective, and, as many commentators have noted, more "romantic," in several senses of the word. As a consequence, she has much less to learn in the course of the novel, less than Emma does, making Anne Elliot a singularly passive heroine and *Persuasion* an actionless book, as, in effect, she waits for Captain Wentworth to come around. Unlike the other novels, *Persuasion* has only one closing, climactic proposal scene (discounting Captain Wentworth's first proposal to Anne, which takes place before the novel begins). Charles Musgrove once proposed, though before the action narrated here, and Mr. Elliot threatens to propose, but no more seriously than Mr. Collins. Captain Wentworth's proposal is what the narrative leads up to, and though it may seem inevitable, it is also made to seem Anne's only hope in dreary and depressed circumstances. In several ways, *Persuasion*'s is Austen's most weighty proposal scene, the least perfunctory, the most significant. In all other respects, in its uses of silence, inexpressibility, and privacy, this scene is the fulfillment of all the elements that Austen has used before.

Persuasion does have two proposal scenes if we count the earlier version of the scene in the canceled chapter 10. Though the first version is much shorter, comparison shows the same devices at work. In the first version, Admiral Croft has brought Anne home, where they meet Captain Wentworth. Having heard that Anne is to marry her cousin, the admiral forces an embarrassed Wentworth to ask Anne whether, when married, she will want to return to Kellynch Hall, and Anne's emphatic denial precipitates their reconciliation:

> [He] looked, with an expression which had something more than penetration in it, something softer;—Her Countenance did not discourage.—It was a silent, but a very powerful Dialogue;—on his side, Supplication, on her's acceptance.—Still, a little nearer—and a hand taken and pressed—And "Anne, my own dear Anne!"—bursting forth in the fullness of exquisite feeling—and

all Suspense & Indecision were over.—They were reunited.
(P 263)

The clumsy narrative device of forced interrogation not only is intrusive, but also gives the mistaken impression that all Wentworth and Anne need is an opportunity to speak with one another.[22] In the final version, however, Anne's overheard conversation with Captain Harville brings to the fore all that Wentworth has misunderstood about her character and about her role as a woman, asserting that it is not simply their failure to meet that has kept them apart, but more importantly, it is their failure to understand one another. The first version, however, contains the rudiments of the much more elaborate, published version, for both scenes involve privacy intruded upon, in an overheard conversation or a family rumor, and both scenes also employ silent supplication and silent acceptance. In *Pride and Prejudice,* Darcy threatens to lapse into silence, and all of the previous proposal scenes have hovered on the edge of silence and inexpressible happiness, but this is the first time that both parties have been able to conduct themselves without words. As a consequence, the first version in *Persuasion* lacks presence; though there are some stage directions concerning Captain Wentworth's chair, "a silent, but a very powerful Dialogue" is too abstract to visualize. Although Austen still refuses to describe their state of mind, the final version is much more complex, detailed, and vivid.

Austen's most significant change in the published version is to stage this delicate event in public, in a crowded room. Anne's family has always intruded into her affairs, and so it is fitting that they should be present here. It is also fitting that the event should be precipitated by overheard remarks. The novel is filled with overheard conversations. Like a Brontë governess, Anne has no status, and so she remains on the periphery of this social world, playing the piano while others dance or nursing a child while his parents dine. On the edge of events, Anne overhears because no one bothers to address her directly, including Captain Wentworth, who earlier was overheard to say that Anne was "so altered he should not have known" her (P 60). Anne also overhears his conversation with Louisa Musgrove, in which Wentworth lectures Louisa on the proper character for women, "the character of decision and firmness" (P 88). It is fitting, then, that Wentworth should overhear Anne's describing the difficulty inherent in the passivity expected from women. In this way, Wentworth's proposal is conducted in a scene of reversal: Anne occupies the center of attention, while he remains at the edge listening, an arrangement that allows Anne to express sentiments she would not ordinarily direct to Wentworth.[23] She directs her thoughts about Wentworth to Captain Harville; Wentworth directs his thoughts about Anne to paper; yet they manage to communicate across the gulf. With five people in the room, formed into three distinct parties that only occasionally interact, this is perhaps Austen's most complicated scene. With Jamesian complexity, messages are passed through intermediaries to interested parties. Beyond the letter itself, all that directly passes between the principals is a look "of glowing entreaty" (P 236). In effect, the two conversations, those of Mrs. Musgrove and Mrs. Croft on long engagements and of Anne and Captain Harville on female patience, perform the same function as Wentworth's question about Kellynch Hall in the first version of the scene. Both conversations metaphorically condense Anne and Wentworth's relationship over nine years, without giving the awkward impression that they have been introduced merely to further the plot. More important, they contribute to the scene's suggestive effect of private business being conducted in public, of powerful emotion communicated while no one else is aware. In this sense, the scene epitomizes Anne Elliot's experience of living at one remove from the social group around her. The scene also epitomizes the essence of Austen's representation of powerful emotion: It is something private, to be enclosed and protected from public scrutiny. As in the first version, Anne accepts Wentworth in silence, with a look, and past this acceptance there is no further dialogue. The narrator recedes into abstraction, and the reader is dismissed into the public crowd of Bath, the "sauntering politicians, bustling housekeepers, flirting girls" (P 241). At this point, we can know no more about them than the strangers passing around them, though as readers we presume to know these characters intimately.[24]

Austen's proposal scenes develop over the course of the six novels, replaying techniques in increasingly complex and sophisticated fashion. The last version in *Persuasion* is a subtle refinement of key elements, reaching what are described as the limits of dialogue and narration itself. Yet to be assessed fully, Austen's scenes need to be compared with novelistic convention in general. In large part, of course, the differences between early eighteenth- and early nineteenth-century representations of marriage in fiction are determined by the changes in the institution of marriage itself. In Defoe, for example, marriage is a much more practical, economic venture than in Austen. Moll Flanders's account of her first marriage is starkly pragmatic: "he would have me, and I was not oblig'd to tell him, that I was his Brother's Whore, tho' I had no other way to put him off; so I came gradually into it, to his Satisfaction, and behold, we were Married." After a single sentence describing the wedding night,

Moll continues: "It concerns the Story in hand very little to enter into the farther particulars of the Family, or of myself, for the five Years that I liv'd with this Husband; only to observe that I had two Children by him, and that at the end of five Year he Died."[25] Not all fictional wives in this period are quite as matter of fact as this, but the lack of particularity noticeable in the phrase, "this Husband," is also apparent, though for different reasons, in *Tom Jones*. In Fielding's novel, the union of Tom Jones and Sophia Western performs more of an ethical service than an emotional one; this marriage is offered as an emblem of the union of practical and speculative knowledge, prudence and wisdom. Indeed, in the vast bulk of eighteenth-century novels, marriage is used as a narrative device of formal closure or morally symbolic closure rather than as an emotional climax. The novels in which romantic interest is of paramount importance, Austen's most influential models, are those of Richardson and Burney, with whose proposal scenes Austen was very familiar.

As with everything else in Richardson, what is immediately noticeable about his proposal scenes is their size: Sir Charles Grandison's proposal to Harriet Byron is ten times the length of Austen's longest scene and is proportionately more detailed. The first person narration of epistolary fiction allows for much more self-examination, the sort of reflection that Austen refuses to render. In *Sir Charles Grandison*, between the hero's declaration of his love and his proposal, Richardson interposes three letters, one, from Harriet's confidant Lady G, anatomizing the declaration. In addition, Richardson does not concentrate marriage proposals into one scene as does Austen, but builds up to the event with a long series of negotiations; Grandison must first approach Harriet's friends to discuss the possibilities of discussing the possibilities of marriage with Harriet herself. In *Pamela* too, a gradual turning of Mr. B. toward the idea of marriage is drawn out, in place of a sudden conversion experience. Even then, half the book has yet to run, for Richardson tracks Pamela and Harriet Byron long after they are married. Richardson is concerned to explore the whole range of courtship and marriage, whereas Austen stops at the conclusion of courtship. The same is true of proposals, in that Austen leads up to the offer itself and then withdraws, whereas Richardson describes the whole scene in vivid detail from entrance to exit, leaving little to the reader's imagination. Pamela's full description relates her every emotion, leading up to this climax of religious transcendence:

> O the Joy that fills my Mind on these proud Hopes! on these delightful Prospects!—It is too mighty for me; and I must sit down to ponder all these Things, and to admire and bless the Goodness of that Providence, which has, thro' so many intricate Mazes,

made me tread the Paths of Innocence and so amply rewarded me, for what it has itself enabled me to do! All Glory to God alone be ever given for it, by your poor enraptur'd Daughter![26]

Not only is *Pamela* more explicitly religious and didactic, but Richardson shows no doubt that even religious rapture can be fully rendered in such scenes.[27]

The proposal scenes in *Clarissa* are even more detailed and more thoroughly anatomized, now by several correspondents.[28] The motives and the responses of each participant can be revealed and explored for the benefit of each confidant, as when Lovelace describes for Belford the effect his sudden offer of marriage has upon Clarissa:

> I never beheld so sweet a confusion. What a glory to the pencil, could it do justice to it, and to the mingled impatience which visibly informed every feature of the most meaning and most beautiful face in the world! She hemmed twice or thrice; her look, now so charmingly silly, then so sweetly significant; till at last the lovely teaser, teased by my hesitating expectation of her answer, out of all power of articulate speech, burst into tears.[29]

Again, there is no suggestion that either Lovelace's or Richardson's pencil cannot do justice to the scene. Such confidence in narration is most apparent in the proposal scenes of *Sir Charles Grandison*, which are many and massive, leisurely in their pace and luxurious in their detail. The novel abounds in proposals, for Harriet Byron is a much pursued woman, and even Sir Charles has his share: Not only does he propose to both heroines, but another woman proposes to him. These scenes are also highly complicated, involving a set of rules and stratagems so intricate that the negotiations for marriage to Lady Clementina take up the central third of the novel. Though his offer to Harriet Byron is less complicated, it too takes up more than a hundred pages. This is, without doubt, the grandest proposal scene in fiction: Richardson and his correspondents savor every moment, and their volubility conveys the impression that nothing has been left out. The only complication to this scene lies in Sir Charles's love for Lady Clementina and the question of his ability to transfer his affections to Harriet, a complication that affords Sir Charles the opportunity to explain himself at length. If the shortest possible rendition of this event is the fairy tale formula used in *Mansfield Park*, "they married and lived happily ever after," *Sir Charles Grandison*'s rendition is the longest possible. Richardson's last novel suggests why these scenes and emotion cannot be successfully clothed in words: The narrative asserts that Harriet Byron can sit down and write at enormous length and in great detail of transcendent emotion. She calmly transcribes her changing complexion, her apprehensions of fainting, her tears, her inability to speak, and her motionlessness. Whole pages intervene between Harriet's beginning a sentence to Grandison and her finishing it. In the end, after some twenty pages of intimate exchange, Grandison finally puts before her a yes or no proposition, and yet it is another full page before she can get her yes out:

> CAN you say, that the man before you is the man whom you CAN, whom you DO, prefer to any other?
>
> He stopt; expecting my answer.
>
> After some hesitations, I have been accustomed, Sir, said I, by those friends whom you so *deservedly* value, to speak nothing but the simplest truth. In an article of this moment, I should be inexcusable, if—
>
> I stopt. His eyes were fixed upon my face. For my life I could not speak; yet wished to be able to speak—
>
> *If, If what*, madam? and he snatched my hand, bowed his face upon it, held it there, not looking up to mine. I could then speak— If thus urged, and by SIR CHARLES GRANDISON—I did not speak my heart—I answer—Sir—I CAN—I DO. I wanted, I thought, just then, to shrink into myself.[30]

Austen knew *Grandison* backward and forward, and she also knew the novel through its many later imitations, the most important of which are Fanny Burney's. Burney's novels come closer to the norm of popular eighteenth-century novels of "love interest," for they are less didactic, less original, and less idiosyncratic than Richardson's, and so it is fair to regard *Evelina, Cecilia,* and *Camilla* as representative of the generation of novels preceding Austen's. *Evelina,* Burney's first and best novel, is a *Sir Charles Grandison* writ small. Evelina is too artless and naive to indulge in the sophisticated self-analysis of Clarissa or Harriet Byron, and so the proposal scenes are substantially shorter, though they are still composed of elevated diction:

> "I esteem and I admire you above all human beings!—you are the friend to whom my soul is attached as to its better half! you are the most amiable, the most perfect of women! and you are dearer to me than language has the power of telling!" . . . I cannot write the scene that followed, though every word is engraven on my heart. . . . he drew from me the most sacred secret of my heart![31]

Much is reminiscent of Richardson here: the superlatives and extravagant language in general, the tears and paralysis (Evelina is "sunk, almost lifeless"), the generosity of the "Patrician Hero," which is matched only by the heroine's gratitude.[32] This style is not naturalistic, but the description does stop when we are told that it cannot be written. In both *Cecilia* and *Camilla,* where Burney shifts from a first person epistolary form to a third person narrative, the proposal scenes grow much longer: *Evelina's* one page turns into seventeen in *Cecilia.* The latter scene is also more elaborate, for it is precipitated by Cecilia's apostrophe to Delville's dog, which is overheard by the master himself, rendering all three "speechless." In this novel as well as in *Camilla,* declarations of love and proposals fall halfway through the story, with much misunderstanding and exigency of plot separating the protagonists before they can be reunited at the end; again as in Richardson, proposals do not function as a concluding goal, but are simply part of a continuing melodrama designed to provoke a flood of emotion at the end. As Austen summarizes the form in her burlesque "Plan of a Novel," "The Tenderest & completest Eclaircissement takes place, & they are happily united" (MW 430). It is a commonplace of Burney criticism that her style gets more artificial with each passing novel, with *Camilla* employing the delicate sensibility of the sentimental novel:

> "O Edgar," she cried, "how little can I merit such a gift! yet I prize it . . . far, far beyond all words."
>
> The agitation of Edgar was, at first, too mighty and too delicious for speech; but his eyes, now cast up to heaven, now fixed upon her own, spoke the most ardent, yet purest felicity; while her hand, now held to his heart, now pressed to his lips, strove vainly to recover its liberty. "Blest moment!" he at length uttered, "that finishes for ever such misery of uncertainty! that gives my life to happiness . . . my existence to Camilla!"
>
> Again speech seemed too poor for him. Perfect satisfaction is seldom loquacious; its character is rather tender than gay; and where happiness succeeds abruptly to long solicitude and sorrow, its enjoyment is fearful; it softens rather than exhilarates. Sudden joy is sportive, but sudden happiness is awful.[33]

This scene repeats *Grandison's* scrutiny of emotion, though here the task of scrutiny has fallen to an omniscient narrator rather than a letter writer/participant. When Camilla herself relates the particulars of this scene to her sisters, her emotion is expressed in tears: "now hiding in their bosoms the blushes of her modest joy, now offering up to Heaven the thanksgiving of her artless rapture, now dissolving in the soft tears of the tenderest sensibility, according to the quick changing impulses of her natural and lively, yet feeling and susceptible character."[34]

The late eighteenth-century novel dissolves in tears, as weeping becomes a sign of inexpressible sentiment; the narrator of *Camilla* asserts that "Tears were the only language that could express the fullness of joy which succeeded to so much sorrow."[35] As sentimental novels attempt to portray the extremes of pathos, reliance on ineffability becomes more and more common; in Mackenzie's *The Man of Feeling*, Harley's response to an act of charity is silence: "There were a thousand sentiments;—but they gushed so impetuously on his heart, that he could not utter a syllable."[36] This novel contains no proposal scene because Harley's feelings are so delicate that he cannot bring himself to speak on such a subject. When such scenes do occur, as in Henry Brooke's *The Fool of Quality*, they are accompanied with "unspeakable ardour," "indescribable sweetness," and "a plenteous shower of tears."[37] Though gothic and sentimental novels would seem to strive for antithetical effects, when it comes to their proposals of marriage, they are similarly weepy; compare Brooke, "kneeling down, I gently took one of her hands, and pressing it between mine, I bathed it in a silent shower of tears,"[38] with Radcliffe's *The Mysteries of Udolpho*, "Valencourt sighed deeply, and was unable to reply; but, as he pressed her hand to his lips, the tears, that fell over it, spoke a language, which could not be mistaken, and to which words were inadequate."[39]

When we look over a century of proposal scenes in fiction, they tend to blend into one another. Most of them seem closer in style to Sidney's *Arcadia* than to Austen's novels, as novels work with little variation in a fixed form.[40] This is not surprising, for there is a limited number of ways to say "come live with me and be my love." Like the elegist, the novelist attempts to break through traditional forms of expression to renew one more time the feeling of grief or love. But where the elegist has the sanction of traditional form, lament, remembrance, and consolation, such a form is not supposed to be available to the novelist. As is signaled by its name, the ideology of the novel celebrates novelty, uniqueness, and individuality; the genre presupposes that its protagonists are unique, though they have a tendency to propose marriage to one another in very much the same language (just as we have a tendency to do in real life, though here too we presuppose the uniqueness of individuals). But in Austen's novels, distinctive character is emerging in proposal scenes, for Emma's frankness to Knightley could not be Fanny's nor even Elizabeth's. In part this variation is due to the different function of marriage in

Austen's novels; unlike Smollett or Burney or Smith or Reeve, Austen does not use marriage solely as the formal closure of a new comic plot. Rather, Austen's marriages are like the "choice of life" in *Rasselas*. They are presented not merely as the reward to a process completed, but rather as a fulfillment; Julia Prewit Brown argues persuasively that Austen's are the first novels to "assert the cultural significance of marriage and family."[41] That is to say, in Austen's fiction, marriage is coming to assume a different ideological burden than it had in novels earlier in the century.

Though Austen focuses more exclusively upon courtship than her predecessors, and though she places much greater importance upon marriage itself, her proposal scenes are much shorter. To some degree, through sentimental and gothic fiction, with their exaggeration of pathos and the consequent admission of ineffability, these scenes had grown much shorter than Richardson's. But Austen's proposals are not just short: the narrators consciously and overtly refuse to tell us what happens. In this practice of refusal, Austen is not alone at the end of the eighteenth century. In Maria Edgeworth's *Belinda*, for example, a novel that Austen goes out of her way to praise in *Northanger Abbey*, the long expected reconciliation between Belinda and Clarence Harvey takes place at the very end of the novel, and neither character is allowed to speak; Lady Delacourt parodies lengthier proposal scenes:

> Fear nothing—you shall have *time* enough to become accustomed to Clarence. Would you choose that I should draw out the story to five volumes more? . . . A declaration of love, you know, is only the beginning of things; there may be blushes, and sighs, and doubts, and fears, and misunderstandings, and jealousies without end or common sense, to fill up the necessary space, and to gain the necessary *time*.[42]

Similarly, in Elizabeth Inchbald's *A Simple Story*, the concluding proposal of marriage is equally curtailed: "Whether the heart of Matilda, such as has been described, *could* sentence him to misery, the reader is left to surmise—and if he supposes that it did not, he has every reason to suppose their wedded life was a life of happiness."[43] Though Sir Walter Scott's *Waverley* hardly qualifies as a domestic novel of courtship and marriage, its proposal scene is equally curtailed: "We will not even trouble the reader with the hum-drum details of a courtship Sixty Years since. It is enough to say, that, under so strict a martinet as the Baron, all things were conducted in due form."[44]

Austen's juvenilia parodies a generation of overblown language of sentimentality from fiction, implying that such novelists had used up the language of emotion. If this most important emotion cannot be expressed well, Austen and contemporary novelists imply, it ought not be expressed at all. Further, there are indications in her novels of cultural or social or perhaps even personal reticence about displaying the extremes of emotion. Women are taught in Austen's generation and in her novels that it is imprudent to expose one's emotion; where women are conventionally prevented from giving any indication of preference until the man makes his choice, how are women, as Fanny Price complains to Edmund Bertram, expected to respond when he does make his choice? The dangers of speaking what one feels are graphically displayed in the unhappiness that is visited upon Marianne Dashwood, and Austen stresses that the Dashwood sisters differ not in the presence of strong feelings, but rather in the expression of strong feelings.

This distinction is clear from what Austen chooses to tell us. That is to say, though it remains hidden from Marianne and from other characters (which could not be the case in an epistolary novel), Elinor's emotion is displayed before the reader by way of free indirect speech.[45] Austen's contribution to narrative form has been attributed by several critics to her development of the technique of free indirect speech.[46] This technique, situated on a middle ground between direct and indirect quotation, enables much of Austen's irony, by mocking or mimicking the speech of such characters as Miss Bates, under the authority of the narrator. But for the present discussion, what is most important about free indirect speech is that it allows Austen's narrator free and fluid access to her characters' consciousness, though it is not often directly signaled either grammatically or syntactically.[47] Because it is often difficult to determine whether a judgment originates with the narrator or with the character, the overall effect of Austen's use of this device is to dissolve the rigid distinctions between narrator and character, between object and subject. In his discussion of a passage from *Mansfield Park*, Roy Pascal demonstrates how Austen uses free indirect speech to convey subjectivity:

> The psychological effect is marked. At first the narrator is her [Fanny Price's] interpreter, and when her own words are given, they only have FIS [free indirect speech] form; we are thus made to feel her modesty and shyness, for it seems that the words have to be coaxed out of her. Even when she speaks up, she seems hardly able to look at Edmund, and can hardly arrogate the self-assertive "I" for herself.[48]

Austen's particular subject, female emotional change, is crucially dependent upon free indirect discourse because of the social insistence on female passivity: men are given full license to express their thoughts (within limits); women must rein in theirs. Austen thus has the narrative technique, the technical wherewithal to expose her heroines' emotions at the climax, and yet she chooses not to, in either direct, indirect, or free indirect discourse. Instead her narrators obtrusively withdraw from the scene, because Austen so values privacy and individuality that she protects her characters from inquisitive readers. Marilyn Butler, however, argues differently of *Emma*:

> Although so much of the action takes place in the inner life, the theme of the novel is skepticism about the qualities that make it up—intuition, imagination, original insight. . . . The technical triumph is to employ the character-centered format, to place the action almost wholly within the heroine's consciousness, to enlist (as in the subjective tradition) the reader's sympathy; and at the same time, largely through the medium of language, to invoke the reader's active suspicion of unaided thought.[49]

Margaret Kirkham raises some problems with this argument: "According to Butler, having discovered how to use the 'indirect free style', Austen found it an embarrassment because it did not fit the moral purpose attributed to her. . . . Austen developed the means of presenting the non-rational aspects of the inner life of individuals, but, because she distrusted them, she found she had invented a technique she did not want."[50] Much of this difficulty can be attributed to the historical and causal assumptions about technical innovation as the means of change: that is, that Austen's novels, themes, and morals are the consequence of the technical innovation, and not the other way around, that it is the emerging individual subject that necessitates a different mode of representation. Free indirect discourse would be of little consequence to Fielding's Tom Jones, who has no consciousness to be presented, by any technique, for he is the creation of, the tool of, and the possession of a supremely authoritarian narrator, who has no need to share that authority with his character. In Austen's novels, however, where the notion of the individual is so powerful, we can see a contradiction at work: Individual character is both valuable and private, exposed and hidden at the same time, showing surface features, while promising depth and complexity. What is most valuable about individual character is located precisely in those interior qualities that cannot be easily exposed to public view, the feelings, sentiments, fineness of character, and perception. We are directed not to judge character by exterior qualities, wealth, and possessions or by female accomplishments picked up at a finishing school; rather we (and the male protagonists) are to discover the delicately valuable qualities of the female protagonist after lengthy familiarity or intimacy that only can lead to gradual understanding. At best, what Austen tries to do with her use of free indirect discourse is to offer us an occasionally brief "sample" of the fineness of her characters' feelings and perceptions, but the narrative will not linger in this interior region, exposing them for long to open air and public view.

If Austen is not "embarrassed" by the technique of free indirect discourse, her use is still quite restrained. Pascal notes that although Austen uses free indirect discourse to convey subjectivity or thought, she rarely does so in an emotionally colored style, as later nineteenth-century writers do: That is, thought is conveyed as rational and objective, in grammatically correct sentences, and not in a broken or confused fashion to represent differing states of mind. Also, Austen does not render her characters' response to their environment, for thought is abstracted from any physical situation.[51] Thus emotion itself is something idealized by Austen, for emotion must always remain something of an abstraction— joy and sorrow—and it has nothing to do with the body. It remains an entirely dematerialized phenomenon.

Thus in the narrative itself, Austen acknowledges the presence of strong feeling but doubts the efficacy of describing or transcribing these emotions. At best she can claim with Anne Elliot and Captain Wentworth that, although her words are earthbound, their emotions are transcendent. Her strategy is to bring her reader to the edge of this scene and merely to outline or sketch broadly what it might contain, but never, as in Burney or Richardson, does she attempt to analyze or explain. I attribute this technique to a conscious rhetorical strategy, rather than to personal repression, because it is consistent with every other formal feature of her novels, all of which place the one happy marriage just outside the narrative, on the verso, as it were, of the last page. The situation of Austen's proposal scenes then is not unlike that of Wordsworth's "The Solitary Reaper." Both writers take their readers to the edge of a prospect, but no further, because to intrude closer would only destroy the intimacy of the scene. The only way to protect the privacy of the scene is to withdraw, preserving it in the imagination or memory:

> The music in my heart I bore
> Long after it was heard no more.

3
Limits of Language

O who has deeply felt, deeply, deeply! & not fretted &
grown impatient at the inadequacy ⟨of Words to Feeling,⟩
of the symbol to the Being?—Words—what are they but
a subtle *matter*? and the meanness of Matter must they
have, & the Soul must pine in them, even as the Lover
who can press kisses only on his this the garment of one
indeed beloved . . . O what then are Words, but articulated Sighs of a Prisoner heard from his Dungeon! powerful only as they express their utter impotence!
                            —Samuel Taylor Coleridge, *Notebooks*[1]

In the first important study of Jane Austen,
Mary Lascelles writes of Austen's language as
an inheritance from Samuel Johnson: "To us Jane Austen appears like
one who inherits a prosperous and well-ordered estate—the heritage of a
prose style in which neither generalization nor abstraction need signify
vagueness, because there was close enough agreement as to the scope
and significance of such terms."[2] With its suggestions of literary inheritance and succession, this is an attractive and comforting metaphor, but
it is also an ambiguous one. On the one hand, it is misleading to think of
language as something to be handed down, for, in this case, at least three
generations intervene between father (Johnson, born 1709) and daughter (Austen, born 1775), and however generous the father, language is
not a static property that can be willed away intact. Rather, as Johnson
discovered writing his *Dictionary*, language is changeable and unfixable,
the very antithesis of real property.[3] On the other hand, there is considerable evidence to suggest that over the course of this period, language did
come to be conceived as a kind of property, for in the hands of school-
masters, booksellers, linguists, and lecturers on elocution, language was
something that could be objectified, packaged, sold, and bought. In
short, along with Wedgwood china, Packwood's razor strops, and other

consumer goods in eighteenth-century England, language came to be commodified.

After Locke, ideas of language underwent considerable revision in eighteenth-century England, a transformation that underscores the inevitable fact of linguistic change and that in turn undermines notions of literary continuity and tradition, as embodied in Samuel Johnson's "well-ordered" verbal estate. We should, therefore, be wary of letting a too hasty identification between one particular writer and her precursor stand in the way of our precise historicizing of concepts of language. From this view, it should not be surprising that in her view of language Austen is closer to her contemporaries, that is, closer to Wordsworth and other early Romantics, than she is to Johnson. Furthermore, assumptions similar to Lascelles's concerning Austen's confident, all-powerful, Johnsonian language underlie some influential misinterpretations of her work. For example, in *Sense and Sensibility*, Marianne Dashwood explains, "sometimes I have kept my feelings to myself because I could find no language to describe them in but what was worn and hackneyed out of all sense and meaning" (SS 97). As with many of Marianne's sentiments, this idea is somewhat suspect, as Stuart Tave claims in *Some Words of Jane Austen*: "To be without the word is to be without the thing. . . . In the reality and in the language of Jane Austen there are degrees of exactness that must be found to meet the purposes of life."[4] But Marianne is by no means the only figure in Austen who cannot find language adequate to her feelings, because all of the heroines and even the narrators at times complain of similar difficulty. This frustration with "worn" language echoes contemporary Romantic poets, who frequently express similar frustration. Throughout the eighteenth century there is a growing sense of "the deficiencies of language," as Wordsworth puts it in his famous note to "The Thorn."[5] This common ground that Austen shares with Romanticism needs to be explored, because to ignore Austen's admission of inexpressibility is to miss as well the ways in which Austen projects emotion that she cannot clothe in words, even while she will attempt obliquely to indicate its existence. In the same way that Austen introduces physical objects only to withdraw them or leads up to proposal scenes in order to defer them, Fanny Price's feelings can only "be half acknowledged" (MP 370), that is to say, indicated but not described.

Later eighteenth-century laments concerning the inadequacy of language to express sentiment are intimately connected with concurrent attitudes toward the individual, interior feeling, and privacy, for these laments reflect the distinction or separation between language and feeling, between an external or social system of language and an interior world of

self and emotion. The larger, more pervasive trends toward interiorization and privatization in this period point out, in any number of ways,
how the significant life of individuals seems to be moving inward, away
from social and communal action, toward a life of distant spectating and
feeling. This exteriorization of language (the dissociation of language and
thought) and interiorization of feeling (the dissociation of feeling and
language) have a great deal to do with the process by which language as a
subject of investigation and discussion came to be reconceived as an
object that could be analyzed, its signs and sounds deciphered and its laws
mastered. Another side to this investigation meant that language as an
object could be sold, that is, language was objectified into something
printed and packaged, sold and bought, in primers, grammars, spelling
books, and lectures on rhetoric and elocution. Of Austen's novels, these
patterns and changes figure most prominently in *Mansfield Park,* to which
we shall turn at the end of this chapter. But first, in order to outline this
Romantic conception of language and Austen's affinity with it, we need
to trace the growing awareness through the century of the limits of
language and, second, show that Austen shares this sense of the inadequacy of language. Both of these ideas can be demonstrated through
changes in the two prominent metaphors used to describe language: the
wealth of language and the ability of language to clothe thoughts in
words.[6]

Murray Cohen chronicles later eighteenth-century writers' anxiety "that
language has been impoverished, . . . that language is too poor for great
literature."[7] From classical times, rhetoricians, poets, and linguists have
characterized the relative wealth or poverty of their language, usually in
order to boast of its riches. But whereas early eighteenth-century writers
routinely commend the wealth or power of their language, later
eighteenth-century writers lament its poverty. The aristocratic vocabulary of Augustan poetics—rich, wealthy, opulent, luxuriant, powerful—
is unlikely to appeal to many Romantic writers, if only because they no
longer seek to identify with and to appeal primarily to the very wealthy,
the Ormands and Howards for Dryden, the Burlingtons and Bathursts for
Pope. This sense of impoverishment, however, is not just a matter of
changing vocabulary, for it suggests a change in the conception of language, which involves a recognition of limits past which words cannot
go.[8] The issue of limits can be discerned in the various measures of linguistic wealth, which range from simple estimates of the stores in the lexi-
con; that is, English has a larger vocabulary capable of more subtle shades
of meaning than French or Latin.[9] Wealth can also refer to less measur-
able estimates of the expressibility of a language. Throughout eighteenth-

century English linguistics, North American Indian languages, for instance, are described as impoverished, not only because they have few words, but also because it is assumed that few ideas can be expressed in these languages. Like the savages who use them, these tongues are incapable of sophisticated utterance.[10] A third yet more abstract measure of linguistic wealth estimates the expressibility of language per se. Instead of comparing one European language with another, or modern with classical languages, late eighteenth-century writers often weigh language against thought. In such comparisons, language is often said to be incapable of fully representing individual thought.

The inability of language to encompass thought is an issue that arises only when it is assumed that the primary function of language is to convey thought. Many seventeenth-century theorists accepted the premise that words represent things and so stand for reality, whereas Locke argued that language forms a mirror for thought. It is only after Locke sought to explain speech as a psychological phenomenon that the capacity of language to contain thought became a consideration. As Hans Aarslef has shown, such questions are intimately bound up with the unending debates over the origin of language and whether word or thought has historical priority.[11] The gradual but thorough abandonment of biblical explanations of speech enabled eighteenth-century linguists to speculate freely about the origin and development of language, especially its "invention," an idea that had hitherto been heretical in the face of the account in Genesis. Whether men first thought or first spoke has bearing on the question of whether thought is dependent upon the structure of language or whether language is dependent upon the structure of thought. In addition, concern with language development encouraged comparison between ancient and modern languages, as well as European and "primitive" (i.e., non-Western) languages, and even human and animal languages. For Hugh Blair, James Beattie, Adam Smith, Thomas Sheridan, Lord Monboddo, and especially Jean-Jacques Rousseau and Gottfried Herder, such pairs lead to a valorized opposition of natural and artificial language, with natural emerging as the ideal from which we have degenerated. Their explanations are entirely different, yet Monboddo and Sheridan concur with Rousseau and Herder that language has degenerated down to the present; all languages are subject to "degeneracy," observes Monboddo, and "our language will necessarily grow worse, and become at last quite barbarous."[12] For Monboddo and Sheridan, corruption succeeds a fall from the perfection of classical culture; for Rousseau and Herder, it follows a fall from the primordial state of nature. But whether the cause is classicism or primitivism, all four argue vigorously that theirs is an age of linguistic decline. Herder and

Rousseau claim that the more sophisticated, artificial, and social languages become, the further words fall from natural and original sincerity. In short, they argue that language is freshest, purest, and best in its infancy, exactly the opposite from what Dryden argued a century earlier. For Herder, language was originally an appropriate medium for the natural expression of passion and poetry, but it is no longer.[13] These philosophic matters may seem quite removed from Austen, who most likely had little familiarity with many of these writers and certainly had no fully articulated theory of language. Nevertheless, *Mansfield Park*, in which "there were emotions of tenderness that could not be clothed in words" (MP 369–70), is a domesticated expression of the same sense of the limits of language that Wordsworth epitomizes in *The Prelude*, of which he writes, "in the main / It lies far hidden from the reach of words" (1805, III, 184–85).[14]

It is often argued that the advent of new science brought on a pervasive distrust of language, and yet Romantic poets, most notably Wordsworth, are far more distrustful of language than their Augustan precursors.[15] Dryden and Pope are closer in time to Sprat, Glanvill, Wilkins, and Locke, writers for whom the deception of language is a regular theme, but nevertheless it is Wordsworth and not Dryden who writes of "the sad incompetence of human speech" (1850 *Prelude*, VI, 593). Dryden celebrates the "riches" of language, whereas in the "Essays Supplementary to the Preface" to *The Lyrical Ballads*, Wordsworth complains of the "Poverty of language."[16] In his *Defense of the Epilogue* (1672), Dryden examines the "improvement of our language," especially its "receiving new words":

> 'Tis obvious that we have admitted many: some of which we wanted, and therefore our language is the richer for them, as it would be by importation of bullion; others are rather ornamental than necessary, yet by their admission the language is become more courtly, and our thoughts better dressed.[17]

Dryden claims that in his day English is "more refin'd" than in the days of Ben Jonson, and most assuredly since the days of Chaucer, just as he asserts that his own translations show an improvement over the "poverty of his [Virgil's] language."[18] Pope similarly commends the richness of English:

> Pour the full Tide of Eloquence along,
> Serenely pure, and yet divinely strong,
> Rich with the Treasures of each foreign Tongue.[19]

Verbal richness for Pope is not synonymous with the classical and medi-
eval idea of *copia,* which in rhetoric and poetics signifies a prized abundance or a cornucopia of words. In the *Essay on Criticism,* Pope does not
recommend a simple lushness in the sense of a fullness or opacity of
language:

> *Words* are like *Leaves;* and where they most abound,
> Much *Fruit* of *Sense* beneath is rarely found.
>
> (I, 274; ll. 309–10)

Many words are not automatically better than few, but still, neither
Pope nor Dryden ever shows concern for the adequacy of language, or its
capacity to express their thoughts; on the contrary, when Pope compli-
ments William Murray, he is "Grac'd . . . with all the Pow'r of Words"
(IV, 239; Epistle I, vi, l. 48). Other Augustans such as Addison clearly
share this confidence in their language and its powers:

> Words, when well chosen, have so great a Force in them, that a
> Description often gives us more lively Ideas than the Sight of
> Things themselves. The Reader finds a Scene drawn in stronger
> Colours, and painted more to the Life in his Imagination, by the
> help of Words, than by an actual Survey of the Scene which they
> describe. In this Case the Poet seems to get the better of Nature.[20]

Augustan pride in the wealth and power of language contrasts sharply
with later eighteenth-century regret for its poverty. Addison claims that
the skilled poet can write a scene better than we can see it for ourselves,
but in "Tintern Abbey" Wordsworth admits, "I cannot paint / What then
I was" (ll. 75–76), just as Sir Walter Scott warns his reader in *Marmion,*
"Expect not . . . / That I can tell such scene in words."[21] Such lines invoke
a tradition of modesty, but many such statements go on to implicate the
adequacy of language itself, from Byron's extravagant compliment,
"how feebly words essay / To fix one spark of Beauty's heavenly ray,"
("Bride of Abydos," ll. 170–71) to *Lara*: "It was not . . . aught / That
words can image to express the thought" (ll. 365–66).[22] The essence of
Romanticism, according to Schlegel, "is that which cannot be described,"
and as a consequence Romantic poetry is filled with references to inexpressible emotion, from Wordsworth's "Thoughts that do often lie too
deep for tears" ("Intimations," l. 204) to Coleridge's "Thoughts all too
deep for words!"[23] It is often claimed that passionate emotion, one of the
principal subjects of Romanticism, is transcendent, existing beyond language. Their lyrics are made up of an "ineffable tale," as in Shelley, or in

Wordsworth, "inarticulate language" (*Excursion*, IV, 1207), "bliss ineffable" (1805 *Prelude*, II, 419), "incommunicable sanctity" ("Tuft of Primroses," l. 117), "incommunicable powers" (1805 *Prelude*, III, 188), "Unutterable love" (*Excursion*, I, 205), and "silence . . . Was best, the most affecting eloquence" (*Excursion*, IV, 414–15). His poems lead into "silent language" (1805 *Prelude*, II, 472), as they tell tales of a "silent Poet" ("When to the Attractions of the Busy World," l. 80) and "mute dialogues" (1805 *Prelude*, II, 283).[24] Wordsworth's assessment of the limits of language is not so defeatist as these selections might imply, for his attitude ranges from regret to confidence that the language of the heart must be known to all:

> Yet wherefore should I speak?
> Why call upon a few weak words to say
> What is already written in the hearts
> Of all that breathe?
>
> (1805 *Prelude*, V, 184–87)[25]

At his most confident, Wordsworth projects a universal language of emotion, not words, which is intuited by all. Of his rural, homely, and unlettered subjects, he asserts:

> Theirs is the language of the heavens, the power,
> The thought, the image, and the silent joy:
> Words are but under-agents of their souls.
>
> (1805 *Prelude*, XII, 270–72)

Although the concept of inexpressibility is certainly not new with Romanticism, nevertheless, the words *inexpressible, unutterable,* and *incommunicable* are absent from the poetic vocabularies of Dryden and Pope. When these words do appear earlier, in all of the *Oxford English Dictionary* examples, they refer to religious transcendence. Earlier, what is unutterable is far above human experience, or, conversely, far below it; that is, only religious and pornographic topics, angelic and bestial, are deemed "unspeakable."[26] I do not mean to suggest that inexpressibility first appears in the 1790s, or that earlier writers such as Johnson do not occasionally invoke the idea. In *Rambler* 5, Johnson writes that "There is, indeed, something inexpressibly pleasing in the annual renovation of the world," just as in *Rasselas* Pekuah and Nekayah are reunited with "transport too violent to be expressed."[27] But such phrases are exceptional in Johnson, whereas they are habitual in Wordsworth. If it is so that during the eighteenth century the language of poetry is assessed first as adequate and later as inadequate, first rich then poor, the question that remains is whether this judgment indicates a distinctly different view of language and its limits, or whether it indicates only a change in the subject of poetry. The oldest saws of literary history state that Augustan poetry concerns itself with general experience and rational behavior in decorous language, yet Romanticism seeks to portray the extraordinary and the irrational. By the late eighteenth century, however, the unutterable appears among much more commonplace human experiences. That is to say, emotion itself or at the least extreme emotion comes to be regarded as inexpressible. Here is Byron again:

> but words—what are they? can they give
> A trace of breath to thoughts while yet they live?
> No—Passion, Feeling speak not—or in vain—
> The tear for Grief, the groan must speak for Pain.
>
> ("Harmodia" ll. 21–24)

This passage does not indicate any sense that the poet feels dispossessed of his language. Indeed, the frequency and the obvious fascination with which Romantic poets claim that things cannot be said suggest that this assertion is a common technique or device similar to the use of the unfinished, fragmentary, or obscure.[28] It is of course essential that the Byronic hero remain private and unexplained:

> By those, who deepest feel, is ill exprest
> The indistinctness of the suffering breast;
> Where thousand thoughts begin to end in one,
> Which seeks from all the refuge found in none;
> No words suffice the secret soul to show,
> And Truth denies all eloquence to Woe.
>
> (*Corsair*, Canto III, 640–45)

Typically, Wordsworth's refusal to describe is at once an invitation and an exclusion, for it draws us in and holds us back at the same time; Margaret's story in Book I of *The Excursion* is offered in such tantalizing fashion:

> 'Tis a common tale,
> An ordinary sorrow of man's life,
> A tale of silent suffering, hardly clothed
> In bodily form.
>
> (ll. 636–40)

Although we are excluded from fully sharing the thought and the feeling of the speaker, the poet often goes on to suggest in brief what cannot be stated in full. The Solitary's remembrance of the grief occasioned by the deaths of his daughter, son, and wife is only suggested:

> What followed cannot be reviewed in thought;
> Much less, retraced in words.
>
> (*Excursion*, III, 681–82)

Later in the poem, this inability calls up the fundamentally Romantic frustration with mortal conditions:

> 'tis a thing impossible to frame
> Conceptions equal to the soul's desires.
>
> (IV, 136)

At other times the poet may deny in order to elicit admiration for how well in fact he does describe his subject. In Austen, as in Wordsworth, there is a vast difference between "will not tell" and "can not tell"; not saying covers a wide range of circumstances, from a rhetorical disinclination, to the failure of language to convey emotion, thought, or experience. In Austen, we find a similar range of denials; *Mansfield Park* includes at least twenty-four separate instances in which the narrator tells us that characters experience feelings that they cannot express or that cannot be clothed in words: Their happiness or gratitude or horror is "indescribable" or "unspeakable" or "indefinable." In both poet and novelist, such passages often encourage the reader imaginatively to create or to re-create his own corresponding understanding or memory of the feeling in question.[29] In an important distinction that Thomas Sheridan draws, the words can name emotion, but they cannot realize it, cannot embody or vivify that feeling for the reader: "But the use of these names [words for emotions], is not to stand as types of the emotions themselves, but only as signs, of the simple or complex ideas which are formed of these emotions"; it is as if words only suggest a surface, past which we cannot penetrate, for when the poet names anger, fear, or love, "he makes use of words only, as the signs of emotions, which it is impossible they can represent."[30]

Inexpressibility clearly has its rhetorical uses, which are not unlike the techniques of indirection, insinuation, and reluctance so prominent in Ciceronian rhetoric. The most popular of late eighteenth-century rhetorics, Hugh Blair's *Lectures on Rhetoric and Belles Lettres*, following Edmund Burke, observes that "Obscurity . . . is not unfavourable to the

Sublime," simply because the moment of sublimity cannot be drawn out, or it "sinks" and becomes "emasculated."[31] It is handy to be able to claim that climactic moments cannot be fully described in words, and no doubt, late eighteenth-century writers' assertions about the inadequacy of language reflect such a strategy. But this "new" subject cannot fully account for the increased dependence on the idea of the unutterable, for poets often attempt the extremes of passion without inevitably suggesting that their language is limited. For example, Ovid's extravagantly emotional *Heroides* remained a popular form for imitation; Pope conveys absolute confidence in his ability to express passion in *Eloisa to Abelard,* which ends on a note of pride: "He best can paint 'em [her woes], who shall feel 'em most" (l. 366). But it is fruitless to attempt to divorce a view of language from its subject, for Romantic poets could believe that they had reached the limits of language in pushing their subjects to unimagined extremes. Furthermore, there is some parallel between this general transition in language from wealth to poverty, infinite to limited, adequate to inadequate in more theoretical discussions of the later eighteenth century.

There is little consistency among eighteenth-century linguists on these issues, though neither Berkeley, Hume, Harris, Monboddo, Sheridan, Blair, Beattie, Smith, Warburton, Campbell, Herder, nor Rousseau claims that language cannot express thought.[32] It is difficult to argue around the fact that the group most interested in theories of language in the eighteenth century are the Scots, and it is hard to find any strong anticipation of English Romanticism in the Scottish Common Sense School. But even with the Scots, in the second half of the century, rhetoric in general and the sublime in particular are discussed in psychological terms as feelings rather than in more traditional terms as a technology of tropes and figures. In his *Lectures on Rhetoric,* Adam Smith refuses to discuss figures of speech, the bread and butter of classical rhetoric, and Hugh Blair's discussion of the subject is similarly perfunctory.[33] This heterogeneous group of writers is noticeably preoccupied with the linguistic problems raised by sentimental literature and the expression of passion. In his opening discussion of taste, for example, Blair insists that taste is a function of sympathy and feeling, not rational judgment or technical achievement (I, 10–11). The primacy of feeling is especially evident in the topic of oratory, which, according to Blair, is synonymous with sincerity: "No kind of Language is so generally understood, and so powerfully felt, as the native Language of worthy and virtuous feelings. He only, therefore, who possesses these full and strong, can speak properly, and in its own language, to the heart" (II, 231). To an unprecedented degree, Blair, Smith, Campbell, and other rhetoricians anatomize this language of the heart, especially Blair and Smith, whose subject, rhetoric and belles lettres, involves a good portion of practical criticism of such genres as tragedy and the novel.

Both Smith and Blair carefully explore the practical limits of the description and expression of impassioned language, in large part by employing a psychology of emotion, as Blair does here:

> No man, for instance, when he is under the strong agitations of anger, or grief, or any such violent passion, ever thinks of describing to another what his feelings at that time are; or of telling them what he resembles. . . . If we attend to the language that is spoken by persons under the influence of real passion, we shall find it always plain and simple . . . never employing those [figures] which belong to the mere embellishment and parade of speech. . . . it [passion] expresses itself most commonly in short, broken, and interrupted Speeches; corresponding to the violent and desultory emotions of the mind. (II, 508–10)

Adam Smith writes similarly on this matter:

> Internal objects, as passions and affections, can be well described only by their effects. These again [are] either internal or external. The best rule that can be given on this head seems to be that if passion is very violent and agitates the person to any high degree, the best method is to describe it by the external effects it produces, and these ought to be enumerated pretty fully and in the most striking and expressive manner. ⟨The sentiments which a violent passion excites in the mind are too tumultuous and rapid for your description to keep pace with.⟩ (p. 71)

For the first time since Locke, the words *natural* and *native* start to creep back into the description of language, in such phrases as Blair's "the native Language of passion" (II, 54). Against the nominal and artificial languages of particular societies is set the universal and intuitive language of nature, in which emotion is truly expressed, for "cries of passion . . . are the only signs which nature teaches all men, and which are understood by all" (I, 101). These signs constitute a whole system because "To every emotion or passion, Nature has adapted a set of corresponding objects," objects that are not words but "tones, looks, and gestures [which] are natural interpreters of the sentiments of the mind" (II, 192 and I, 136).[34]

As Blair indicates in a note, his notion of the language of nature comes from Thomas Sheridan, whose popular *Lectures on Elocution* were billed as an attempt to revive the classical art of oratory.[35] To that end, Sheridan separates spoken from written language, to the disparagement of the latter: "they have each their several offices and limits belonging to them," the limit of writing being that it is designed to convey ideas, whereas "the passions and the fancy have a language of their own, utterly independent of words."[36] Sheridan distinguishes carefully between the province of "living tongue" and that of "dead written language": "Words are, by compact, the marks or symbols of our ideas; and that is the utmost extent of their power. Did nothing pass in the mind of man, but ideas," words would be sufficient:

> But as there are other things which pass in the mind of man, beside ideas; as he is not wholly made up of intellect, but on the contrary, the passions, and the fancy, compose great part of his complicated frame; as the operations of these are attended with an infinite variety of emotions in the mind, both in kind and degree; it is clear, that unless there be some means found, of manifesting those emotions, all that passes in the mind of one man cannot be communicated to another.[37]

The means (which offer cold comfort to the poet or novelist) lie in the language of nature, "by which the emotions of the mind are discovered, and communicated from man to man, [and] are entirely different from words, and independent of them."[38] Sheridan promotes nothing short of a millenarian and logocentric revival of the language of presence: "we have given up the vivifying, energetic language, stamped by God himself upon our natures, for that which is the cold, lifeless work of art, and invention of man, and bartered that which can penetrate the inmost recesses of the heart, for one which dies in the ear, or fades on the sight."[39] This valorized opposition is analogous to Rousseau and Herder's priority of the original, natural, emotional, musical, and expressive language of nature over the rational, artificial, and stultifying language of society. As with Sheridan, Herder argues that speech was once alive and passionate, only to be displaced by a moribund written language of ideas:

> It was unschooled sublimity of imagination that worked out such feelings in such words. But now, as used by stale imitators without such feeling and without such occasion, alas, they are vials of words which the spirit has left; and that, in later times, has been the fate of all the languages in which the first forms were so bold.[40]

Hence, Herder's description of the "inadequacy" and "inertia" of modern languages, in which a "law of economy" infuses "parsimony" through-out.[41] In Herder's contemptuous formulation, we are left with a language not fit for poetry but only for philosophy.[42] The hegemony of reason, in Rousseau's words, substitutes "exactitude for expressiveness," ideas for feelings, and prose for poetry, depriving "language of its vital, passionate quality."[43] Individuals, in short, have been alienated from this original and expressive language of nature and are forced to speak a language with which they feel no natural or inherent connection: Their present language is not a part of them but rather an external, impersonal, and artificial system that they use.

Later eighteenth-century visions of this deprivation of language are nicely illustrated in the transformation of the metaphor of language clothing thought in words, a transformation that is indicative of a changing conception of language. The locus classicus is Quintilian, though it is found in Horace, Erasmus, and countless Renaissance and seventeenth-century rhetoricians. The same comparison is found everywhere in Augustan literature, from Robert Boyle to Sir William Temple, Dryden, Pope, Addison, and Berkeley.[44] This example from Dryden is typically commonplace: "As the words, etc., are evidently shown to be the clothing of the thought, in the same sense as colours are the clothing of the design, so the painter and the poet ought to judge exactly when the colouring and expressions are perfect, and then to think their work is truly finished."[45] Though casual and commonplace, the comparison is not always unambiguous, for, as Addison would be the one to note, both clothes and words depend upon fit: a "true" reader has "the Judgment discerning, to know what Expressions are most proper to cloath and adorn them [images] to the best advantage."[46] Also potential in the clothing metaphor are implications of veiling or concealing, as can be seen in this dazzling conceit from George Berkeley:

> It were, therefore, to be wished that everyone would use his utmost endeavors to obtain a clear view of the ideas he would consider, separating from them all that dress and encumbrance of words which so much contribute to blind the judgment and divide the attention. In vain do we extend our view into the heavens and pry into the entrails of the earth, in vain do we consult the writings of learned men and trace the dark footsteps of antiquity—we need only draw the curtain of words, to behold the fairest tree of knowledge, whose fruit is excellent and within the reach of our hand.[47]

Pope's elaborate comparison in his *Essay on Criticism* is representative of
Augustan citations in that it is substantially the same as Quintilian's:

> Expression is the *Dress* of *Thought,* and still
> Appears more *decent* as more *suitable;*
> A vile Conceit in pompous Words exprest,
> Is like a Clown in regal Purple drest;
> For diff'rent *Styles* with diff'rent *Subjects* sort,
> As several Garbs with Country, Town, and Court. . . .
> In *Words,* as *Fashions,* the same Rule will hold;
> Alike Fantastick, if *too New,* or *Old;*
> Be not the *first* by whom the *New* are try'd,
> Nor yet the *last* to lay the *Old* aside.
>
> (ll. 318–23, 333–36)

By 1814, however, when Wordsworth refers to the same metaphor in
his third *Essay on Epitaphs,* it has been radically subverted:

> Words are too awful an instrument for good and evil to be trifled
> with: they hold above all other external powers a dominion over
> thoughts. If words be not (recurring to a metaphor before used) an
> incarnation of the thought but only a clothing for it, then surely
> will they prove an ill gift; such a one as those poisoned vestments,
> read of in stories of superstitious times, which had power to
> consume and to alienate from his right mind the victim who put
> them on. Language, if it do not uphold, and feed, and leave in
> quiet, like the power of gravitation or the air we breathe, is a
> counter-spirit, unremittingly and noiselessly at work to derange,
> to subvert, to lay waste, to vitiate, and to dissolve. (II, 84–85)

In between Pope and Wordsworth, this central metaphor has been
thoroughly inverted. Rosemond Tuve has shown its importance to Elizabethan and Jacobean poetics, in which the dress of expression suggests
not a mere cover to thought but a bodying forth or manifestation, a
giving life to or realizing thought.[48] Yet when Wordsworth employs the
garment metaphor, it is to suggest that ordinary thoughts may be clothed
in words, but extraordinary thoughts may not:

> Not seeking those who might participate
> My deeper pleasures (nay, I had not once,
> Though not unused to mutter lonesome songs,
> Even with myself divided such delight,

> Or looked that way for aught that might be clothed
> In human language), easily I passed
> From the remembrances of better things,
> And slipped into the weekday works of youth,
> Unburdened, unalarmed, and unprofaned.
>
> (1805 *Prelude*, III, 237—45)

When Austen refers to words clothing thought, the figure is also employed negatively, to assert that some feeling or thought cannot be expressed.[49] It is a figure of denial for Austen, used only when the ability to narrate or to describe breaks down. Even with her most conventional usage, in *Northanger Abbey*, Austen employs it to set language against feeling: "The General, accustomed on every ordinary occasion to give the law in his family, prepared for no reluctance but of feeling, no opposing desire that should dare to clothe itself in words" (NA 247).

By the late eighteenth century, then, the clothing metaphor points up the limits of what can be expressed, an inversion that may be seen as part of the general shift during the eighteenth century from physical, spatial, or visual analogies for language to a conception of language as "function, process, and activity"; Gerald Bruns demonstrates that in some Romantic theories of language a "word [is] conceived not as an object but as a presence."[50] And indeed, in the same passage from the *Essay on Epitaphs*, Wordsworth connects language with "Energy, stillness, grandeur, tenderness, those feelings which are the pure emanations of nature, those thoughts which have the infinitude of truth, and those expressions which are not what the garb is to the body but what the body is to the soul, themselves a constituent part and power or function in the thought" (II, 84).[51] A model of language as process comes to replace older "traditions in which language is conceived explicitly as a 'thinglike being.'"[52] The dominant image for language has passed from concrete and stable, to intangible, from clothing to feeling. Whereas the literature of the earlier eighteenth century is full of clothing comparisons, the literature of the second half of the century is not: The figure does not appear in Beattie, Harris, Smith, Herder, Rousseau, Tooke, or Sheridan.[53]

Through this metaphorical transformation of language from garments to presence, the vehicles have changed from material to ideal, yet it is clear that at the same time language was being objectified. Language as a subject of study was reconceived as an object that could be sold on the open market; that is to say, language per se was both objectified and reified, turned into an object, a thing that could be, as never before; packaged, printed, sold, and bought, both in book and in lecture form. The process of the objectification of language is already apparent in the commercial schemes for universal languages such as those of George Dalgarno and Bishop John Wilkins in the late seventeenth century.[54] There language comes to be conceived, not as something inherent and internal to all men and women, but rather as something appropriated from the outside, and so it could be replaced at will as soon as linguists perfected or synthesized a better language.[55] Murray Cohen has shown a pervasive trend in eighteenth-century linguistics toward the tabular or graphic or visual presentation of printed language, the "techniques of printed visualization," particularly with regard to phonetic alphabets and other schemes for the transcription of spoken language.[56] What such ventures have in common with the elocutionary movement, and Thomas Sheridan in particular, are ways to reify or objectify language so that it could be sold for individual profit, whether printed in book form or delivered in the form of lectures for foreigners, Scots, Irish, and Welsh who could, by attending his lectures, purchase standard British pronunciation and thereby render themselves employable in England. The massive eighteenth-century outpouring of dictionaries, secret code schemes, spelling books, grammar books, pronunciation books, and lectures demonstrates the degree to which language had become commodified, something objectified and sold again and again.[57] By attending Sheridan's lectures, one could obtain what had once been regarded as one's birthright: the "native" English tongue. Now standard English was no longer the exclusive possession of Londoners and those who could afford regular education, because it could be reproduced in books by phonetic transcription and sold to just as many through the lectures. Following the general pattern of consumer goods in the eighteenth century, such as fashion or Wedgwood china, objects that had once been characterized by exclusivity now were purchased through the social patterns of emulative spending or conspicuous consumption, imitating one's betters by buying copies of what they owned, including their once distinctive speech.[58] As language becomes a commodity to be sold and bought, simultaneously it becomes characterized by exchange value, not use value, and as such it loses connection with inherent properties or essences and is characterized instead by what it costs. And so, as with all commodities language becomes alienated from traditional social relations.[59] As is painfully evident in Wordsworth's comparison to poisoned vestments, language is but one aspect of social relations from which individuals become alienated in the course of the eighteenth century. Hence language is something external, something that is learned or bought from the outside, not something internal and inherent, a capacity with which one is born. At the same time, by means of the central ideological contradiction of bourgeois culture, in effect, personal or private, individual emotion comes to be conceived as existing "inside" language, that is, cut off or hidden from expression, and by means of the supreme privileging of the private, interior emotion can be regarded as transcendent.

By the end of the eighteenth century, then, a roughly parallel sense of the (in)capacity of language is found in both philosophy and literature. Moral philosophers, linguists, rhetoricians, as well as poets and novelists, all comment regularly on the limits of language. Jane Austen shares this view, and her use of the clothing metaphor, along with her other appeals to inexpressibility, suggest what can and cannot be expressed in her novels. Of all Austen's characters Fanny Price suffers the greatest impediments to speech, but the inability to speak is not confined to Fanny, for Edmund, Sir Thomas, and even Mary Crawford are at times unable to express themselves. Some of these moments are, of course, conventional and commonplace: Mary Crawford writes to Fanny at Portsmouth: "I miss you more than I can express" (MP 423).[60] From everything that is shown of Mary's feelings for Fanny, and also of Mary's often inexact speech, this expression sounds formulaic and shallow—with a little effort, one assumes, Mary could say how much she misses Fanny. Inexpressibility also occurs when it is social circumstances that inhibit speech, through embarrassment or reticence. For example, Fanny is unable to speak of Crawford's proposal before her formidable uncle, Sir Thomas: "Fanny's colour grew deeper and deeper; and her uncle perceiving that she was embarrassed to a degree that made either speaking or looking up quite impossible, turned away his own eyes" (MP 313–14). At other times, this phrase calls up a rather ordinary inability to find words or argument: In a discussion with Edmund, "Fanny could not answer him" (MP 154), just as Edmund "could not answer" an inane remark of Rushworth's (MP 139). Usually Austen makes it clear when the failure or inability is momentary: at Henry Crawford's proposal of marriage, we are told that Fanny "was exceedingly distressed, and for some moments unable to speak" (MP 301). At other points, however, similar phrases are designed to suggest more than just a circumstantial inability to reply. At Edmund's appearance in Portsmouth, for example, the reader is shown a condition in which speech is impossible: "She found herself pressed to his heart with only these words, just articulate, 'My Fanny—my only sister—my only comfort now.' She could say nothing; nor for some minutes could he say more" (MP 444). There are as well times when the narrator is quite explicit that particular emotions lie outside the possibility of speech: When Edmund and Fanny return to the Park at the close of the novel, the narrator flatly says that Edmund's unhappiness "did not admit of speech" (MP 453).[61] Fanny's concluding happiness is similarly indescribable: "But there was happiness elsewhere which no description can reach. Let no one presume to give the feelings of a young woman on receiving the assurance of that affection of which she has scarcely allowed herself to entertain a hope" (MP 471).

Such expressions are not, of course, unique to Austen and can be found in earlier novels; there is no need to claim that these figures are significant in Austen but trivial in preceding novelists, for it is impossible to plot exactly when the idea and use of inexpressibility begin to change. Our examination of marriage proposals in eighteenth-century novels shows a steadily increasing dependence upon ineffability; after Richardson, in the 1770s and beyond, with the rise of sentimental fiction and the increasing inclusion of overwhelming emotion, novelists such as Burney, Mackenzie, Brooke, and Radcliffe routinely extricate themselves from narrative difficulties by declaring their characters' emotions indescribable. It is difficult to determine the significance of a specific instance of commonplace; we are left to evaluate the poet's ability to make us believe him when he says, "I cannot paint what then I was." Still, it will not do simply to assert that this figure is a cliché when found in lesser writers, but important in Austen and Wordsworth; rather, we should see that the trope of inexpressibility was in self-conscious and effective use by a whole series of writers around the turn of the nineteenth century.[62] In *Camilla,* and in *Udolpho,* such figures show up with apparently formulaic regularity, in stories that again and again build up to emotional climaxes that are inevitably declared indescribable. Austen is obviously self-conscious about her language (novels are celebrated in *Northanger Abbey* when they "are conveyed to the world in the best chosen language," NA 38) and always careful to point out "novel slang," such that one is confident in concluding that at the least Austen is aware of when she claims that something cannot be said.

A revealing instance of the precision with which Austen uses these expressions can be found in the revisions to *Persuasion,* in which the narrator originally reports Captain Wentworth's saying that Anne "had *gained* inexpressibly in personal Loveliness" (P 264). In the final version, however, the inexpressibility has been reassigned from the material to the ideal, from Anne's appearance to Anne's feelings about Wentworth's perception of her:

> It is something for a woman to be assured, in her eight-and-twentieth year, that she has not lost one charm of earlier youth: but the value of such homage was inexpressibly increased to Anne, by comparing it with former words, and feeling it to be the

result, not the cause of a revival of his warm attachment. (P 243; Captain Wentworth's former words are "Altered beyond his knowledge," P 60).[63]

Another excellent index of Austen's self-consciousness about ineffability can be found in the many times she uses such expressions with unmistakable irony, always in connection with her shallowest characters, thus indicating her awareness of the potential for cliché. In *Pride and Prejudice*, at a point when Mr. Collins is overcome with his self-importance, the narrator tells us that "words were insufficient for the elevation of his feelings; and he was obliged to walk about the room" (PP 216). Similarly, in *Sense and Sensibility* when John Dashwood gives an account of the hateful Fanny's selfish display of hysterics, his sisters "looked their assent; it seemed too awful a moment for speech" (SS 265). When Austen toys with this figure in her correspondence, as she writes to Cassandra, she is plainly aware of its commonplace nature: "Your silence on the subject of our Ball, makes me suppose your Curiosity too great for words" (L 257). Additionally, that Austen is aware that this expression is a cliché associated with Romanticism is also clear from Sir Edward's remarks about Wordsworth and Scott in *Sanditon*, which Charlotte describes as "Nonsense": He "ran with Energy through all the usual Phrases employed in praise of their [the Sea & the Sea shore's] Sublimity, & descriptive of the *undescribable* Emotions they excite in the Mind of Sensibility" (MW 398 and 396). In earlier novels inexpressibility sometimes is invoked in order to dismiss the work of description, as in Fielding's portraits of Fanny or Sophia or Sterne's of the Widow Wadman; Austen herself alludes to such tricks at the end of *Northanger Abbey*, in order to avoid explaining Eleanor Tilney's suitor, a character who is never mentioned previously: He is "to a precision the most charming young man in the world. Any further definition of his merits must be unnecessary; the most charming young man in the world is instantly before the imagination of us all" (NA 251).[64]

Inexpressibility, however, is more commonly invoked in Austen's novels when emotion is carefully examined and almost always in connection with female characters, those whose speech is most subject to social inhibition. In the following passage, in which Fanny Price contemplates a return to her original family in Portsmouth after an absence of ten years, Austen employs the clothing figure not to dismiss but rather to anatomize with great care the range and degree of inexpressible emotion:

Had she ever given way to bursts of delight, it must have been then, for she was delighted, but her happiness was of a quiet, deep, heart-swelling sort; and though never a great talker, she was always more inclined to silence when feeling most strongly. At the moment she could only thank and accept. Afterwards, when familiarized with the visions of enjoyment so suddenly opened, she could speak more largely to William and Edmund of what she felt; but still there were emotions of tenderness that could not be clothed in words—The remembrance of all her earliest pleasures, and of what she had suffered in being torn from them, came over her with renewed strength, and it seemed as if to be at home again, would heal every pain that had since grown out of that separation. To be in the centre of such a circle, loved by so many, and more loved by all than she had ever been before, to feel affection without fear or restraint, to feel herself the equal of those who surrounded her, to be at peace from all mention of the Crawfords, safe from every look which could be fancied a reproach on their account!—This was a prospect to be dwelt on with a fondness that could be but half acknowledged. (MP 369–70)

Fanny's emotion here can "be but half acknowledged," that is to say, indicated but not described, in the same way that Austen introduces physical objects only to whisk them away or leads up to proposal scenes in order to collapse them. The presence of the emotion is announced, but because it is not described or enacted in any way, we cannot see it—we are told but not shown. This particular passage is narrated entirely by an external authority; because Austen does not use free indirect discourse here, we can see none of Fanny's thoughts directly, but only in their indirect presentation by a highly protective narrator. (Like Edmund within the novel, Austen and her narrator present Fanny as a character to be protected and defended from the ordinary roughness of others.) Such passages as this one capitalize upon Fanny's desire in order to bolster her otherwise dubious authority as a character. The most cursory familiarity with the secondary literature on this novel shows the distaste that the character of Fanny Price can engender in readers. Given the difficulties of creating sympathy for a "creepmouse," as Tom calls her (MP 145), it is important that Austen expose Fanny's emotions, at the same time Austen makes it clear why they are never publicly expressed. This paragraph does so by succinctly reiterating that Fanny's emotional needs are minimal, for family and for affection. And again we are reminded why Fanny cannot repine against such deprivation in her present situation. That almost all of these prospects are ruined by her visit only underscores the poignancy of her desire.

The many instances of ineffability in *Mansfield Park* may be explained in part by the fact that this is primarily a novel of education, and so it dramatizes Fanny's developing speech. The novel's first episode sets this development in motion; when Edmund helps Fanny write to her brother, "Fanny's feelings on the occasion were such as she believed herself incapable of expressing; but her countenance and a few artless words fully conveyed all their gratitude and delight, and her cousin began to find her an interesting object" (MP 16). For a good portion of the novel, the protagonist is both inarticulate and unwilling to express herself, at least compared with the likes of Elizabeth Bennet: In contrast to the endless deference shown to an Emma, Austen writes of Fanny Price, "Few young ladies of eighteen could be less called on to speak their opinion than Fanny" (MP 48). Much of the experience of the novel is shown from within Fanny Price in order to convey the sense that there is much that is felt but not uttered. Because much of her reaction is narrated through free indirect discourse, the narrator is free to suggest or to indicate emotions that are then declared indescribable. Fanny's closeness of speech also functions in the extended contrast that is drawn between her and Mary Crawford. If Fanny feels much but says little, we are shown that Mary says much that ought to remain unsaid: Mary "wished she had not spoken so warmly in their last conversation. . . . She wished such words unsaid with all her heart" (MP 286); "When she had spoken it, she recollected herself, and wished it unsaid" (MP 295). Throughout the novel a verbal prudence associated with *reserve,* as is exemplified by Sir Thomas, contrasts with *easy* speech and manners, as is exemplified by Henry Crawford or Yates. Verbal prudence is reflected in such phrases as "delicacy of language" (MP 293) or "She might scruple to make use of the words" (MP 390).[65] Fanny is characterized by a delicacy of feeling and speech that Mary Crawford lacks. Early on Edmund excuses Mary, claiming that "She does not *think* evil, but she speaks it" (MP 269); his account of his last interview with Mary indicates that he has come to believe that Mary Crawford does indeed speak and think evil.

Austen has complicated speech itself in this novel. By focusing on a young, poor, shy, and female dependent, the novelist stresses a whole host of social, economic, and sexual inhibitions to Fanny's speech. This novel takes speech as one of its central concerns—the inability to speak in the face of social and class pressures, as well as emotional and private strictures against speech. Fanny continually withdraws into silence while the others around her speak too much, as scrupulous and reticent words are contrasted with rash and impetuous ones.[66] The opposition of speech and silence governs not only Fanny and Mary, but Edmund and Henry and Lady Bertram and Aunt Norris. A similar contrast is evident in property itself, in the very houses, as Fanny compares the noise and discord of Portsmouth with the quiet and harmony of Mansfield Park: "Let us have the luxury of silence," Edmund tells Fanny (MP 278). Again, the discord and noise in Portsmouth are things that obtrude: Like the filth in the food, they are things that Fanny notices only because they are not supposed to be there. In Portsmouth we are shown that silence is an expensive luxury produced by a host of servants who labor to make the domestic work painless, silent, and invisible for their employers, a luxury that the Prices obviously cannot afford.

Here, as in countless eighteenth-century texts of aesthetics and morality, from Shaftesbury and Addison, through Hutchison and Burke, the issues of decorum, delicacy, and taste are consciously presented in terms of class difference: Only the well-bred and the well-educated understand the importance of delicacy. In the absence of delicacy, Austen implies, a Mary Crawford is as vulgar as a Mrs. Price. At the same time, however, Austen plainly shows, and has Sir Thomas painfully come to recognize at the end, that Julia's and Maria's education to accomplishments, taste, and delicacy is based on class privilege and superiority that mask a kind of moral deficiency. When the little girls complain of Fanny's inadequacy (Fanny does not know "all the Metals, Semi-Metals, Planets, and distinguished philosophers"), their Aunt Norris responds:

> "To be sure, my dear, that is very stupid indeed, and shows a great want of genius and emulation. But all things considered, I do not know whether it is not as well that it should be so, for, though you know (owing to me) your papa and mamma are so good as to bring her up with you, it is not at all necessary that she should be as accomplished as you are;—on the contrary, it is much more desirable that there should be a difference." (MP 19)

Though Sir Thomas's conclusion is obscured by a kind of hardship morality ("the advantages of early hardship and discipline, and the consciousness of being born to struggle and endure," MP 473—they ought to pull themselves up by their bootstraps), the fineness and delicacy that even Fanny has imbibed from Mansfield Park are invigorated by an infusion of energy from below, from the working class, in the persons of William and Susan. In short, Austen seems aware that silence, decorum, and fine feelings, along with the leisure and the privacy to enjoy them, are luxuries that only the wealthy can afford.

From beginning to end, there is much that Fanny cannot say, starting with her affection for Edmund; it is dangerous to acknowledge, and so ought not be uttered. *Mansfield Park* is filled with emotions that can be said but should not, as well as emotions that cannot be expressed at all. These gaps between feeling and saying contribute to an unusually difficult presentation of character for Austen, so that it is very hard to determine, for example, just how attractive the Crawfords are meant to be. There is no consistently omniscient narrator to explain what transpires; instead, the narrator passes in and out of the characters' thoughts with deceptive ease. The narrative shifts so often and so unobtrusively that it is often difficult to attribute a particular judgment to either character or narrator. We are treated to a collection of partial and conflicting views; we are shown, for example, just enough of Mary Crawford's thoughts to think that Fanny is unfair in her condemnation of the Crawfords.[67] Along these lines, Avrom Fleishman has observed that Fanny's internal judgments tend to overcompensate for what she cannot say.[68] In the same way, Fanny's overblown raptures about nature and gardening may reflect the fact that her only safe expression of emotion can be directed toward an animated landscape.

Inexpressibility is most common in the novels with dependent or repressed heroines. The more self-possessed characters such as Elizabeth Bennet and Emma Woodhouse are presented as disinclined to admit that there is much that they cannot express, though they too are forced to come to this admission. Also, the same topoi, such as inexpressibility, silence, and reserve, are put to different uses in different novels. Anne Elliot is as much a silent observer as Fanny, but Anne is presented as older and more capable, one for whom the ability to speak is never questioned, just the occasion. *Persuasion* is a novel in which characters do not speak in large part because their emotion can be communicated by the means Thomas Sheridan celebrates: "the features . . . the voice, or the turn of sentiment and expression" (P 48). In a number of ways, Austen's last is her most visual novel, with an extraordinary emphasis placed on "looks," in the sense of Sir Walter's vanity, but also in Anne's "bloom"; her blushes, which are carefully described a dozen times; Mr. Elliot's "look" at Anne in Lyme, which is referred to on four separate occasions; on up to the climactic mutual "look" with which Wentworth proposes and with which Anne accepts: He "only looked. Anne could command herself enough to receive that look" (P 239). In a novel in which so little conversation takes place between hero and heroine, feeling is passed in a look; as Mrs. Smith observes of Anne Elliot's blush, "Your countenance perfectly informs me . . ." (P 194). Just as Sheridan argues, physical presence here is supposed to be far more expressive of emotion than words, because the action is precipitated "by manner, rather than words" (P 176). When Anne reflects on one of the very few conversations she has with Wentworth, his words are the least important part of the experience: "His choice of subjects, his expressions, and still more his manner and look, had been such as she could see in only one light" (P 185). Unlike any of Austen's earlier couples, these two know one another well enough to interpret each other's looks: Mary Musgrove "received no other answer, than an artificial, assenting smile, followed by a contemptuous glance, as he [Wentworth] turned away, which Anne perfectly knew the meaning of" (P 86). Again and again, Anne is able to read private thoughts in Captain Wentworth's face, which remains masked to others, as here, when Wentworth responds to Mrs. Musgrove's remarks about her son:

> There was a momentary expression in Captain Wentworth's face at this speech, a certain glance of his bright eye, and curl of his handsome mouth, which convinced Anne, that instead of sharing in Mrs. Musgrove's kind wishes, as to her son, he had probably been at some pains to get rid of him; but it was too transient an indulgence of self-amusement to be detected by any who understood him less than herself. (P 67)[69]

Anne Elliot's question of Captain Wentworth, "how were his sentiments to be read?" (P 60), is the central question in all six novels, for Austen writes about feelings that are not fully communicable to others. Again, as the narrator of *Emma* insists, "Seldom, very seldom, does complete truth belong to any human disclosure" (E 431). The social and moral dimensions of speech and particularly their limits represented in Austen's domestic fiction naturally differ from the more purely theoretical issues in linguistics and philosophy with which we began this chapter. Although a general sense of the limited capacity of language had become commonly accepted, Austen's particular focus is on individual or personal relations and the bars between them. Most often she stresses social impediments to speech, but these impediments are seen within a larger frame of the limits to language itself. *Mansfield Park* attempts to represent only as far as is necessary the private world of Fanny Price, much of which is hidden beyond the reach of public language, a situation not unlike that of the poet and the Solitary Reaper, whose song he hears, but which he still cannot understand. So too, as Austen's characters become more complex from Catherine Morland to Anne Elliot, the more it is suggested that communication of individual experience and feelings in their entirety is not possible. Often, as eighteenth-century rhetoricians maintain, a language of gesture can mediate, as does Edmund's embrace in Portsmouth, but for the most intense emotions, Austen asserts again and again that words do not suffice. Just as with her contemporary Wordsworth, words are at best a halfway measure, which distorts and conceals as much as it clothes. In a passage not directly about language but curiously suggestive of it, Austen objectifies and naturalizes her descriptive technique of "half-acknowledgment"; the avenue to Mansfield Park is described as Edmund and Fanny return from her prolonged stay in Portsmouth: "the trees, though not fully clothed, were in that delightful state, when farther beauty is known to be at hand, and when, while much is actually given to the sight, more yet remains for the imagination" (MP 446–47). Like these leaves, Austen's words fill out and give form to an imaginative world of inner experience, by claiming a presence beyond the limits of language. Inner experience, then, is represented in Austen's fiction much in the same manner as the material world, for it too is but "half-acknowledged," offered only to be withdrawn.

4
Character and Interpretation

How vain it is to think that words can penetrate the mystery of our being! Rightly used they may make evident our ignorance to ourselves, and this is much.
—Shelley, *Essay on Life*[1]

In *Persuasion,* when Anne Elliot and Captain Wentworth meet after eight years' separation, Anne wonders, "how were his sentiments to be read?" (P 60), a question that takes the whole of the novel to answer. The action of Austen's novels revolves around reading or interpreting others' sentiments, and reading others' thoughts turns out to be such an absorbing process because the natures of Austen's protagonists are only gradually revealed over time. Like Austen's representation of things and emotions, her characters are "half acknowledged" (MP 370), briefly exposed and then withdrawn from view again. In this way, Austen's characters are presented as complicated enough to need interpretation, and their intriguing complexity has been the most popular topic in Austen studies. In an enduring essay on the subject, Reuben Brower locates the appeal of Austen's fiction in this very feature: "What most satisfies us in reading the dialogue in *Pride and Prejudice* is Jane Austen's awareness that it is difficult to know any complex person, that the knowledge of a man like Darcy is an interpretation and a construction, not a simple absolute." Brower goes on to argue that it is the business of the novel as a whole to facilitate the interpretation of character, distinguishing Bingleys from Darcys, simple from intricate ones: "a reasoned judgment of character

[is] reached through long experience and slow weighing of possibilities."[2] More recently, the interpretive activity of Austen's characters is explored in phenomenological terms by Gerald Bruns in his acute study of Austen's "hermeneutics of human social life": "the world of *Pride and Prejudice* is a world of hidden meanings which require to be recovered by interpretation."[3] The obstacles that Austen places in the way of interpretation have been studied at length by Darrel Mansell, who explores the heroines' "epistemology of projection," a subject that, in turn, Susan Morgan has connected with the main currents of Romanticism: "The subject of Austen's fiction, like that of the major poets of her time, is the relation between the mind and its objects."[4]

All of these studies, in one form or another, ask again the question "how were his sentiments to be read?" In so doing, they follow traditional assumptions of novel reading: that character is a representation of unique or individual personality; that there are sentiments to be read; and that these sentiments can be read and understood by other characters as well as by the reader. As Brower asserts, character is a complex matrix of possibilities, yet it is possible and rewarding to interpret character; it is rewarding in novels such as Austen's because here readers can join in the same intellectual activity as the characters—interpreting, weighing, and judging one another. There is little point in arguing that these assumptions are false or that they are not the appropriate ones to apply to Austen, for they are clearly the ones her fiction promotes. Nevertheless, one should recognize these a priori assumptions about character as historically determined concepts, rather than regarding these novels in terms of technical or literary achievement—a natural portrayal of what people are really like.[5]

Analysis of character in Austen's fiction, which seems like the simplest and most common exercise in literary studies, becomes considerably more complex if her work is not seen in progressive and technical terms—that is, how best to represent people accurately or realistically. Analysis of conception and representation of character in Austen's fiction is complicated by the fact that between her time and ours theories of character or psychologies have changed.[6] (As we have observed before, such a problem is exacerbated by the fact that Austen's view of the world appears deceptively similar to ours, a similarity that has encouraged too many commentators to enjoy the "timeless" quality of her fiction.) The theoretical issue raised is not an unfamiliar one: how to use, moreover how to historicize, the insights of contemporary psychology.[7] Either personality is natural and unchanging over time, and so it has always been essentially the same since time immemorial, or "self" and "identity" are abstractions that are subject to invention, use, change, and abandonment, just as is any other idea.[8] The psychoanalyst Roy Schafer puts the problem this way:

> Self and identity are not facts about people; they are technical ways of thinking about people; and they have become ways in which many people think about themselves. Still they are not outside of and above the realm of self-representation and object representation; each is merely one type of representation or one way of representing. . . . There is, I submit, a claim to unity and stability of self-representation in the way terms of this sort are used or understood that is not supported by observation.[9]

If this view of identity is correct, then contemporary models of personality and identity are questionably accurate or appropriate for characters written much earlier. The issue is further complicated because Austen is the beneficiary of a century's speculation about the nature of character, and so we cannot expect to find in Austen or her contemporaries a fully articulated, consistent, and coherent model of evolving concepts of self and identity. Finally, it is as difficult to get around our own models of identity as it is to recover those of the past, such that the attempt to understand the ways in which people may have conceived of themselves and others in the remote past is the most difficult effort for the historical imagination. If it is not possible to abandon fully our own assumptions about character and identity, and I see no way that we can, then we can only hope to extrapolate backward from what we think we already know, in a kind of psychological archaeology. Therefore, to explore these matters in Austen systematically and comparatively, in this chapter we shall proceed to survey the interpretation of character in terms of late eighteenth-, late nineteenth-, and late twentieth-century psychologies. Austen's presentation of character will first be examined in terms of eighteenth-century psychology, specifically David Hume's and Wordsworth's. Next, the difficulty of interpreting character in traditional Freudian terms, a descendant of Romantic characterization, will be examined.[10] Freudian procedure, in turn, will be compared with a post-Freudian view from the vantage of the revisionist psychoanalyst Heinz Kohut and his theory of narcissism.

In employing psychology and psychoanalysis we are not departing from the social and historical explanation that we have followed thus far, but rather, we need to understand the psychological within the social and historical. Leo Bersani makes explicit the correlation between social order and psychological models in realistic novels of the nineteenth century:

The formal and psychological reticence of the most realistic fiction makes for a secret complicity between the novelist and his society's illusions about its own order. . . . Perhaps the surest guarantee of social order is psychological coherence, and the nineteenth-century novelist, in his commitment to significant structures of character, is providing his readers with more than just an intellectual satisfaction with well-drawn patterns. In spite of his troubling heroes and heroines, he has opted for, he is in fact insisting on, the readability of the human personality.[11]

To put this another way, in the most general terms, the subject under examination here is object relations, whether in Hume's concept of identity as a "convenient fiction," Freud's mechanism of transference, or Kohut's theories narcissistic transference. Within the category of object relations these three psychologies generally concur that object relations are inevitably beset with impediments or fictions, from transference and idealization, to projection and introjection, a whole host of forces or mechanisms that prevent the subject from seeing the object clearly. Psychology is the science of object relations, but still it is a relatively new science, one whose history roughly parallels that of advanced capitalism, for object relations had no need of such minute, exacting, and complex explanations before the onset of the objectification of social relations under capital. A unique inner life is the essential presupposition of psychology, and this inner life was invented simultaneously with a psychology that was thought necessary to explain it: There are obvious correlations among material accumulation, a morality of improvement, and personal development, as opposed to older, more static views of property, class, and character. These object relations are not natural and eternal, but rather are part of what Lukács terms the antinomies of bourgeois thought: "between subject and object, freedom and necessity, individual and society, form and content"; as the privileged term in each of these pairs shifts from the second to the first, psychology is the discipline promulgated to investigate and understand the interiorized self.[12] Characterization in the novel, in short, must be connected with the objectification of social relations under capital. As J. M. Bernstein writes, under capital and the objectification of human relations, "Freedom and value must hence retreat into subjectivity," and the novel is the form pre-eminently suited to represent the narcissistic retreat into self-absorption and subjectivity.[13]

To begin to explore the nature of character in Austen's novels, it is helpful to extend Robert Langbaum's inquiry into the *Mysteries of Identity* backward a bit.[14] Langbaum begins with Wordsworth, as the first Romantic writer to focus on questions of personal identity. We shall see that similar concerns pervade Austen's fiction. That her characters can appear so complicated, and be so self-conscious about this complexity, may be attributed to the progress of eighteenth-century psychology as well as to the "rise of the novel." Elizabeth Bennet seems considerably more three-dimensional than Tom Jones, not only because of Austen's realism of presentation, as opposed to Fielding's more plainly allegorical form, but also because of rich and prolonged eighteenth-century speculation on the nature of personal identity.[15] Patricia Meyer Spacks formulates the contrast quite neatly:

> The characters in eighteenth-century fiction show less capacity for essential change than we like to believe is possible in life, and the limited possibilities for change they have depend upon external kinds of learning about the world outside themselves. Jane Austen's heroines, in contrast, through undergoing their confined and decorous experience, alter in minute but important ways: Emma's final capacity to admit herself wrong does not, like Tom Jones' prudence, constitute a quality added to her earlier characteristics, but an actual reversal of a previous set of assumptions, and it derives from her increased understanding of what lies within.[16]

In between Fielding and Austen, personality itself was coming to be envisioned as a more complex structure, enduring ever more precariously in time. Under the influence of Locke and then Hume, and the privileged status of individuality, privacy, mobility, and development, the idea of simple and fixed identity had been under considerable assault in English philosophy, literature, and society for some time before Elizabeth Bennet was conceived.[17]

The origin of this assault has traditionally been located in David Hume's *A Treatise of Human Nature*, which would, no doubt, have profoundly shocked eighteenth-century audiences had it been much read. Yet coming well before Hume and much more influential is Locke's *Essays Concerning Human Understanding*, which, though it does not directly address the concept of fixed identity, nevertheless goes a long way toward its dissolution by questioning and thereby complicating the nature of individual essences and their extension in time, as weell as our ability to apprehend them.[18] It is still Hume, though, who in the *Treatise* reduces personal identity and its continuity over time to a convenient "fiction."[19] Throughout eighteenth-century English empiricism, time is brought to bear on identity, as character or personality comes to be conceived as dynamic and developmental, rather than as a fixed state or essence. Hume's discussion of personal identity in the *Treatise* forms but one small part of his whole program of radical skepticism, which is finally directed at dogmatic concepts of morality.[20] Here Hume proceeds to undo personal identity in the same fashion that he earlier dismantled causality, beginning with the question,

> whether in pronouncing concerning the identity of a person, we observe some real bond among his perceptions, or only feel one among the ideas we form of them. This question we might easily decide, if we wou'd recollect what has been already prov'd at large, that the understanding never observes any real connection among objects, and that even the union of cause and effect, when strictly examin'd, resolves itself into a customary association of ideas. For from thence it evidently follows, that identity is nothing really belonging to these different perceptions, and uniting them together; but is merely a quality, which we attribute to them, because of the union of their ideas in the imagination, when we reflect upon them.[21]

In short order, identity is reduced, as is causality, to a fiction of continuity that we impose on all external phenomena including other persons and ourselves: Individuals "are nothing but a bundle or collection of different perceptions, which succeed each other with an inconceivable rapidity, and are in a perpetual flux and movement."[22] And so Hume concludes that "The identity, which we ascribe to the mind of man, is only a fictitious one, and of the like kind with that which we ascribe to vegetables and animal bodies."[23] Hume's radical view of character and personality contrasts with Samuel Johnson's more conservative view; in his *Life of Pope,* for example, Johnson writes as if Pope never knew his own character, as if character is a stable condition, something into which one is born and which endures over a lifetime. Later, Wordsworth's notion of self at work in *The Prelude* is substantially more dynamic and developmental, as he chronicles "the growth of a poet's mind," a consciousness that is created over time and therefore subject to change. But such contrasts are by no means clear and categorical, because in the writers of this period, particularly in Wordsworth and in Austen, we can detect tensions and contradictions between stable and dynamic visions of character.[24] Much of their representation of character is ambiguous as to whether character is, in fact, changeable and, if so, to what degree. Yet what is certain in late eighteenth- and early nineteenth-century literature is the degree to which the profound split between subject and object has determined the ground of psychological speculation in the period.

Conflict between stable and dynamic visions of character can be seen quite clearly in *Pride and Prejudice*'s original title, *First Impressions*, a title that foregrounds the interpretive action of the novel: the retention and dissolution of first impressions. Both Elizabeth and Darcy are presented as holding fast to their first impressions of one another, long after these original impressions ought to have been modified or abandoned. Elizabeth expects Darcy to continue to conform to the first impression that she formed of him at the dance, as if his character had been indelibly imprinted in her memory. At a few significant intervals, we are allowed to see Darcy as he alters his original assumptions about Elizabeth. But both characters begin with static concepts of character, assuming that the other is not subject to change, that they are not subject to error, and that they have every right to expect the other to remain consistent with the first impression. (At one point, Elizabeth asserts, "people themselves alter so much, that there is something new to be observed in them forever" [PP 43], but her confidence in her own judgment and penetration belies this.) Elizabeth's belief in the continuity of character is evident throughout; she claims, for example, that an interchange between Miss Bingley and Darcy is "exactly in unison with her opinion of each" (PP 47), and the same certainty underlies her response to Jane's doubt about Darcy: "I beg your pardon;—one knows exactly what to think" (PP 86). With Emma-like complacency, Elizabeth sums up and fixes her expectations of the visit to Hunsford and with "a lively imagination soon settled it all" (PP 158). In the following dialogue between Elizabeth and Darcy at the Netherfield ball, the interpreters compete directly with one another. Here, the subject's assurance of her skill is played off against her acknowledgment of the object's impenetrability:

> "I remember hearing you once say, Mr. Darcy, that you hardly ever forgave, that your resentment once created was unappeasable. You are very cautious, I suppose, as to its *being created*."
> "I am," said he, with a firm voice.
> "And never allow yourself to be blinded by prejudice?"
> "I hope not."
> "It is particularly incumbent on those who never change their opinion, to be secure of judging properly at first."
> "May I ask to what these questions tend?"
> "Merely to the illustration of *your* character," said she, endeavoring to shake off her gravity. "I am trying to make it out."
> "And what is your success?"

> She shook her head. "I do not get on at all. I hear such different accounts of you as puzzle me exceedingly."
>
> "I can readily believe," he answered gravely, "that reports may vary greatly with respect to me; and I could wish, Miss Bennet, that you were not to sketch my character at the present moment, as there is reason to fear that the performance would reflect no credit on either."
>
> "But if I do not take your likeness now, I may never have another opportunity." (PP 93–94)

This exchange builds upon the earlier discussion in which Elizabeth distinguishes between a transparent character, such as Bingley, and "a deep, intricate character," such as Darcy (PP 42). In both conversations, the simple skill of plumbing the other is complicated by the quarry's possibility of change, and it is time and change that both characters have to reckon with in their assessment of each other. At first, though, both Darcy and Elizabeth cannot see that they themselves change, any more than they are able to see change in others. Just as Darcy and Elizabeth begin with the assumption that the other remains the same over time, so each one assumes that he or she possesses a stable self. Darcy draws special pride from the fixity of his family name, home, and library, all metonyms for the endurance of his self, in contrast to the lamentably changeable Bingley, who lacks the necessary family, library, and estate.[25] Yet, even for Darcy these vestiges of the feudal estate, with all of their assurance of familial and genealogical continuity, are unable to supply the requisite sense of stability and continuity. Darcy must value his aristocratic upbringing and heritage, and yet he must acknowledge that he needed Elizabeth's correction to become what he is by the end of the novel. Both Darcy and Elizabeth, it is inferred, become worthy, or lovable, through the agency of the other, when they have left familial control and status. In the scene at Pemberley, the house and land are beautiful, but Austen is at pains to show that what is most impressive is the change in Darcy himself, that he can be nice to Elizabeth and the Gardiners, a change that she is supposed to have wrought in him.

The two halves of this novel, up to and following Darcy's first proposal to Elizabeth at Hunsford, contrast initial assumptions of fixity with an emerging sense of change. Darcy's first proposal marks the culmination of these notions of the stability of self, for both of the protagonists have to be proved wrong in their interpretation of the other before they can begin to accept the possibility of change or improvement. The first and second halves of the novel then contrast the denial or fear of change with signs of the acceptance of and desire for change. (To employ different terms for a moment, such a transition can be seen in terms of the mature acceptance of change and growth, in place of the more childish conviction of permanence or immortality.) The changes are most clearly seen in their acknowledgments at the end of the novel concerning how much the other has done; without Elizabeth, Darcy admits that he would have remained just as he was, but that constancy or stability is something that is no longer desirable.

Austen, however, is neither clear nor consistent about the desirability of change. Wickham, for example, is a classic confidence man, cheerful, amusing, gallant, and obliging in different ways to everyone he meets, one apparently capable of infinite, though by no means desirable, variation, especially in contrast to Darcy's stiffness and fixity. And yet, it also is suggested that he has been willful and wicked from childhood. Austen is unclear about the degree to which individuals are capable of change, but she is far more ambiguous about the causes of both moral character and change. As Mary Poovey notes, Austen makes no consistent attempt to account for the difference between siblings, for in *Sense and Sensibility* Austen attributes the difference between Edward and Robert Ferrars to their education, but the differences between Elinor and Marianne seem to require no such explanation.[26] The moral excellence of the elder Price children is credited to the early hardships they endured, but what accounts for the difference among them is never addressed. For instance, Austen never explains how Susan can survive as an unpolished jewel in the Price household. The best one can conclude is that Austen is at least consistent about what can go wrong with upbringings: Consistently her most distasteful characters are those who have had things too much their own way as children, usually eldest children who have been "spoiled."

The most positive view of character in *Pride and Prejudice* incorporates both fixity and change, permanence and transience. Hume had presented a frightening view of changeable character in his dissolution of personal identity, wherein the self was viewed as nothing more than a collection of impressions that have no inherent coherence or continuity, but only mental and therefore fictitious association. But by the end of the century, change, development, growth, and maturity in character are all concepts that have acquired positive connotations. Austen makes it quite clear that fixity also has its dangers in *Pride and Prejudice,* for Darcy and Elizabeth are surrounded with figures who are incapable of change or improvement. Humours characters such as Mrs. Bennet are presented as ossified. Mrs. Bennet has a simple, transparent, and stagnant personality and is ridiculed for all of these features: "*Her* mind was less difficult to develope. She was a woman of mean understanding, little information, and uncertain temper" (PP 5).

If by arguing for complete fluidity or even dissolution of character, Hume threatens the very notion of personal identity, the antithetical dangers of extreme fixity in this period can be epitomized by the memorable picture Wordsworth draws of a blind beggar in London:

> And once, far-travelled in such mood, beyond
> The reach of common indications, lost
> Amid the moving pageant, 'twas my chance
> Abruptly to be smitten with the view
> Of a blind Beggar, who, with upright face,
> Stood, propped against a wall, upon his chest
> Wearing a written paper, to explain
> The story of the man, and who he was.
> My mind did at this spectacle turn round
> As with the might of waters, and it seemed
> To me that in this label was a type,
> Or emblem, of the utmost that we know,
> Both of ourselves and of the universe;
> And, on the shape of the unmoving man,
> His fix'ed face and sightless eyes, I looked,
> As if admonished from another world.
>
> (1805 *Prelude* VII, 607–22)

One of Wordsworth's most arresting descriptions, this pathetic man is made all the more disturbing by the continual stress on his changeless state. His story, like the sentence of a condemned man, is affixed to his surface, as his static face and sightless eyes call up an infernal world of poverty, mutilation, and death. In an earlier version of these lines, the implication for personal identity is made even terrible:

> and I thought
> That even the very most of what we know
> Both of ourselves and of the universe,
> The whole of what is written to our view,
> Is but a label on a blind man's chest.[27]

In this earlier version, though not so clearly in the 1805 text, Wordsworth has fleshed out a grim pun of character as personality and character as written sign, here savagely condensed into the note on the poor man's chest. The cold and absent writing, lacking the warmth and presence of living speech, epitomizes the inability to interpret or penetrate the fixed story, which for this man has already been told.

In an entirely different fashion and tone, a similar distress at the idea of character as a simple, fixed, or tale already told and finished is evident in *Pride and Prejudice,* beginning in the scene at Netherfield in which the subject of complexity and interpretation of character is addressed; complex characters are more rewarding for the persistent interpreter, as Elizabeth tells Bingley:

> "I understand you perfectly."
>
> "I wish I might take this for a compliment; but to be so easily seen through I am afraid is pitiful."
>
> "That is as it happens. It does not necessarily follow that a deep, intricate character is more or less estimable than such a one as yours. . . .
>
> "I did not know before," continued Bingley immediately, "that you were a studier of character. It must be an amusing study."
>
> "Yes; but intricate characters are the *most* amusing. They have at least that advantage." (PP 42)[28]

In examining the interpretation of Austen's characters, so far we have considered the opposition between static and dynamic concepts of characters, which is closely related to the opposition between simple and complex characters: Intricacy of characters can only be found in those capable of change. It is as if Austen works with three sets of coordinates of character, constant and changeable, simple and complex, knowable and unknowable, and the changeable are often complex and dangerously unknowable, whereas the fixed are usually simple and obvious. These factors are, of course, related, but we can clarify the relationship further. Complexity is the direct consequence of change or development. Darcy becomes interesting because he seems different from moment to moment: There is more to know, more to figure out, more depth to plumb. In addition, he generates interest because he appears to be different from those around him, from others Elizabeth has known, and so she cannot easily figure him out. His intricacy is another word for what has traditionally been called "individualism," the belief that each one is original, unique, special, and no one else is quite like any other. Such assumptions of complexity are, in turn, related to the issue of knowability: If complexity has become a value, a good in and of itself for Austen, then the consequent risk is unknowability. There can be no value without risk or threat of loss, for what is the worth of any gain that anyone can have without exertion? The fineness or delicacy of sentiment and inner feeling that we have explored previously, and the inability of language either to reach it or to convey it, underscore what a scarce and therefore precious commodity intricacy of personality has become. Austen's fiction centers on these interior values of the individual subject, values that can only be mined with scrupulous care, with the greatest skill, to figure out what Darcy is "really like." Like all other objects, the more difficult to acquire, the rarer and scarcer, the more valuable intimate knowledge of the other becomes.

Elizabeth (and the reader) must figure out the enigma of Darcy, and as such, the riddle of his personal nature is quite different from the sort of hermeneutic code of character evident in earlier novels.[29] Compare, for example, the questions posed by Darcy with those by Lord Orville in Fanny Burney's *Evelina*. Although it is true that we must figure out why Lord Orville wrote such an *outré* note to Evelina, the question turns on how this could have happened (was he perhaps drunk?), not on what sort of man he is. Similarly, the hermeneutic code of *Tom Jones* turns on his parentage and external, social questions, not on his internal nature, of which, such as it is, we have been assured from the beginning. Defoe's novels as well do not pose Austen's sort of riddles about what character is "really like"; rather the questions that remain after we wonder how Crusoe or Moll or Jack or Singleton will survive are what their place will be in the social scheme, what kind of status they will achieve, and whether they have the claim to the social distinction from which they always feel that they have been unfairly excluded. Even in *Clarissa*, which contains the most complex characters in eighteenth-century fiction, the reader has been exposed to Lovelace's black heart very early in the novel, even if Lovelace manages to conceal his villainy from Clarissa for a few thousand pages. What remains in suspense, then, is not the essential nature of his character, but rather the question of his willingness to reform, again more an external, social question than an internal, psychological question. In short, such novels concern themselves with what will become of the protagonist, but not with what the protagonist essentially is.

Austen's novels, however, are devoted to determining just what the protagonist essentially is, and the questioning of character is not confined to the complex. Jane Bennet is obviously presented as a simple character, but she is still not easy to decipher: Darcy and Bingley, and to a lesser degree even Elizabeth herself, are unable to read Jane fully.[30] Early on, Charlotte Lucas comments on Jane's habit of concealment and enclosure: "If a woman conceals her affection with the same skill from the object of it, she may lose the opportunity of fixing him; and it will then be but poor consolation to believe the world equally in the dark" (PP 21).

Charlotte Lucas goes on to assert the grave difficulty of fully knowing others:

> I wish Jane success with all my heart; and if she were married to him to-morrow, I should think she had as good a chance of happiness, as if she were to be studying his character for a twelve-month. Happiness in marriage is entirely a matter of chance. If the dispositions of the parties are ever so well known to each other, or ever so similar before-hand, it does not advance their felicity in the least. They always continue to grow sufficiently unlike after-wards to have their share of vexation; and it is better to know as little as possible of the defects of the person with whom you are to pass your life. (PP 23)

These remarks are directed at marriage, a subject about which Charlotte Lucas is a fatalist. But the point has wider significance; it is not possible to know the other fully or finally, for when the object is in flux, any knowledge is evanescent. Knowledge of others, like marriage, could be a matter of chance, not of time and exertion. Darcy is the novel's most opaque character, and Elizabeth has consistent difficulty penetrating his nature; he remains a cipher until he decides to reveal himself in the letter that he gives to Elizabeth at Hunsford. Later, when she has become considerably more interested in his affairs and wishes to know how much they depend upon her, she is still unable to tell.[31] With two such complex characters, knowledge seems impossible without consent. Even so, Elizabeth's wish at Pemberley—"she longed to know what at that moment was passing in his mind" (PP 253; compare *Emma*: "He looked at her, as if wanting to read her thoughts," E 260)—is a desire that will be perpetually frustrated.

Yet despite her flirtation with such frustrations and implicit bars to knowledge, Austen never asserts that it is impossible to know the other. Rather, she works a fine line between intricacy or complexity of character and readability. In these novels, knowledge of others is not so much achieved as it is given as a reward for newly discovered knowledge of self, and the process of knowing others is interiorized. In the second half of the novel, Elizabeth and Darcy have very little commerce with each other, but they are shown to be continually reassessing one another in absentia. This reassessment is acted out by Elizabeth, whom the narrative follows. After Darcy's first proposal and consequent letter, she is shown to be increasingly isolated from her previous confidants, becoming more secretive and self-enclosed; upon return from Hunsford, she summarizes the events of her stay by reflecting upon "how much I shall have to conceal" (PP 217). Secrets destroy the intimacy Elizabeth previously enjoyed with Jane, for now in their conversation "there was still something lurking behind, of which prudence forbad the disclosure" (PP 227), and until disclosure can be made, "she had rather be without a confidante" (PP 320). Jane remains ignorant of Elizabeth's most immediate thoughts: "Elizabeth had sources of uneasiness which could not be suspected by Jane" (PP 334). Elizabeth is unable to confide in Mrs. Gardiner, or even, when Collins's last letter arrives, to share jokes with her father as formerly. This pattern of increased self-enclosure and self-absorption is accompanied by words such as *guarded, suspicions,* and *sly* (PP 258, 261, 292, 325), a vocabulary that underscores the fact that Elizabeth's feelings toward Darcy are formed when she is very much by herself.

Elizabeth's attitude to Darcy changes most dramatically when he is absent; she is forced to respond, not to him, but to signs of him: to his and Mrs. Gardiner's letters, as well as to his portrait at Pemberley. As everyone knows, *Pride and Prejudice* was at one time an epistolary novel, and even in the final version some forty-four letters are mentioned or produced. It is in these letter-reading scenes that the struggles for interpretation take place most clearly. Darcy's letter to Elizabeth is the most obvious example, but the scene in which Elizabeth and Jane try to decipher Miss Bingley's letter offers the best instance of interpretive difficulty. The two sisters trade and compare various readings, all of which are finally proved wrong:

> "What do you think of *this* sentence, my dear Lizzy?"—said Jane as she finished it. "Is it not clear enough?—Does it not expressly declare that Caroline neither expects nor wishes me to be her sister; that she is perfectly convinced of her brother's indifference, and that if she suspects the nature of my feelings for him, she means (most kindly!) to put me on my guard? Can there be any other opinion on the subject?"
>
> "Yes, there can; for mine is totally different.—Will you hear it?" (PP 118)

When he writes to Elizabeth about the enigma of Jane, Darcy describes the method of interpretation that the novel endorses, that of a conscious struggle against subjectivity and projection: "I did not believe her to be indifferent because I wished it;—I believed it on impartial conviction, as truly as I wished it in reason" (PP 197–98). Close inspection like this is of course impossible with a letter, around which the novel's most crucial scenes of interpretations revolve. Again, the pun of character as sign/

character as personality is relevant, because in this novel the other remains an indecipherable sign, its meaning always determined by often dubious interpretation. The most plainly suspect character/sign is Wickham, in whose face and first impression women read "truth" and "veracity" (PP 85 and 86). But Darcy is no more readable; Elizabeth and Darcy arrive at their understanding of one another independently because the other remains so unreachable.[32]

Throughout her acute exploration of all the impediments to knowing others fully and accurately, Austen never suggests that character is unknowable, but only that knowledge of complex persons, as Reuben Brower puts it, is exceedingly difficult, laborious, and fraught with error. Tracing the errors to which interpretation of others is prone makes up the central plot of each of her novels. This tracing is made up not so much of external and epistemological impediments to understanding as of internal or psychological impediments: that is to say, not so much *First Impressions* as *Pride and Prejudice.* In the first half of the novel, Elizabeth's ability to see Darcy is impeded by antipathy, and in the second half by her growing attraction. To analyze such matters, Freud is our most ready guide because our understanding of psychology is formed by the assumptions of Freudian psychoanalysis. The distance between Austen and Freud is also helpful; because Freud's analysis of the state of being in love and of transference is technical and consciously less judgmental than Austen's, his clinical vocabulary helps to demystify what Austen calls love. On the overall topic of the difficulty of interpreting others, Freud's theoretical and metapsychological discussions of transference are most relevant, those in which he argues that one's ability to see and know others is always clouded by transference. In "Dynamics of Transference," Freud writes of need:

> If someone's need for love is not entirely satisfied by reality, he is bound to approach every new person whom he meets with libidinal anticipatory ideas; . . . a cathexis which is held ready in anticipation . . . will have recourse to prototypes, will attach itself to one of the stereotype plates which are present in the subject; or, to put the position in another way, the cathexes will introduce the doctor into one of the psychical series which the patient has already formed.[33]

Response to others is colored by the residue of previous figures, prototypes that merge with or are projected upon the present figure. Analysis brings to the surface these dominant prototypes by transferring the responses they provoke to the figure of the analyst. In this fashion, analysis is said to mobilize or reactivate responses to the powerful figures of the analysand's childhood, early or primitive parental images, which continue to dominate the analysand's object relations into the present. Freud's remarks on transference are usually directed toward the analytic situation, but it is his more general remarks about transference that are the most suggestive for Austen's fiction: "Transference is merely uncovered and isolated by analysis. It is a universal phenomenon of the human mind, it decides the success of all medical influence, and in fact dominates the whole of each person's relations to his human environment" (SE, XX, 42).

The terms of transference provide us with a model for discussing Elizabeth's changing attitudes toward Darcy, Wickham, and her father. As we have seen, Elizabeth is unable to see Darcy as he is and as he changes, in large part because she is changing as well. She begins to recognize her failure to do Darcy justice upon reading his letter:

> Had I been in love, I could not have been more wretchedly blind. But vanity, not love, has been my folly.—Pleased with the preference of one, and offended by the neglect of the other, on the very beginning of our acquaintance, I have courted prepossession and ignorance, and driven reason away, where either were concerned. Till this moment, I never knew myself. (PP 208)

Predisposed to dislike Darcy, as she is to like Wickham, Elizabeth misinterprets both until the crucial letter enables her to adjust her response. This alteration is no simple matter, though, for although Elizabeth may rapidly change her view of Wickham, her recalculation of Darcy takes up the rest of the story. With Darcy, Elizabeth must begin all over again, not only in reassessing him, but in reexamining her methods of interpretation as well. The second half of the novel chronicles Elizabeth's steadily growing attraction to Darcy, but here, too, the focus remains on the subject and not the object of affection, for little of the reprocessing concerns the man himself; rather it relates to the internal adjustments that she herself must make. Although it has been suggested that this latter part of the novel is unnecessarily long, Austen's most subtle treatment of character is at work here.[34] In the second half of her novel, Austen carefully presents Elizabeth's growing absorption in Darcy, as he begins to acquire all of the qualities that Elizabeth comes to admire: "She began now to comprehend that he was exactly the man, who, in disposition and talents, would most suit her. His understanding and temper, though unlike her own, would have answered all her wishes" (PP 312). The process by which he acquires value is that of transference, which

Freud analyzes in "Being in Love and Hypnosis," where he writes, in the "question of being in love, we have always been struck by the phenomenon of sexual overvaluation":

> The tendency which falsifies judgment in this respect is that of *idealization*. But now it is easier for us to find our bearings. We see that the object is being treated in the same way as our own ego, so that when we are in love a considerable amount of narcissistic libido overflows on to the object. It is even obvious, in many forms of love-choice, that the object serves as a substitute for some unattained ego ideal of our own. We love it on account of the perfections which we have striven to reach for our own ego, and which we should now like to procure in this roundabout way as a means of satisfying our narcissism.
>
> If the sexual overvaluation and the being in love increase even further, then . . . the ego becomes more and more unassuming and modest, and the object more and more sublime and precious, until at last it gets possession of the entire self-love of the ego, whose self-sacrifice thus follows as a natural consequence. The object has, so to speak, consumed the ego. Traits of humility, of the limitation of narcissism, and of self-injury occur in every case of being in love. . . . The whole situation can be completely summarized in a formula: *The object has been put in the place of the ego ideal.* (SE, XVIII, 112–13)

Austen's portrayal of the progress of love in all her novels conforms to this formula, for each of her heroines, not just Emma, must be humiliated before her love can be rewarded—each of the heroines follows the pattern of idealizing the other while abasing the self. Elizabeth's re-evaluation of Darcy begins with her declaration "How despicably have I acted. . . . How humiliating is this discovery!" (PP 208); the subsequent action can be glossed by her own summary, "For herself she was humbled; but she was proud of him" (PP 327). From this perspective, Elizabeth's view of Darcy in the second half of the novel is no more accurate than in the first half, because, as Freud argues in "Observations on Transference-Love," all love is determined by transference. After exploring the "genuineness" of love generated by analytic transference ("can we truly say that the state of being in love which becomes manifest in analytic treatment is not truly a real one?"), the paper ends by calling into question the genuineness of all love:

> it is true that the love consists of new editions of old traits and that it repeats infantile reactions. But this is the essential character of

every state of being in love. There is no such state which does not
reproduce infantile prototypes. It is precisely from this infantile
determination that it receives its compulsive character, verging as
it does on the pathological. Transference-love has perhaps a degree less of freedom than the love which appears in ordinary life
and is called normal; it displays its dependence on the infantile
pattern more clearly and is less adaptable and capable of modifica-
tion; but that is all, and not what is essential. (SE, XII, 168)[35]

Suggestive as it is, this explanation of love as transference can be
further particularized through the use of revisionist, post-Freudian work
on transference. More than forty years ago, Geoffrey Gorer observed that
Austen's heroines marry figures similar to their fathers: Each of the six
novels follows a "girl who hates and despises her mother and marries a
father-surrogate."[36] Although there may be some truth to this generalization, it has the effect of reducing Austen's heroines to psychoanalytic
stereotypes. In order to examine the specific nature of transference love
in these novels, we should turn to the theory of self-psychology developed by Heinz Kohut, the contemporary psychoanalytic authority on
narcissism, solipsism, and narcissistic transference.[37] Kohut sees narcissism as developing as a compensation for an insufficiently developed
sense of self or identity, and this sense of inner lack is manifested by a
dependence on self-objects, transitional objects with which the subject
tries to supplement her defective concept of self. In Kohut's précis, "The
essential psychopathology in the narcissistic personality disorders is defined by the fact that the self has not been solidly established, that its
cohesion and firmness depend on the presence of a self-object (on the
development of a self-object transference), and that it responds to the
loss of the self-object with simple enfeeblement, various regressions, and
fragmentation."[38] Kohut's theories of narcissism provide a very compelling explanation for a number of features in Austen's fiction, but as is the
case with all psychological models, his theories need to be balanced
against a more concrete social and historical understanding of the individual subject.

The presence of narcissism in Austen's novels has already been no-
ticed. In *The Female Imagination*, Patricia Meyer Spacks characterizes
Elizabeth Bennet as a kind of adolescent narcissist; Elizabeth's "struggles
with her narcissism" reflect a condition common to adolescent females
when they are socialized to perform as reflections of male love.[39] Maturation in *Emma*, according to Spacks, involves a transcendence of adolescent narcissism and solipsism: "Emma must learn to transcend her own
kind of selfishness," just as "at the novel's end she [Elizabeth] and Darcy

both transcend solipsism."[40] These two figures, Emma and Elizabeth, are Austen's most egotistical characters, who experience the world as a reflection of the self. Emma especially is selfish, self-centered, and egotistical; to employ Kohut's clinical description of narcissistic behavior, Emma appears to entertain "grandiose fantasies" of unrealistic power, to manifest a "recurrent theme of being 'special,' 'unique,' and very frequently, of being 'precious'. . . . [one who commonly expresses] the archaic need for certainty of success and for limitless achievement and limitless acclaim."[41] Because Elizabeth is a more likable character, the usually pejorative term *narcissist* may seem unnecessarily harsh when applied to her. But if Elizabeth is not so vain, she too is presented as a figure inclined to measure the world in terms of her self:

> "There are few people whom I really love, and still fewer of whom I think well. The more I see of the world, the more am I dissatisfied with it; and every day confirms my belief of the inconsistency of all human characters, and of the little dependence that can be placed on the appearance of either merit or sense." (PP 135)

Here we can see Elizabeth's similarity to the more obviously haughty Emma, both of whom are like those who, in Kohut's words, embrace "narcissism by concentrating perfection and power upon the self—here called the grandiose self—and by turning away disdainfully from an outside to which all imperfections have been assigned" (*Analysis* 106). At the outset, both lack, and therefore must learn, what Kohut calls a sense of "realistic imperfections and limitations of the self" (*Analysis* 108). If Elizabeth does not quite have Emma's "grandiose self image which is rigidly defended by hostility, coldness, arrogance, sarcasm, and silence," Elizabeth does exhibit some of Emma's "painful narcissistic tensions experienced as embarrassment, self-consciousness, and shame" (*Analysis* 135–36 and 262). For both, the climactic realization of emotional dependence can be seen in terms of Kohut's description of the narcissist's "gradually increasing awareness of the intensity of her demands and of her need for their fulfillment, a recognition which she resisted vigorously because she now could no longer deny the presence of an extreme neediness in this area which had been covered for a long time by a display of independence and self-sufficiency," a passage that aptly fits Emma's sudden realization of her need for Knightley (*Analysis* 293).

A model of narcissism seems fitting for two such assertive, self-confident, and aggressively egotistical characters, but Kohut's theory is most useful because it is appropriate for the likes of Fanny Price as well. Austen writes of two sorts of heroines, one kind brash, aggressive, self-confident, witty, egotistical, and proud (Emma, Elizabeth, and, to a lesser degree, Elinor), the other timid, withdrawn, vulnerable, lacking in self-esteem (Anne, Fanny, and, to a lesser degree, Catherine). All six of Austen's heroines fit Kohut's description of narcissistic personality structure. Emma and Elizabeth conform to Kohut's profile of the grandiose type of narcissism, and Fanny and Anne conform to his profile of idealizing narcissism, which, according to Kohut, is characterized by an "intense hunger for a powerful external supplier of self-esteem and other forms of emotional sustenance" (*Analysis* 17). Much more fragile and easily wounded than Emma, in their "search for an external object of perfection," Fanny and Anne display "a great vulnerability of . . . [their] self-esteem," seeking praise and always wounded when they think it is insufficient (*Analysis* 44 and 57). Fanny in particular is a character marked by what Kohut identifies as narcissistic symptoms: "vague and diffuse depression, disturbed work capacity, and irritability . . . self-consciousness, shame propensity, hypochondriacal preoccupations, and ill-defined physical discomforts" (*Analysis* 86). This description of symptoms would have little use but for the fact that both types are fundamentally related by the same underlying narcissistic personality structure. Such personalities often swing back and forth from one to the other, that is, between these two basic manifestations of narcissism: Emma's, the grandiose state, called *mirror transference* and epitomized by the assumption " 'I am perfect,' " and Fanny's, called *idealizing transference* and epitomized by the assumption " 'You are perfect, but I am part of you' " (*Analysis* 27). The relationship between the two can be summarized as follows: these "two basic narcissistic configurations . . . are, of course, antithetical. Yet they coexist from the beginning and their individual and largely independent lines of development are open to separate scrutiny" (*Analysis* 27). They are "two facets [object/subject] of the same developmental phase, or, in other words . . . they occur simultaneously" or in "parallelism" (*Analysis* 107).

These characters correspond to Kohut's profile of narcissism, as do the causes of narcissistic personality disorders: They occur when parents fail to supply the needs of the child from the original state of primary narcissism, when the child still experiences parents as part of himself, as a "self-object," that is, when the mother mirrors the child, and then later when the child attempts to idealize a parent, usually the father:

> the child has two chances as it moves toward the consolidation of
> the self—self disturbances of pathological degree result only from
> the failure of both. . . . The two chances relate, in gross approx-
> imation, to the establishment of the child's cohesive grandiose-

exhibitionistic self (via his relation to the emphatically responding merging-mirroring-approving self-object), on the one hand
[e.g., the mother], and to the establishment of the child's cohesive
idealized parent-imago (via his relation to the emphatically responding self-object parent who permits and indeed enjoys the
child's idealization of him and merger with him), on the other
[e.g., the father]. (*Restoration* 185)[42]

   In Austen's novels, parents are inadequate at best and hateful at worst.
If mothers are not dead, as in *Emma* and *Persuasion*, they are distant and
callous, as in *Mansfield Park*; ineffectual and vain, as in *Sense and Sensibility*; or foolish and stupid, as in *Pride and Prejudice*. (The only sensible
parents are Catherine Morland's in *Northanger Abbey*, so sensible, in fact,
that Austen must remove Catherine from their good influence for the
bulk of the novel and substitute a type of Mrs. Bennet.) Inadequate
mothers appear frequently in Austen's fiction, and ineffectual fathers are
just as numerous.[43] Mr. Bennet is more vivacious and witty than the
imbecile Mr. Woodhouse, but in the end Elizabeth's father appears
comparably indolent, withdrawn, weak, and morally irresponsible. Mr.
and Mrs. Bennet are typical Austen parents: Both are selfish, vain, and
self-absorbed. In reaction to her foolish mother, Elizabeth has plainly
turned to her father, who also fails her. Rather than see Elizabeth's
response to her father's failure merely as the repetition of universal
Oedipal desire, as Gorer does, we can instead describe her search for
external ideals in Kohut's terms: she "was convinced that the maternal
self-object would not provide her with self-esteem-enhancing acceptance and approval . . . [and so] she had attached herself with great
intensity to her father. . . . The relation to her idealized father, in other
words, provided her with the outlines of an internalized structure—a
paternal ideal—which was a potential source of sustenance for her self"
(*Restoration* 61). Elizabeth's recognition of her love for Darcy occurs
simultaneously with her disappointment in her father, for she rejects the
father as she accepts the lover, following the narcissistic "need to attach
themselves to powerful figures in their surroundings in order to feel that
their life had meaning, indeed, in order to feel alive" (*Restoration* 146).

Though the evidence is slight (from memoirs by relatives written after
Austen was dead and from the letters that her sister Cassandra did not
burn) and the argument highly speculative, this pattern of narcissism
must have had part of its origin in Jane Austen herself. Such an argument
can also become circular, moving out of the novels to the life and back
again, looking for evidence of a family life not dissimilar from that

portrayed in the novels. There is little factual evidence about Austen's childhood, but from the patterns established in Kohut's clinical evidence, Austen's parents ought to have been distant and withdrawn. There is no direct criticism of the mother in her letters, except for some suggestive hints of hypochondria. Jane Austen writes to Cassandra: "My mother continues hearty, her appetite & nights are very good, but her Bowels are still not entirely settled, & she sometimes complains of an Asthma, a Dropsy, Water in her Chest & a Liver disorder" (L 39). The tone of private letters is often difficult to decipher, but it is clear that this list of ailments is being ridiculed, whether the list originated with mother or daughter. Later she writes to Cassandra:

> It began to occur to me before you mentioned it that I had been somewhat silent as to my mother's health for some time, but I thought you could have no difficulty in divining its exact state— you, who have guessed so much stranger things. She is tolerably well—better upon the whole than she was some weeks ago. She would tell you herself that she has a very dreadful cold in her head at present; but I have not much compassion for colds in the head without fever or sore throat." (L 57)

Austen it seems has no compassion for sickness that lacks symptoms. George Holbert-Tucker concludes of the mother, "By the 1790's, when Mrs. Austen was nearing sixty, she seems . . . to have developed a tendency towards hypochondria."[44] (It is perhaps no accident that Austen's first published novel, *Sense and Sensibility*, involves a heroine, Elinor Dashwood, who suffers considerably at the hands of a weak and foolish mother who adores another, rival sister, and so the good, dutiful daughter must provide all the sense and direction that the mother lacks.) Whatever the source of her ailments, in her very old age, Mrs. Austen shows an indolence worthy of *Mansfield Park*'s Lady Bertram, telling her grand nephew, " 'Ah, my dear, you find me just where you left me,—on the sofa. I sometimes think that God Almighty must have forgotten me.' "[45]

If Mrs. Austen did suffer from hypochondria when Jane Austen was younger, the family situation corresponds to the pattern that Kohut describes, and to that found in the Bennet family as well. When the mother is withdrawn and unable to provide the child with sufficient mirroring, in compensation the child seeks to idealize the other parent. Narcissistic personality structures arise when the second parent fails to satisfy the child's needs. Jane Austen appears to have idealized her father, seeking to share his love of words, as she was free to roam in his study. In the "Biographical Notice of the Author" introducing *Persuasion*, Jane Austen's brother characterized their father as having "a most exquisite taste in every species of literature."[46] Kohut outlines such a pattern in which literary interests are traced to a desire "to share the father's power in the realm of language" or "artistic activities were an attempt to live up to a paternal ideal of perfection" (*Restoration* 14 and 61). For narcissism to develop, however, the second parent has to fail as well, after the child has turned to him with a heightened need. If this pattern occurred, some oblique evidence may lie in Jane Austen's apparent hysteria that followed her father's abrupt and financially unfortunate decision to retire and leave the family home at Steventon. Though conjectural, this projection of Austen's early family history parallels that of the Bennet family, with its vain, foolish, and self-absorbed mother and idealized father who grievously disappoints an adoring daughter.

Kohut's prototypical narcissist manifests "a faulty integration of the grandiose self, which led to swings between states of anxious excitement and elation over a secret 'preciousness' that made her vastly better than anyone else (during times when the ego came close to giving way to the hypercathected grandiose self) and states of emotional depletion (when the ego used all its strength to wall itself off from the unrealistic grandiose substructure)."[47] Such swings can be seen in the very structure of *Emma* and *Pride and Prejudice*, swings from well-being, euphoric grandiosity to depressive depletion and humiliation. This oscillation, on a larger scale, is evident in the pattern of the composition of the novels themselves, from *Pride and Prejudice* to *Mansfield Park* to *Emma*.[48] As Meredith Skura writes in *The Literary Use of the Psychoanalytic Process*,

> The analyst is always concerned with the relationship between the fictional story and the narrator to whom it ultimately refers. The relation is not always a matter of substitution, in which the patient makes up a substitute self as an alternative to the real one. The location of the self is not that simple and may be present in the entire narrative.[49]

Thus, Austen's personality can be seen as condensed into the six novels and miniaturized in each of the novels, with their obsessive swings from pride to humiliation and back again, from grandiose inflation to vulnerable deflation, such that the very moral lesson embedded in each of the novels has its origin in the psychic history of the author.

Nonetheless, I do not want to overemphasize the personal origin of this narcissism or to insist that Austen's characters are narcissists. Rather, we should see that the nature of character in Austen's fiction is narcissistic, for hers is a fiction marked by privatizing strategies, by constant withdrawals, and by a sense of the preciousness and specialness of character. Narcissism in Austen's fiction is not merely a function of Jane Austen's personal neurosis, but it is a cultural, historical, and generic phenomenon as well, the historical result of a culture whose highest narrative form focuses on the individual's self-recognition: As Lukács observes, "the inner form of the novel has been understood as the process of the problematic individual's journeying towards himself."[50]

The moral lesson of humble chastisement (as in the humiliation of Emma Woodhouse) has sources and explanations outside the personal history of Jane Austen as well as inside. What is most notable about Austen's pattern of composition is the fact that her novels, and their differing heroines, seem to alternate from celebration to condemnation of individualism and subjectivity. This oscillation can be ascribed only in part to the different sides or phases of narcissism, for we ought to see that this oscillation is endemic to the period itself, and particularly to this class, the gentry or pseudo-gentry, for the subject/object phases that Kohut writes about can also be understood in terms of the nostalgic and progressive views of the gentry. Austen embodies a backward-looking code of noblesse oblige, social obligation in estate management, and genealogical as well as social continuity in figures such as Darcy and Knightley, but also in the more rigidly moral heroines such as Elinor and Fanny, with their dependence upon and vigorous approbation of traditional social form and obedience to external authority. More mobile figures such as Captain Wentworth, however, bespeak a "morality of improvement," which, in Wentworth, is pictured as something quite different from the voracious acquisition of that speculator in real estate, John Dashwood, and so in *Persuasion,* as many have noted, Austen is far less certain and insistent about the value of traditional, fixed social hierarchy. And with a character such as Emma ("whom no one but myself will much like") or Elizabeth Bennet, Austen is decidedly ambivalent, at once rebuking and celebrating Emma's and Elizabeth's wayward but winning individualism.[51]

The phenomenon of *Pride and Prejudice*'s rhythmic alternation between pride and humiliation can thus be attributed to history—eighteenth-century social or religious lessons that the novel embodies (the abasement of pride); or to ideological contradiction inherent in turn-of-the-century landed gentry; or to psychology—to the pattern of idealization Freud analyzes or those patterns Kohut finds in narcissistic personalities. As different as these explanations appear, they are not necessarily contradictory and mutually exclusive. Rather, as we have suggested, social and political history lay the ground for individual psychology, personal explanation, and models. The apparent embrace of and repudiation of subjectivity and individualism is dramatized in Elizabeth Bennet's personal story, and Austen presents this story as a moral fable. Nevertheless, we can see that this opposition has its roots in cultural and ideological contradiction, between allegiance to a vestigial inherited code of social obligation and to an endorsement of a morality of improvement that is only partially recognized by Austen. The need for psychological explanations of change, growth, and maturity itself has its roots in a society increasingly and publicly dedicated to accumulation and its morality of improvement. We need always to balance the individual explanations that psychoanalysis provides with the larger, collective explanation of history. The best analysis is capable of showing the relationship between these two types of explanation. Bersani gives us a glimpse of this connection by showing the social reasons behind Austen's and other nineteenth-century novelists' commitment to the notion of the psychological integrity:

> Psychological complexity is tolerated as long as it doesn't threaten an ideology of the self as a fundamentally intelligible structure unaffected by a history of fragmented, discontinuous desires. . . . The literary myth of a rigidly ordered self contributes to a pervasive cultural ideology of the self which serves the established social order. Personality is shown to have the coherent, hierarchical wholeness suitable to a social system of sharply distinct ranks. A rigid social hierarchy reproduces, in political structures, the form of the self.[52]

In exploring the question of self-knowledge and knowledge of others in Austen, we have passed from Hume's "convenient fiction"; through Freud's explanation of the source of the fiction, which for him is transference; and on to Kohut's more specific source in narcissistic transference. Having followed this chronological sequence, it is now necessary to repudiate a sense of progress, as if we are getting closer to the truth, or at least closer to a more accurate or scientific analysis. It would be useful here to consider Roy Schafer's critique of Kohut, whose theories of the self in a post-Freudian period of psychoanalysis Schafer regards as "one of the problematic stopgap concepts . . . transitional to new modes of psychoanalytic conceptualization." Not only is Kohut a transitional figure on the way to some place else, betwixt and between ego psychology and the psychology of the self, but more importantly, Kohut's central concept, the "self," is itself a changeable and volatile term.[53] Though he does not go on to make the point, Schafer's argument implies that notions of self and identity are quintessentially historical and, we should add, ideological formations. The latter is a point that Louis Althusser has made with great penetration in his Lacanian essay, "Ideology and Ideological State Apparatuses." The function of all ideology is to provide just such a frame for identity or self: "the category of the subject is only constitutive of all ideology insofar as all ideology has the function (which defines it) of 'constituting' concrete individuals as subjects. . . . all ideology hails or interpellates concrete individuals as concrete subjects."[54]

At this point, to pass on to yet another theorist, on to a Lacanian concept of the fragmentary and decentered self, "the self's radical excentricity to itself," will not solve the fundamental difficulty, for again, we have come back to the problem of applying contemporary psychology to characters conceived much earlier.[55] Narcissism is particularly problematic in this regard, for although Freud may have presented hysteria, his prototypical pathology, as transhistorical, theorists of narcissism, including Kohut, suggest that this is a peculiarly contemporary issue. As Lasch, Kovel, and others have argued, narcissism has come to seem like an unavoidable consequence of life under capital, with its overwhelming split between public and private, and the consequent privileging of interior experience. The difference in manifestations of narcissism between Austen's and our own day, then, suggests the differences between early and late capital, between the beginning of industrial and late monopoly capitalism.[56] There is no question but that Austen does not easily or willingly privilege subjectivity and interior experience (and as we have seen, she does her best to repress or chastise the manifestations of narcissism): Self-absorption is nevertheless a necessary if unrecognized consequence of her estranged and alienated view of social relations and her uneasy combination or contradiction between social morality and private fulfillment.

Thus, even though Austen appeals to a conservative view of the stability of personality, the "problem of discontinuous selves," in Langbaum's words (following Hume), is not an idea that is necessarily anachronistic for Austen.[57] As Spacks puts it, "If novelists like Richardson and Fielding assert the stability of identity, Boswell insists on the converse. Identity, he suggests, is made."[58] John O. Lyons argues that a concept of self was invented in the second half of the eighteenth century, replacing older notions of soul. Jane Austen's lifetime coincides with these changes, but even though "self" and "identity" were abstractions that differ from ours, we have no reason to assume that they were any less elusive than they are today. Analysis of character from earlier periods seems irrevocably caught betwixt and between. It is of course necessary to recognize and comprehend the fact that concepts of identity change, as much as forms of representation change, for otherwise we are left with the blindly unhistorical results of conventional psychoanalytic inter-pretation. Nevertheless, this is an endeavor in which historical positivism is least likely to succeed, because attempts to deny one's own contempo-rary notion of character (depth psychology in particular) in order to reconstruct some distant and different historical idea proceed with the rejection of the complexity and variety of experience in favor of a neces-sarily simplified model. Such a deceptively narrow "historical" recon-struction can be seen in Kenneth Moler's discussion of Emma's "iden-tity," a discussion that begins by questioning Lionel Trilling's claim that *Emma* is about the problems of identity in a confusing world. Moler insists, on the contrary, that Emma has always been clearly defined by her family and her social position:

> It is very difficult to find, either in Emma herself or in the opinions of the other characters in the novel, the slightest doubt about who Emma is, what she is, or why she exists. Their religion and their social organization provide Emma and her neighbors with an-swers to these questions. . . . What is occasionally questioned in the novel—by others and eventually by Emma herself in her moments of self-knowledge—is not Emma's position or function in life, but whether something has prevented her from filling her known position properly and performing her given function well.[59]

This is a reasonable and persuasive argument, based as it is on evidence from eighteenth-century devotional literature, which defines self-knowledge in religious or moral terms of duty. But it is also a simplifying argument, which uses one area of historical study, here religion, to provide the total explanation of the culture, effacing complication and contradiction. In effect, Moler takes Austen's word for it, and in so doing he provides a narrowly traditional view of the historical moment, while he fails to recognize the social changes and consequent ideological con-tradictions that Austen's fiction embodies even if she does not fully recognize them. Established social forms and hierarchy should serve to define Emma adequately, but my point is that these forms do not fully serve, particularly at this historical moment when social form is coming to be seen as external to the individual self and alienated from it. Moler's argument conceives of identity entirely in social and external terms and therefore can only proceed by minimizing the considerable anxiety Emma suffers at the revelation of Harriet's attraction to Knightley. Then, when undefined by external powers, father or lover, Emma's sense of purpose as well as her sense of identity is clearly and painfully in doubt. Certainly Austen goes on to exert all of her narrative skill to assuage and efface this pain and confusion, but to remember only the comic solution in Austen's novels is to belittle her achievement in representing and preserving the contradictions of her culture. This type of interpretation is finally an instance of the practice Raymond Williams repeatedly warns against: "the reduction of the social to fixed forms. . . . Thus we speak of a world-view or of a prevailing ideology or of a class outlook, often with adequate evidence, but in this regular slide towards a past tense and a fixed form suppose, or even do not know that we have to suppose, that these exist and are lived specifically and definitively, in singular and developing forms."[60]

Following the persuasive argument of Skura, that psychoanalytic literary studies should be modeled on the analytic situation, we can draw an analogy between the endeavor to interpret character and Schafer's notion of psychoanalysis, which attempts to "construct life histories of human beings":

> Thus, when psychoanalysts speak of insight, they necessarily imply emotionally experienced transformation of the analysand, not only as life history and present world, but as life-historian and world-maker. It is the analysand's transformation and not his or her intellectual recitation of the explanations that demonstrates the attainment of useful insight. The analysand has gained a past history and present world that are more intelligible and tolerable than before, even if still not very enjoyable or tranquil. This past and present are considerably more extensive, cohesive, consistent, humane, and convincingly felt than they were before. But these gains are based as much on knowing *how* as on knowing *what*. Insight is as much a way of looking as it is of seeing anything in particular.[61]

In short, we should rather aim for a dialectical process, mediating between psychoanalysis and history, to preserve our recognition of the characters of the past and of their difference.

5
Courtship, Marriage, and Work

For the whole endeavor of both parties during the time of courtship is to hinder themselves from being known, and to disguise their natural temper and real desires, in hypocritical imitation, studied compliance, and continued affectation. From the time that their love is avowed, neither sees the other but in a mask, and the cheat is managed often on both sides with so much art and discovered afterwards with so much abruptness that each has reason to suspect that some transformation has happened on the wedding night, and that by a strange imposture one has been courted and another married.
— Samuel Johnson, *Rambler* 45[1]

At the end of *Emma*, we are told that Emma Woodhouse and Mr. Knightley marry and live happily ever after: "the wishes, the hopes, the confidence, the predictions of the small band of true friends who witnessed the ceremony, were fully answered in the perfect happiness of the union" (E 484). Such fairy-tale formulae occur at the end of all Austen's novels, and it is difficult to ascertain what relation these promises of perfect happiness have to the often suspicious or even jaundiced view of marriage evident throughout the rest of the novels. Consider Austen's other Emma, the sheltered younger sister of *The Watsons*, whose eldest sister counsels her: "you know we must marry.—I could do very well single for my own part—A little Company, & a pleasant Ball now & then, would be enough for me, if one could be young for ever, but my Father cannot provide for us, & it is very bad to grow old & be poor & laughed at" (MW 317). Is it only wealth that separates the perfect happiness of the one Emma from the misery that threatens the other? The stories of the two Emmas were composed ten years apart, in different places, and Austen nowhere asks us to reconcile the brutality of *The Watsons* with the gentility of *Emma*. But nevertheless the presence of poverty is felt even in the luxurious world of *Emma*, for the unenviable condition of Miss Bates is ample reminder that "it is very bad to grow old & be poor & laughed at."

In novels, marriage can always perform the formal function of closure, or it can serve as a "mirror of morality," celebrating and marking fruitful union.[2] Marriage can also be seen as the reward of self-knowledge for heroines such as Emma or Elizabeth Bennet.[3] But whatever moral purpose that marriage serves in her narrative, Austen never lets us forget that marriage is also an economic institution. The complex ways in which the moral or emblematic as well as emotional and financial dimensions of marriage interrelate want explanation, for the impulses, motives, and needs of marriage in Austen's fiction are complex and contradictory: The desire of romance is inevitably complicated by financial necessity.[4] *Sense and Sensibility* provides the most interesting example for investigation because Austen's representation of marriage is most hard-nosed there, and so it is most ambivalent. Her portrayal has softened considerably by the time of *Persuasion;* but although romantic idealism is more clearly portrayed as desirable at the end of her career than at the beginning, Austen never minimizes the illusions that accrue to romantic expectations—in all her fiction, marriage is an endeavor ever fraught with danger and disappointment.[5] From first to last in these novels, marriage is closely tied to money, as well as to social status. It is often difficult to explain the relationship between the two poles of love and money, whether we call the opposition romantic and pragmatic or idealist and realist or idealist and materialist. It is particularly difficult to fix their relationship in Austen's fiction because one has not been clearly valorized above the other, though it is hard for modern readers not to assume that they have been hierarchized; nevertheless, the relationship between love and money is neither hierarchical nor dialectical, even while they are always found together and affect one another. Austen summarizes the situation of Edward and Elinor in a typically qualified statement: "they were neither of them quite enough in love to think that three hundred and fifty pounds a-year would supply them with the comforts of life" (SS 369).

No one would deny that a novel such as *Sense and Sensibility* is a comedy that perforce culminates with a celebration of marriage. As Tony Tanner observes in *Adultery and the Novel, Contract and Transgression,* "it is a truism that the majority of bourgeois novels either conclude with marriage (e.g., Jane Austen) or—if they start with marriage—inevitably go on to explore the very *inquiétudes* that are engendered by the married state."[6] Yet although *Pride and Prejudice* celebrates Elizabeth and Darcy's marriage, as well as Jane and Bingley's, these are set alongside Lydia and Wickham's marriage, as well as Charlotte Lucas and Mr. Collins's, whose unions offer no cause for celebration. It is possible that, as with many comedies, marriage serves as a reward for protagonists, and as a punishment for antagonists, but then Charlotte Lucas is not an antagonist. Furthermore, the only marriage that is shown in detail is the Bennets', and this marriage is abysmal. Austen's novels move toward a climactic marriage by anatomizing the failures of marriage along the way. Thus, although they celebrate a handful of individual marriages, they do not celebrate the institution per se, as the disaster of the Rushworths, to call up an extreme example, indicates:

> In all the important preparations of the mind she [Maria Bertram] was complete; being prepared for matrimony by an hatred of home, restraint, and tranquillity; by the misery of disappointed affection, and contempt of the man she was to marry. The rest might wait. The preparations of new carriages and furniture might wait for London and spring, when her own taste could have fairer play. (MP 202)

To paraphrase Raymond Williams, marriage in these novels is not seen flatteringly. Yet, to return to Tanner, a double reading of marriage is not uncommon:

> although the eighteenth- and nineteenth-century novel may be said to move toward marriage and the securing of genealogical continuity, it often gains its particular narrative urgency from an energy that threatens to contravene that stability of the family on which society depends. It thus becomes a paradoxical object in society, by no means an inert adjunct to the family décor, but a text that may work to subvert what it seems to celebrate.[7]

This paradoxically subversive celebration is historically determined by the function or structure of marriage in bourgeois society:

> marriage is *the* central subject for the bourgeois novel; not marriage as a paradigm for the resolution of problems of bringing unity out of difference, harmony out of opposition, identity out of separation, concord out of discord—as it is, for instance, in *A Midsummer Night's Dream*, where marriage is not only social but magical, mythical, metaphysical—but just marriage in all its social and domestic ramifications in a demythologized society. Or rather a society in which marriage *is* the mythology (at least the socially avowed one; it would be possible to say that money and profits made up a more secret mythology). Marriage, to put it at its simplest for the moment, is a means by which society attempts to

bring into harmonious alignment patterns of passion and patterns of property; in bourgeois society it is not only a matter of putting your Gods where your treasure is (as Ruskin accused his age of doing) but also of putting your libido, loyalty, and all other possessions and products, including children, there as well. For bourgeois society marriage is the all-subsuming, all-organizing, all-containing contract. It is the structure that maintains the Structure, or System (if we may use that word, for the moment, to cover all the models, conscious and unconscious, by which society structures all its operations and transactions). The bourgeois novelist has no choice but to engage the subject of marriage in one way or another, at no matter what extreme of celebration or contestation. He may concentrate on what makes for marriage and leads up to it, or on what threatens marriage and portends its disintegration, but his subject will be marriage.[8]

Comparison between *A Midsummer Night's Dream* and *Sense and Sensibility* is instructive, for it suggests the vast difference between earlier comic drama and the novel; marriage in Austen is no longer presented as a sacred emblem or sacramental ritual, but rather it has been entirely secularized. Unlike the image of a cosmic dance of harmony in Sir Thomas Elyot's *The Governour* or the emblematic union of practical and speculative wisdom in *Tom Jones*, marriage for Austen is entirely a matter of earthly choice. Though it may refer to or serve or run parallel to other thematic or didactic patterns found in these novels (reward for self-knowledge, for example), it is not represented in emblematic fashion. Marriage in these six novels is presented as a social, domestic, legal, and economic event and condition. This is not to say that it is "natural" or that it is demythologized, for it certainly is not. In order to understand thoroughly Austen's use of marriage, that is, the way in which she manages simultaneously to idealize and to undermine, we need to try to extricate the material and institutional dimensions of marriage from its mythological or emotional dimensions—the myths of rightness, uniqueness, appropriateness—the reward of romantic love. At the heart of her technique lies a presentation of idealized aspiration that resides alongside an often harsh portrayal of the inadequacies of particular examples. That is to say, marriage is portrayed as both work and reward. Because it is not possible to explore such questions entirely from within a single text, we shall proceed comparatively, by measuring Austen's representation of marriage in *Sense and Sensibility* with her remarks in her letters, particularly those to her favorite niece, Fanny Knight, which were written when Fanny was considering an offer of marriage. In addition, the reconstruction and interpretation of marriage made possible by historians of the family such as Lawrence Stone in *The Family, Sex and Marriage in England 1500–1800* and other more recent revisionist historians provide indispensable tools to measure private and possibly idiosyncratic visions against larger social and historical patterns.

The five extant letters of Jane Austen to Fanny Knight compose a remarkably clear statement about marriage.[9] These letters are all that could be desired, for they are lucid, to the point, not patronizing, but in all appearances, careful and thoughtful statements presenting a considered opinion on what to look for and expect in a marriage partner. These are, in fact, the most compelling letters in the whole collection, in part because of their sense of urgency, and in part because they are not composed in the elliptical shorthand more common in Austen's letters to her sister Cassandra. It is apparent from all of the letters (as well as from the later memoirs by family members) that after Cassandra, Fanny Knight was the woman with whom Austen was most intimate.[10] Throughout the collection, from the time when Fanny was still a child, up till the letters just prior to her death, Austen displays a marked affection for Fanny; in 1808, when Jane was thirty-three and Fanny eleven, Austen writes to Cassandra that Fanny is "almost another Sister,—& [I] could not have supposed that a niece would ever have been so much to me. She is quite after one's own heart; give her my best Love, & tell her that I always think of her with pleasure" (L 217). Nine years later, in the midst of the debate over a suitor for Fanny, Austen writes even more pointedly, "You are the delight of my Life. . . . It is very, very gratifying to me to know you so intimately. You can hardly think what a pleasure it is to me, to have such thorough pictures of your Heart.—Oh! what a loss it will be when you are married" (L 478–79). I belabor this point not merely to emphasize Austen's sense of responsibility over these matters, but also to suggest the great sense of idealization and desire Austen invested in her niece, as in one's own children. Austen seems to have participated in Fanny's courtship as a kind of wish fulfillment. Their relationship then is not unlike that of Mrs. Gardiner and Elizabeth Bennet in *Pride and Prejudice*, but more importantly, I think, it gives a hint of what Austen's attitude toward her creation Elizabeth Bennet might have been like.

These letters, then, present Austen's theory of marriage, and it is a theory that is consistent with her novels and with her other letters.[11] In 1808 Austen writes to Cassandra, "Lady Sondes' match surprises, but does not offend me; had her first marriage been of affection, or had there been a grown-up single daughter, I should not have forgiven her; but I consider everybody as having a right to marry *once* in their lives for love, if they can" (L 240).[12] Much like the sentence describing Edward and Elinor, who were not so much in love as to marry without sufficient income, this statement is formed of contrasts and qualifications; Austen offers her sanction for this obviously imprudent match only after weighing a series of questions on propriety (how this reflects on or affects husband and daughter), only to end with that characteristically turned expression: Love is a natural right, if you can procure it. Such turns characterize all of Austen's pronouncements on marriage.[13] Concerning Fanny's first proposal, Austen writes of this "perfect match," "such a person may not come in your way [again], or if he does, he may not be the eldest son of a Man of Fortune. . . . Anything is to be preferred or endured rather than marrying without Affection" (L 409–10; compare Jane's advice to Elizabeth: "do any thing rather than marry without affection," PP 373). Whether the statement begins with love or with money, the other is sure to follow by the end of the sentence. In the last letter of advice to Fanny that we have, Austen ends with this romantic exhortation: "Do not be in a hurry; depend upon it, the right Man will come at last . . . [and then] you will feel you never really loved before" (L 483). This sentence, which would not seem out of place in a Harlequin Romance, is found on the same page as the following warning: "Single Women have a dreadful propensity for being poor—which is one very strong argument in favour of Matrimony" (L 483). Just as Elinor Dashwood argues in *Sense and Sensibility*, Austen invariably insists that both love and a competent income are necessary for marriage.

The opinions about marriage in the letters are not dissimilar from the view in her novels, nor are they dissimilar to the general pattern of change in the later eighteenth-century that has been detailed by social historians. Lawrence Stone reports a growing "demand" for affection, as Austen counsels Fanny: "nothing can be compared to the misery of being bound *without* Love" (L 418), and again, "I could not wish the match unless there was a great deal of Love on his side" (L 482). These qualifications to marriage correspond to what Stone labels the "companionate marriage." (Sir Walter Scott offers an exemplary definition of the companionate marriage in *Waverley*: "Although Flora was sincerely attached to her brother . . . she was by no means blind to his faults, which she considered as dangerous to the hopes of any woman, who should found her ideas of a happy marriage in the peaceful enjoyment of domestic society, and the exchange of mutual and engrossing affection.")[14] Of the four possible motives for marriage that Stone distinguishes, monetary gain, personal affection, sexual attraction, and romantic love, Austen regularly portrays the first as common but corrupt.[15] Such marriages abound in *Sense and Sensibility*, from Colonel Brandon's brother's voracious acquisition of the pathetic Eliza, to Willoughby, whose attraction to Miss Grey is reported to lie in her "Fifty thousand pounds" (SS 194). Alternately, Austen thinks as little of physical attraction, as is evident in Elizabeth's condemnation of Lydia and Wickham: "But how little of permanent happiness could belong to a couple who were only brought together because their passions were stronger than their virtue, she could easily conjecture" (PP 312). The other two categories, personal affection and romantic love, are not easily separated, but Austen's novels are built around the attempt to distinguish them. Of the latter, she appears to affirm its attraction while she doubts its efficacy, if not its reality. Elinor warns Marianne: "after all, Marianne, after all that is bewitching in the idea of a single and constant attachment, and all that can be said of one's happiness depending entirely on any particular person, it is not meant—it is not fit—it is not possible that it should be so" (SS 263).

Here Elinor does not deny the appeal of romance, only the likelihood of its producing lasting happiness. As with Austen's remark on Lady Sondes, everyone has a right to marry for love *once* in her life, *if* she can. Throughout *Sense and Sensibility*, Austen again and again validates the type of attachment that Edward and Elinor develop, with all their reticence to declare love, and their use of the word *esteem* instead, which so infuriates Marianne (SS 21). Elinor and Marianne exemplify this opposition between the gradual development of friendship and affection versus what amounts to romantic "love at first sight" (Austen may indulge in a little joke here, having Marianne fall in love as she falls down the side of the hill). Elinor is disturbed by the rapidity with which Marianne and Willoughby establish their intimacy, a rapidity that is facilitated by romantic expectations: "His person and air were equal to what her fancy had ever drawn for the hero of a favourite story"; "Willoughby was all that her fancy had delineated in that unhappy hour and in every brighter period, as capable of attaching her" (SS 43 and 49).

Austen's letters and novels also convey obvious disapproval of arranged marriages, of the type that Stone describes as prevailing. Almost all of her novels proceed in a programmatic way through a series of variations on marriage arrangements; typically, in *Pride and Prejudice*, Elizabeth endures her mother's choice of Mr. Collins and Darcy's independent choice, before finally achieving a successful union of mutual consent with parental approval. Of the four types of arrangement—entirely of the parents' making, parental choice subject to the child's veto, the child's choice subject to the parents' veto, and entirely the child's determination—Austen shows no sympathy for the first.[16] The long-term plans of Darcy's mother and Lady Catherine to marry their children together come to nothing, and Mrs. Ferrars's plans for her son Edward and Miss Morton are similarly ridiculed. Mrs. Ferrars proceeds on the assumption of "interchangeability," which, though Stone says is characteristic of a much earlier period, is still evident in these novels.[17] Personal affection is so negligible that one son can substitute for the other equally well, as John Dashwood informs his sisters:

> "We think *now*"—said Mr. Dashwood, after a short pause, "of *Robert's* marrying Miss Morton."
> Elinor, smiling at the grave and decisive importance of her brother's tone, calmly replied,
> "The lady, I suppose, has no choice in the affair."
> "Choice!—how do you mean?"—
> "I only mean, that I suppose from your manner of speaking, it must be the same to Miss Morton whether she marry Edward or Robert."
> "Certainly, there can be no difference; for Robert will now to all intents and purposes be considered as the eldest son." (SS 296– 97)

Although this respect and concern for class status or social position over any personal or interior characteristics are clearly represented as outmoded, this attitude is not confined to the Ferrars in *Sense and Sensibility*, for Charlotte Palmer shows a similar confidence in her mother's duty and ability to arrange her marriage to someone or other. Here she confides to Elinor her indifference to her mother's choice of mate for her:

> "I believe," she added in a low voice, "he [Colonel Brandon] would have been very glad to have had me, if he could. Sir John and Lady Middleton wished it very much. But mama did not think the match good enough for me, otherwise Sir John would have mentioned it to the Colonel, and we should have been married immediately."
> "Did not Colonel Brandon know of Sir John's proposal to your mother before it was made? Had he never owned his affection to yourself?"
> "Oh! no; but if mama had not objected to it, I dare say he would have liked it of all things. He had not seen me then above twice, for it was before I left school. However I am much happier as I am. Mr. Palmer is just the kind of man I like." (SS 116–17)

Charlotte Palmer is an unreliable authority on Colonel Brandon's desires, but her expectations concerning marriage arrangements run a lot closer to the norm in *Sense and Sensibility* than do Marianne's ideas of high romance. In the end, Marianne succumbs to substantially the same process that Charlotte Palmer describes, for the match with Colonel Brandon is, in very large part, arranged by her friends:

> Marianne Dashwood was born to an extraordinary fate. She was born to discover the falsehood of her own opinions, and to counteract, by her own conduct, her most favourite maxims. She was born to overcome an affection formed so late in life as at seventeen, and with no sentiment superior to strong esteem and lively friendship, voluntarily to give her hand to another! (SS 378)

Although parental tyranny in arranging marriages meets with little approval from Austen, management entirely by children is not recommended either. Edward attributes the mischief of his engagement with Lucy Steele, the chief complication of the plot, to too much leisure and independence: "I returned home to be completely idle, and . . . I had therefore nothing in the world to do, but to fancy myself in love" (SS 362). Mutual consent of child and parent is the only arrangement that is likely to succeed in Austen's novels. Complete independence is often dangerous in these novels, as can be seen in the likes of Willoughby and Henry Crawford and Lucy Steele and Isabella. Throughout Austen's novels there is a consistent disapproval of the idle leisure class; Frank Churchill, Yates, Henry Crawford, Robert Ferrars, Willoughby, Wickham, all vicious young men with too much time on their hands, are set against the likes of Edward, Edmund, Henry Tilney, Captain Wentworth, all active workers, as well as the wealthy but conscientious manager Mr. Knightley. In general, Austen is suspicious of those who do not work for a living.[18]

We have to conclude, then, that some of the changes in attitude that Stone, Trumbach, and other progressivist social historians describe as having occurred by the end of the eighteenth century are not fully evident in Austen's novels.[19] Or, more precisely, the changes that Stone describes as complete appear in her novels as changes in attitude, though perhaps not in practice. Stone writes that "the late eighteenth century sees the full development of the romantic novel, whose central theme was the struggle of love and personal autonomy against family interest and parental control."[20] This pattern, however, does not fit very well Jane Austen (or Fanny Burney or Charlotte Smith or Maria Edgeworth or Elizabeth Inchbald or Sir Walter Scott, for that matter), whose novels portray personal autonomy as being as dangerous as rigid parental control. Whether this ill fit is due to the fact that Austen is a conservative social thinker, an anti-Jacobin, as Marilyn Butler puts it, or that she is particularly attuned to the difficulties unmarried women faced, or that Stone is perhaps too optimistic in his conclusions is difficult to determine. On the basis of the evidence found in Austen's writings, the companionate marriage of affective individualism remained more an ideal than a common social practice.[21] Judging from Jane Austen's view, the actual situation seems to have been one of far more flux and confusion than any of the social historians suggest; after all, it is their business to make order out of the chaos of history. Austen's plots, of course, are designed to exploit such confusion, for without conflict, there can be no story. Following a good many eighteenth-century novelists, Austen sets her heroines on their own, with little parental support on which they can rely. Often Austen's parents and parental surrogates create active difficulties for the children, as do Sir Walter Elliot or Mrs. Norris. Yet compared with more traditional types of parental opposition in the earlier novel, which derives from dramatic sources, such as Mr. Harlowe in *Clarissa*, Squire Western in *Tom Jones*, Madame Duval in *Evelina*, or Schedoni in *The Italian*, parental interference in Austen's novels is pretty mild. In *Sense and Sensibility*, Elinor is portrayed as being more mature and responsible than her mother, but even in *Pride and Prejudice*, Mrs. Bennet functions as a minor irritant, an embarrassment rather than a serious obstacle to the heroine's marriage.

These heroines are not beset by heavy fathers or scheming mothers so much as they are threatened with financial insecurity, for Austen is more concerned with financial than familial conflict. *Northanger Abbey* employs the most conventional romantic plot, with a paternal blocking figure in the general, yet here this plot is openly parodic. All of her heroines occupy "comfortable" social positions (higher, it would seem, than Austen's own), and with the notable exception of Emma, at the story's opening find themselves in straitened or fallen or threatened circumstances. Only in *Emma* and *Northanger Abbey* are the family fortunes secure, and in *Northanger Abbey* their financial stability is threatened by rumor. We are given considerable detail about the personal finances of the heroines: Catherine Morland has £3,000; Elinor, Marianne, Elizabeth, and Jane have £1,000 apiece; Emma has £30,000; and Anne £10,000 (which her father cannot spare). Fanny has nothing, but presumably Sir Thomas can provide for her. Only one, then, clearly has sufficient resources to marry into the class into which she was born.[22] The situation in *The Watsons* may be the most melodramatic, as the preservation of the impoverished family is set against the odious Lord Osborne's attentions to Emma, but at bottom this plot is not so different from that of the other novels. Without fortune in the form of a marriage portion, these characters are set out in the world to preserve themselves by their wit and personal beauty, both perishable commodities, as the officious John Dashwood observes after being informed that Marianne has been ill:

> "I am sorry for that. At her time of life, any thing of an illness destroys the bloom for ever! Her's has been a very short one! She was as handsome a girl last September, as any I ever saw; and as likely to attract the men. There was something in her style of beauty, to please them particularly. I remember Fanny used to say that she would marry sooner and better than you did; not but what she is exceedingly fond of *you*, but so it happened to strike her. She will be mistaken, however. I question whether Marianne *now* will marry a man worth more than five or six hundred a-year, at the utmost, and I am very much deceived if *you* do not do better." (SS 227)

On another occasion Charlotte Lucas describes marriage as "the only honourable provision for well-educated young women of small fortune, and however uncertain of giving happiness, must be their pleasantest preservative from want" (PP 122–23). Austen writes about well-educated young women of small fortune, whose only preservative from want is marriage. The war with France and its blockade resulted in a period of high inflation, one in which the ratio of marriage portion to dower (marriage portion is the sum paid by the bride's family at marriage in return for jointure, the compensating widow's annuity) was steadily going up—in short, a bad market in which to be a marriageable woman.[23] The father of a son was inherently in a better bargaining position than the father of a daughter; sons brought money into the family, but daughters only took money out. As Miriam Slater puts it, "the father of the prospective bride negotiated under the disadvantage of a buyer's market whereas the father of the prospective groom normally enjoyed the advantage of a seller's market."[24]

Marriage, then, remained a business. Despite the prevalence of romantic novels, and a nascent ideology that celebrated personal fulfillment through marriage of affection, it is evident that marriage as a financial transaction had by no means disappeared (or has ever disappeared). Marianne speaks scornfully of an imagined compact between Colonel Brandon and some "woman of seven and twenty" (Anne Elliot's and Charlotte Lucas's age), as a union between nurse and patient: "It would be a compact of convenience, and the world would be satisfied. In my eyes it would be no marriage at all, but that would be nothing. To me it would seem only a commercial exchange, in which each wished to be benefited at the expense of the other" (SS 38). Marianne's scorn echoes the language of Mary Wollstonecraft, who writes regularly of marriage as a business: "The mighty business of female life is to please."[25] So, too, the first page of Maria Edgeworth's *Belinda* announces, "her aunt had endeavoured to teach her [Belinda] that a young lady's chief business is to please in society, that all her charms and accomplishments should be invariably subservient to one grand object—the establishing herself in the world."[26] Though heavily ironic, the concluding passage on Lucy Steele's marriage to Robert Ferrars uses similar vocabulary of business and prosperity as the reward of labor:

> The whole of Lucy's behavior in the affair, and the prosperity which crowned it, therefore, may be held forth as a most encouraging instance of what an earnest, an unceasing attention to self-interest, however its progress may be apparently obstructed, will do in securing every advantage of fortune, with no other sacrifice than that of time and conscience. (SS 376)[27]

The point to be made about this business or market or labor vocabulary is not that marriage had become more of an economic event, but rather that this economic vocabulary seems obtrusive and angry precisely because marriage was coming to raise such different expectations. In other words, conflicts between love and money, romance and reality, had, if anything, become more exacerbated and more visible than they had been earlier in the century. The metaphor comparing marriage to business or to work suggests the degree to which marriage really was a form of labor, and so examination of this point should expose the nature of the antagonism between the economic reality of marriage and the romantic mythology that obscures it.

Julia Prewit Brown has shown how marriage in this period was for women what the choice of profession was for men, and this is a point that Mary Wollstonecraft almost comes to in her comparison between men's education to profession and women's education to marriage:[28]

> In the middle rank of life, to continue the comparison, men, in their youth, are prepared for professions, and marriage is not considered as the grand feature in their lives; whilst women, on the contrary, have no other scheme to sharpen their faculties. It is not business, extensive plans, or any of the excursive flights of

ambition, that engross their attention; no, their thoughts are not employed in rearing such noble structures. To rise in the world, and have the liberty of running from pleasure to pleasure, they must marry advantageously, and to this object their time is sacrificed, and their persons often legally prostituted.[29]

Though it does not suit the present needs of Wollstonecraft's argument, which is to assert the limiting and degrading nature of women's education, nevertheless the logical extension of her comparison here is that women work toward marriage in the same way that men work toward a profession, as a kind of preferment or sinecure, for she writes elsewhere that "Before marriage it is their [women's] business to please men."[30] Austen's heroines understand equally well that courtship is female business, particularly if they have mothers such as Mrs. Bennet for whom "The business of her life was to get her daughters married" (PP 5). Mrs. Bennet, however, does not get her daughters married—they have to do that work for themselves; if marriage or courtship is a business, late eighteenth-century women are more self-employed than they are employed by another. That is to say, affective individualism and the rise of personal autonomy in choosing mates meant that young women had to do work that, in their mothers' time, would have been done for them. Young women had to assume a burden that parents used to bear for them. At the least, the limits of responsibility were unclear. In *Persuasion*, after the engagement of Anne and Captain Wentworth is disrupted by parental interference, neither knows how to resume the initiative to address the other again. Austen's heroines are sent out to do business in a bad market, without adequate direction and without adequate training, on the shifting ground between a compact of affection and a transfer of property. Such uncertainty may be seen as the cause of much of Elizabeth Bennet's trouble and anxiety: Though she is brought up by her father to respect her own intelligence and worth, nevertheless she finds herself in a marriage market in which she is evaluated not by some measure of intelligence or individual or inner worth but by wealth and beauty. These characters find themselves in a marriage market without their choosing to be, even before they seem to be aware that they have been put up for sale. Elinor and Marianne are assumed to be angling for husbands by all they meet, from Fanny Dashwood to Sir John Middleton to Mrs. Jennings. Sir John tells them that Willoughby "is well worth catching," a phrase that Mrs. Dashwood finds objectionable: " 'I do not believe,' said Mrs. Dashwood, with a good humoured smile, 'that Mr. Willoughby will be incommoded by the attempts of either of *my* daughters towards what you call *catching him*. It is not an employment to which they have been brought up. Men are very safe with us, let them be ever so rich' " (SS 44). This denial has no effect, for shortly thereafter Sir John insists to Marianne,

> "You will be setting your cap at him now, and never think of poor Brandon."
>
> "That is an expression, Sir John," said Marianne, warmly, "which I particularly dislike. I abhor every common-place phrase by which wit is intended; and 'setting one's cap at a man,' or 'making a conquest,' are the most odious of all. Their tendency is gross and illiberal; and if their construction could ever be deemed clever, time has long ago destroyed all its ingenuity."
>
> Sir John did not much understand this reproof; but he laughed as heartily as if he did. (SS 44–45)

Despite their objections, the women of Austen's fiction are considered "out" or nubile whether they will or no. Emma's suddenly finding herself wooed by Mr. Elton, though it is comic testimony to her blindness, also attests to the fact that she is considered available for marriage, in much the same way that Elizabeth is pursued by Mr. Collins. Though it is often said that there is no real work nor any real laborers in Austen's fiction, in fact, her novels are full of both, young women working at courtship, laboring toward marriage, their pleasantest preservative from want.

That the work of courtship had become more burdensome than it had been a few generations earlier is clear from the remarks of Mary Wollstonecraft. Though one might expect her to be more sympathetic to the conflicting pressures felt by young women, at times she blames them for exactly the sort of prudence and circumspection that parents had exercised earlier: "Girls marry merely to *better themselves,* to borrow a significant vulgar phrase, and have such perfect power over their hearts as not to permit themselves to *fall in love* till a man with a superior fortune offers."[31] This is just the sort of prudence that Austen recommends to her niece Fanny. In this period it would seem as if the children of the propertied classes were educated to contradictory sets of values, romance and finance, told to expect or hold out for affection in a world ruled by commodity. If the "finishing" education to female accomplishments was, as Wollstonecraft insists, directed toward the "business to please men," then the practice of female education remained focused on courtship, while the ideology of romantic attachment, which is supposed to be natural and spontaneous, necessarily contradicted the need for rules and instruction, art and artifice:[32]

Women are told from their infancy, and taught by the example of their mothers, that a little knowledge of human weakness, justly termed cunning, softness of temper, *outward* obedience, and a scrupulous attention to a puerile kind of propriety, will obtain for them the protection of man; and should they be beautiful, every thing else is needless, for, at least, twenty years of their lives.[33]

In short, women were expected to abide by strict rules of propriety, exert their training in pleasing, while living in both ideal and material worlds of romance and commodity. For characters such as Elinor Dashwood and Elizabeth Bennet, who are presented as being especially intelligent, it is no wonder that they find the whole process of "setting one's cap" abhorrent. Neither is shown to be comfortable or happy or at ease displaying herself as available, being "out." Both Stone and Wollstonecraft liken being displayed in Bath or London to marketing: "what can be more indelicate than a girl's *coming out* in the fashionable world? Which, in other words, is to bring to market a marriageable miss, whose person is taken from one public place to another, richly caparisoned."[34] "A Young Lady's Entrance into the World," Burney's phrase for the prototypical female plot, is accompanied in the fiction of this period, by grandmothers in Burney, aunts in Edgeworth, and the likes of Mrs. Jennings in *Sense and Sensibility,* who, like real estate agents, superintend their charges' entrance onto the marriage market. In such a market, where women are no longer valued solely by family connections or portion, stress on beauty exacerbates the tendency to reify or objectify women into a commodity. The best example of commodification in Austen's fiction is found in Marianne Dashwood: As her brother so clearly sees, in sickness she is scarcely worth £400 or £500 a year; this estimate of her worth has no relation to her character, her nature, or any internal quality, but only to her looks, her "bloom." In such circumstances, it is easy to see why Elinor Dashwood, Elizabeth Bennet, Emma Woodhouse, and the others are so alienated from the work of courtship: When the process itself objectifies one into a commodity and results in loss of self-determination or autonomy, the whole event is dispiriting and dehumanizing—"the worker sinks to the level of a commodity"; "the worker is related to the *product of his labor* as to an *alien* object."[35]

In this respect, marriage is no different from other social relations that were undergoing extreme change as a consequence of industrial capitalism, which Marx described as a " 'reification' of human relationships," through which patriarchal and feudal traditions of authority, structure, stability, and hierarchy were reduced to their exchange value.[36] As

Wordsworth complains in a famous letter, "Everything has been put up to market and sold for the highest price it would bring."[37] That is to say, objects became valued, not for some traditional values or some natural, unalienable properties they possessed, use value, but rather for their exchange value, for what they would fetch. The object itself becomes meaningless, beyond what it can bring in the market, much as in the real estate boom in California in the 1970s. As Clifford Siskin argues, mass production transformed the value of exclusivity: "the object of desire as value is transferred from the product, *whatever* its associations, to the act of possession."[38] Austen confronts these changes in *Mansfield Park,* when Mary Crawford celebrates that "true London maxim, that every thing is to be got with money" (MP 58).[39] In its most extreme form, these new practices of consumption seem to pass beyond the desire for possession to acquisition in and of itself. For example, to John Dashwood, land has been divorced from estates and inheritance and is now merely a commodity to be bought and sold. Here he is complaining to Elinor of his cash flow problems:

> "And then I have made a little purchase within this half year; East Kingham Farm, you must remember the place, where old Gibson used to live. The land was so very desirable for me in every respect, so immediately adjoining my own property, that I felt it my duty to buy it. I could not have answered it to my conscience to let it fall into any other hands. A man must pay for his convenience; and it *has* cost me a vast deal of money."
>
> "More than you think it really and intrinsically worth."
>
> "Why, I hope not that. I might have sold it again the next day, for more than I gave: but with regard to the purchase-money, I might have been very unfortunate indeed; for the stocks were at that time so low, that if I had not happened to have the necessary sum in my banker's hands, I must have sold out to very great loss." (SS 225)

Despite the vestiges of the aristocratic values exemplified by the hereditary estate, Dashwood's interest is that of a speculator, a prototype prefiguring *Sanditon*'s real estate developer/profiteer, Mr. Parker; the land is purchased, not to expand or buttress the hereditary estate, but to make a cash profit, for it can be exchanged for more than he paid for it.[40] The attitude that John Dashwood displays toward the land is analyzed by Marx in his *Economic and Philosophical Manuscripts of 1844*:

> It is necessary that this appearance [the idealized view of feudal allegiance to the hereditary estate and its master] be abolished—

that landed property, the root of private property, be dragged completely into the movement of private property and that it become a commodity; that the rule of the proprietor appear as the undisguised rule of private property, of capital, freed of all political tincture; that the relationship between proprietor and worker be reduced to the economic relationship of exploiter and exploited; that all personal relationship between proprietor and his property cease, property becoming merely *objective,* material wealth; that the marriage of convenience should take the place of the marriage of honor with the land; and that the land should likewise sink to the status of a commercial value, like man.[41]

Early industrial capitalism leads to a general dissociation of possession from acquisition, which can be seen in marriage practices as well. If wives are chosen not on the basis of their lasting family connections and power, but simply for their portion or for their beauty, then marriage too comes to be regarded as acquisition but not possession, that is to say, as an act, but not as a condition—marriage is something performed once, not an ongoing responsibility. In the case of a wife chosen for her beauty (a wife who cannot, of course, be easily discarded or exchanged for another), she may become like Lady Middleton, purely ornamental. Unlike a valuable painting that can be exchanged for more than was given, a wife is rather more like wallpaper, attractive, perhaps, but of no exchange value, as Mr. Bennet finds to his cost when he marries solely on the basis of looks.[42] If, on the other hand, a wife is chosen for her portion, as Willoughby is supposed to do with Miss Grey's £50,000 portion (SS 194), then the ostensible object, Miss Grey, is valueless from the start: As he complains later, "She knew I had no regard for her when we married" (SS 329). Unlike conditions in laboring classes, where mates may be attractive for tangible and presumably lasting skills such as weaving, spinning, or household economy, besides their looks and/or possessions, or unlike the upper classes, in which birth and title remained substantial values, conditions from the middle classes to the lower gentry seem to conspire to make a wife useless when once acquired, as is clear from this bizarre exchange between Mrs. Jennings and her son-in-law:[43]

> "Aye, you may abuse me as you please," said the good-natured old lady, "you have taken Charlotte off my hands, and cannot give her back again. So there I have the whip hand of you."
> Charlotte laughed heartily to think that her husband could not get rid of her; and exultingly said, she did not care how cross he

was to her, as they must live together. It was impossible for any
one to be more thoroughly good-natured, or more determined to
be happy than Mrs. Palmer. The studied indifference, insolence,
and discontent of her husband gave her no pain: and when he
scolded or abused her, she was highly diverted. (SS 112)

In short, in this period young women seem to have had to endure the
duties, responsibilities, and blame of courtship, without much of the
benefits. We can draw a general analogy between women working
toward marriage and the laboring classes. The latter may eventually have
benefited from the industrial and capitalist revolutions, but nevertheless,
in the period when patriarchy was disintegrating, so was the sense of
moral responsibility, and with the loss of responsibility went all of the
patronizing institutions of patriarchy. As a consequence, for a time,
between 1790 and 1820 (these are the years during which Jane Austen
was writing novels), for the laboring classes, conditions became much
worse before they became better (without any poor relief, in some cases,
or in the workhouses and poorhouses the most miserable conditions
imaginable).[44] Austen focuses on this period in which the working
conditions, as it were, declined for young women engaged in the work of
courtship.

These issues concerning the conditions of courtship and marriage are so
deeply infused in *Sense and Sensibility* that it almost seems as if the novel
proceeds as a systematic exploration of the possibilities. Its title and its
heroines are so schematically set up that it is easy to be distracted by the
thematic oppositions that seem to govern it. With so many contrasting
pairs, the novel suggests a couplet structure of balance and antithesis;
yet, as has been argued over the thematic contrast so visible in the title,
pairs do not necessarily lead either to neat, valorized oppositions or to
any happy syntheses. In terms of marriage, the multiplicity of contrasting
examples serves more to confuse and distract than to suggest any clear
recommendation. Elinor's sense and Marianne's sensibility are not finally reducible to restraint and excess nor to prudence and folly, nor does
Austen offer us any easy Horatian mean between the two.

   The many marriages anatomized in *Sense and Sensibility* are not set into
simple oppositions of approved and disapproved behavior, but rather
they are arranged in increasing complexity of choice. Elinor and Marianne form only one of the contrasting pairs around which the story is
built, for these two sisters are matched by the two brothers, Edward and
Robert Ferrars. As further contrast, Austen includes the two Steele sisters, as well as the two daughters of Mrs. Jennings, Mrs. Palmer and Lady

Middleton, and finally the two Elizas. This pattern suggests that Austen chooses to focus not on the individual choice but rather on the family, so that marriage remains a familial, not an individual, affair. We are invited to examine marriage possibilities, not so much in terms of the separate marriages, but through the contrast of five family situations, and also five different kinds of parental pressure: the Dashwoods, the Ferrars, the Jennings, the Steeles, and the Brandons. From this point of view, it is not surprising that the marriages of the Dashwood sisters ultimately are relatively similar, as are the Jennings sisters', and so on. Austen employs this method of contrasting marriages in all of her novels, though less so in the later ones: *Northanger Abbey* compares Catherine Morland and Henry Tilney's marriage with that proposed between James Morland and Isabella; *Pride and Prejudice* compares Elizabeth and Darcy's marriage with those of Wickham and Lydia, Charlotte Lucas and Mr. Collins, and Jane and Bingley; *Mansfield Park* contrasts Maria Bertram and Rushworth's marriage with that of Fanny and Edmund. (In *Emma*, although two brothers marry two sisters, Harriet's, Elton's, and Jane's marriages are all of a different order and so do not seem to be presented any longer as explicit parallels. And in *Persuasion*, there is nothing to compare with the union of Captain Wentworth and Anne Elliot, which suggests how much stronger is the individualist and romantic ideology at the end of Austen's career.) In Austen's first few novels, the multiplicity of contrasts has the effect of removing the motives for marriage from an individual plane onto a familial or social plane: That is, the various choices do not represent individual styles or decisions, so much as they represent the range of available forms.

In *Sense and Sensibility*, however different their beginnings may be, in the end the matches made by Elinor and Marianne are quite similar to each other, in contrast to the matches made by Mrs. Jennings's daughters, which also resemble each other. For the former we are told, "It was contrary to every doctrine of her's [Mrs. Dashwood's] that difference of fortune should keep any couple asunder who were attracted by resemblance of disposition" (SS 15). Judging from the results of her matchmaking, it would appear that it was contrary to every principle of Mrs. Jennings's that difference of disposition should keep any couple asunder who were attracted by resemblance of fortune. Neither the Palmers nor the Middletons have anything in common save similar economic status. Yet compared to the undisguised greed of Fanny and Robert Ferrars, who are continuously exposed by the narrator to satiric ridicule, the marriages of Mrs. Jennings's daughters are presented not as corrupt or disgraceful or even regretful, but rather as normative. That is, if in the matters of love and marriage the Dashwoods are idealized, and the Ferrars and Steeles satirized, the Jenningses may represent Austen's sense of ordinary practice. The norm here is determined by class: It was only the propertied classes in which parents could exert strong influence over children's marital choices; this pattern indicates that Austen exploits a kind of betwixt and between status, in order to set up a conflict of influence and autonomy. Furthermore, within these contrasts and oppositions, the choices seem governed by parental control, which is, in turn, environmental or educational (the Dashwoods of one mother are romantic, of another are pragmatic). The Dashwoods, Jenningses, Steeles, and Ferrars all follow a familial pattern, with the exception of Edward Ferrars, who, we are told, has been educated quite differently from his foppish brother. Colonel Brandon is similarly presented as being the romantic opposite of his voracious brother, though in his case, the difference appears to be that between older and younger sons, wherein the younger, paradoxically, can afford to indulge himself in romantic dreams because he has nothing to lose.

Because Marianne's romantic notions of attachment most conform to our own, readers are likely to identify hers as the central values of the novel as a whole, the ones by which the others should be judged. Even when readers accept the "authority" of Elinor's more prudent and practical view, it is common to find muted expressions of disappointment at what happens to Marianne, disappointment that she has to be penalized with Colonel Brandon, chastised under a policy of reduced expectations. It would be a mistake, however, to evaluate all these marriages by the standard of the most idealized vision. We may judge that few are shown to be successful, in our narrow sense of leading to some domestic comfort, if not some variety of happiness, yet in her terms of acquisition and social mobility, Lucy Steele's marriage to Robert Ferrars is wildly successful. Willoughby is the only one to complain that his marriage is a failure, and even then he does so only to elicit sympathy from Elinor, and, indirectly, from Marianne. Only the marriage of the first Eliza breaks down into public scandal and divorce: Again, the marriages of the Middletons and the Palmers are more typical. Although the Middletons have nothing in common, and seem ill suited to one another, there is no indication of discontent. The Palmers hardly fulfill romantic expectations of companionate union, but they are by no means unhappy, and Mrs. Palmer shows every sign of being content with her lot. Although Marianne most obviously is forced to soften her harsh judgment of Mrs. Jennings and family, it is significant that Austen also has Elinor change her view of Mr. Palmer, who seems to be a preliminary sketch for Mr. Bennet—Mr. Palmer is similarly disappointed in marrying an attractive but silly woman. However, when Elinor observes him at his home, he too is not displeased with his domestic lot.

Sense and Sensibility argues that romantic expectations have little likelihood of producing either domestic tranquility or personal happiness. Marianne's attraction to Willoughby, which amounts to a restrained version of "love at first sight," is viewed with suspicion from the first. Austen represents such love not as some natural or spontaneous action, but a result of mediated desire, the result of romantic longing or expectation or desire, for "something evermore about to be" in Wordsworth's phrase. As Austen makes clear, Willoughby conforms to what Marianne's "fancy had delineated."[45] Marianne's precipitous attraction to Willoughby, then, is set in explicit contrast to the slow growth of Elinor's esteem for Edward. Elinor's courtship is characterized by labor or exertion, in short, work, whereas her sister's is characterized by laxity and lassitude. One method leads to security and happiness, the other to disappointment, which is followed by exertion, security, and (qualified by an indeterminately troubling policy of lowered expectations) happiness. All of this returns us to the sense that in Austen's view courtship must involve some sort of work to develop affection and respect.

From *Northanger Abbey* to *Persuasion,* Austen makes it clear that it is not enough that the two protagonists like or even love each other. In several of the novels, including *Northanger Abbey* and *Mansfield Park,* the heroine's affection for the man she will marry is established early on, from childhood in the case of Fanny Price. In others, including *Pride and Prejudice* and *Emma,* it is the male protagonist's affection that develops first, though of course this is not revealed until near the end of *Emma.* Either way, both characters spend the length of the novel learning enough about the other to venture into a lifelong compact of dependence. In *Northanger Abbey,* Austen is quite explicit that Catherine and Henry do not know one another well enough to marry safely: His father's "unjust interference [and the delay occasioned by it], so far from being really injurious to their felicity, was perhaps rather conducive to it, by improving their knowledge of each other, and adding strength to their attachment" (NA 252). This is an idea that Austen returns to again at the end of her life, in *Persuasion,* where Anne Elliot and Captain Wentworth "returned again into the past, more exquisitely happy, perhaps, in their re-union, than when it had been first projected; more tender, more tried, more fixed in a knowledge of each other's character, truth and attachment; more equal to act, more justified in acting" (P 240–41). If the romance plot of these works is based on some sort of trial or *agon,* that trial is resolved only through knowledge of the other, the sine qua non of successful marriage according to Austen. At the onset, Captain Wentworth and Anne Elliot may have enough affection for one another, but they do not have sufficient knowledge of one another to risk marriage. In *Sense and Sensibility,* Willoughby's confession shows that Marianne was not deceived by his affection for her, but she had no adequate knowledge of his character. In this novel, the issue of knowledge is underscored by the emphasis on mystery and secrecy.[46] Lucy Steele hoards and selectively (and punitively) divulges secrets about Edward. Mrs. Jennings has an unseemly interest in Colonel Brandon's unknown "business" that takes him away to London so mysteriously. Marianne seems to conceal a secret engagement to Willoughby, and Elinor takes it upon herself to spy on her sister and her correspondence when they are in town (see, for example, SS 156–57 and 167).

Within the highly constrained and structured rituals of courtship, the task set for both man and woman, but chiefly for the woman, since she is the one who gives up most, is to find out enough about the other to venture her independence. As with any other important investment, but most especially with this one in which one's very person is invested, one does as much research as possible to minimize risk; that research is what the labor of courtship involves for Austen's heroines: not only angling or setting one's cap in the business of pleasing, but rather more studying a potential, all-important investment. However much research one does, Austen still makes it clear that marriage is a high-risk investment, for it is by very definition a bad business practice—sinking all of one's working capital into one single venture. As Mary Crawford observes to Fanny Price after recounting a horrific series of marital disasters among her London acquaintances ("I look upon the Frasers to be about as unhappy as most other married people"), "This seems as if nothing were a security for matrimonial comfort!" (MP 361). But nonetheless, courtship and marriage remain the only real work open to women in this period and class.

All this emphasis on work, labor, money, interest, and investment may seem far more appropriate to the hard-nosed and angry *Sense and Sensibility* than it does to *Persuasion,* which is considerably more romantic. Yet here too Anne Elliot and Captain Wentworth must also work at courtship. Financial considerations may seem less prominent because both are relatively wealthy by the end, but Austen underscores the fact that it was Wentworth's lack of fortune that was the principal reason for their parting seven years earlier. Although Anne's sisters and father stand out for their greed for social and material superiority (something of the reverse of Elinor and her mother), nevertheless, his original lack of cash is never forgotten. At the end, when he inquires of Anne, she makes it clear that "a few thousand pounds" would have enabled them to marry:

> "Tell me if, when I returned to England in the year eight, with a few thousand pounds, and was posted into the Laconia, if I had then written to you, would you have answered my letter? would you, in short, have renewed the engagement then?"
> "Would I!" was all her answer; but the accent was decisive enough. (P 247)

As the last chapter sums up, "Captain Wentworth, with five-and-twenty thousand pounds, and as high in his profession as merit and activity could place him, was no longer nobody" (P 248). Once again, Austen insists that affection is not sufficient means on which to marry. This insistence is perhaps more forcefully asserted in *Persuasion* than in any other of the novels, for it is inevitable that any romantic plot, with its idealization of marriage, in a realistic treatment is bound to make normative practice seem all the worse—the grander the expectations, the worst common practice will appear. The more perfection is held out for admiration and desire and reward, then by consequence, the more wanting normal practice will seem. On the one hand, the harsh judgment of "ordinary" marriage is the direct consequence of idealization, but on the other hand, the idealization is always called into question as well.

Finally, in all of Austen's novels, quite unlike more traditional comedy, such as Goldsmith's *She Stoops to Conquer*, love and money are not opposites, around which conflict a plot is fashioned. In order to read Austen's work aright, we must rid ourselves of the romantic preconception that only love matters, that love conquers all, that love is transcendent. Although it is important to recognize the demands of both, love is neither privileged over money in a hierarchy, nor are they synthesized in a dialectic. Love and money are not presented as antinomies, enemies, or antitheses: In Jane Austen's novels they are simply unrelated. Or they are related only by the fact that individuals must deal with both, that is, by consequence or effect but not by mythological or ideological or even narrative structure. To assert that money and love are antithetical or that one is the enemy or nemesis of the other is to imply a structure that is not of Austen's making or even of her reflecting: In short, to call money the antithesis of love is to endorse an ideology of romantic love. One affects the other, or qualifies the other, and they both have to be dealt with, but in and of themselves; they are not related, except in accidental or incidental ways, no more than love and health or love and work are related.

Although Austen can present love and money in this parallel fashion, it is by no means clear that she either resists or is fully conscious of the ideology of romantic love. We note that Austen is unwilling or unable to recognize alternatives to marriage. In all her works, she sets marriage for security against the single life of poverty, but nowhere in her letters or in her novels does Austen seriously consider the obvious alternative, that which she may have enjoyed toward the end of her life: a single life of financial independence. On the single life, we can compare Anne Elliot, the one character who comes closest to living alone, a fate that she faces in considerable distress, with Charlotte Brontë's Lucy Snowe, whose independence is so painfully but triumphantly achieved at the close of *Villette*. The closest Austen ever comes to considering the alternative is in *Emma*, when Emma herself amusingly, if cruelly, distinguishes for Harriet the difference between poor and wealthy old maids:

> "Never mind, Harriet, I shall not be a poor old maid; and it is poverty only which makes celibacy contemptible to a generous public! A single woman, with a very narrow income, must be a ridiculous, disagreeable old maid! the proper sport of boys and girls; but a single woman, of good fortune, is always respectable, and may be as sensible and pleasant as anybody else." (E 85)

Yet this distinction is explicitly repudiated, in several ways: most obviously, in that Emma herself cannot resist the lure of marriage, and also in that poor spinsters are eventually declared exempt from sport, Emma's in particular. In a more telling category, content widows are not very common in Austen. Mrs. Jennings, Mrs. Dashwood, and Lady Russell seem content, if not fully sketched in, but more common are the Mrs. Bateses in Austen: Mrs. Thorpe, Mrs. Smith, Lady Catherine de Bourgh, Mrs. Norris, all of whom are either poor or disagreeable or both. Widowers, who include General Tilney, Sir Walter Elliot, Captain Benwick (of a sort), Mr. Weston, and Mr. Woodhouse, obviously have a better time of it than do the likes of Mrs. Smith in *Persuasion*. Perhaps we can only conclude that the ideological pressure toward marriage is so powerful and so pervasive that Austen can neither recognize nor resist it.

All the same, in those passages in which Austen recommends marriage, financial security is often offered as the most pressing reason. In several significant passages—in the letter that speaks of "the dreadful propensity for being poor"; in *The Watsons*, in which it is terrible "to be poor and old and laughed at"; in Charlotte Lucas's "pleasantest preservative from want"; in Emma's banter about old maids—poverty is the major threat to the single life. We are not told that unmarried women will be lonely or unfulfilled or inadequate—we are only told that they are likely to be poor. Austen never says this directly (and the structure of *Emma* actively belies it), but the logical, though silent, conclusion is that a secure single life might be just fine. Given the social role of women, however, which is practically defined by dependence, it seems that happily unmarried women are as rare in fact as in her fiction.[47] But happily married women are rare in Austen's fiction as well, leaving the companionate marriage of affection something of a longed-for ideal, infinitely desirable and infinitely rare.

Marriage in Austen is representative of her technique of simultaneously undermining and idealizing, a kind of satiric apposition between the depressingly debased common run of things and the idealization of an exceptional alternative: the many versions of Mr. and Mrs. Bennet versus the singular match of Darcy and Elizabeth. In this respect, marriage lies at the very heart of ideological contradiction in Austen's fiction, for it is both, at one and the same time, problem and solution. Pierre Macherey's explanation of the peculiarly Marxist sense of contradiction is helpful here, in which ideology is seen as the (surface) effacement or repression of real social conflict:

> By definition, an ideology can sustain a contradictory debate, for ideology exists precisely in order to efface all trace of contradiction. Thus, an ideology, as such, breaks down only in the face of the real questions: but for that to come about, ideology must not be able to hear these questions; that is to say, ideology must not be able to translate them into its own language. In so far as ideology is the false resolution of a real debate, it is always adequate to itself *as a reply*. Obviously the great thing is that it can never answer the question. In that it succeeds in endlessly prolonging its imperfection, it is complete; thus it is always equally in error, pursued by the risk that it cannot envisage—*the loss of reality*. An ideology is loyal to itself only in so far as it remains inadequate to the question which is both its foundation and its pretext.[48]

In Austen's class, the practices and procedures of marriage reveal the objectification of social relations unusually clearly.[49] Prospective mates are chosen as if they were objects, as if marriage itself is not a relation between people, but rather assumes "the fantastic form of a relation between things." The opening of *Pride and Prejudice* dramatizes the humiliation involved in this process, as Austen shows Darcy first responding to Elizabeth, "quizzing" her as if she were some kind of horse or other animal on show: "She is tolerable; but not handsome enough to tempt *me*" (PP 12).[50] Like people shopping for consumer goods in the market, the men look over the women at the assembly as if they are all on display for purchase. Through the course of this novel, Austen attempts the difficult task of transforming Darcy from a jaded shopper who sees only the physical object before him, to one who can see *within* Elizabeth, beyond exchange value, to see finally what she really is, inside. This process spans the two poles of marriage in Austen, from the angry exposure of the courtship as relation, not between individuals, between people, but between things, to the idealization of romantic intimacy. If middle-class marriage practices do not seem quite the same as the worker's sale of her labor on the market for wages, nevertheless many conditions are similar: The nubile female must part with her independence on the open market, taking what the market will bear. And so the marriage market is, from this view, like all other social institutions in that it has become externalized and objectified, transformed into an institution that always precedes the individual, is external to her and alienated from her, such that she seems to have no say in its rules or organization, but is merely subject to it. As Lukács writes of the worker entering the labor force and the monolithic factory, "the personality can do no more than look on helplessly while its own existence is reduced to an isolated particle and fed into an alien system."[51] Like wage laborers, women in a marriage market become subject to a larger circulating system, as Gayle Rubin has argued in her suggestive study of "The Traffic in Women."[52]

Yet despite suggestions of these practices in Austen, marriage is never fully represented as an institution, but rather is represented only as an individual practice, something at which the Bennets have failed, and not something that is corrupt at its heart. Herein lies the other side of the contradiction. Whenever marriage is imaged as an institution (as, very briefly, in Charlotte Lucas's statement about preservatives from want), a system or "factory" in which women must enter and work for others who set the rules and control them, it is always seen as cruel and unjust. At the same time, however, rather than dwell on its institutional and social nature, Austen portrays marriage as a flight from and refuge from commodification and the objectification of social relations. If men and women interact as if they were things, the conception of marriage as a private act becomes the solution to this alienation, providing love, support, and presence in the face of the terrible reification of all other social realms. The problem, the dehumanizing nature of marriage as capital exchange, thus by the process of ideological contradiction becomes the solution, the refuge, the harbor from a terrifyingly externalized world.

One aspect of this treatment of marriage as harbor appears in particularly vivid form in *Emma*, as several times it is suggested that marriage is a "safe" station for women, notably for Harriet Smith and Isabella, but also, by implication, for Emma herself. In marriage, the first two rather weak, or, it is implied, feebleminded, women will be kept out of trouble, and they will not have the opportunity to run amuck. Early on, Mr. Knightley says of Harriet, "Let her marry Robert Martin, and she is safe, respectable, and happy for ever" (E 64), and the idea of safety is repeated at the end: Upon marrying, Harriet "would be placed in the midst of those who loved her, and who had better sense than herself; retired enough for safety, and occupied enough for cheerfulness" (E 482). The same terms are used of Emma's sister Isabella, who, "passing her life with those she doated on, full of their merits, blind to their faults, and always innocently busy, might have been a model of right feminine happiness" (E 140). These passages, of course, can be interpreted as Austen's muted or veiled critique of marriage, or, on the other hand, as ideological assumptions about marriage as a "natural" or an appropriately safe state for women. Unlike the suggestion in Charlotte Brontë's *Villette*, that Lucy Snowe wants "keeping down," something the heroine resists strenuously, Jane Austen's *Emma* would rather seem to promote the suggestion that its heroine does need to be repressed by male authority.

In these various individualizing or privatizing ways, then, Austen portrays marriage, on the one hand, as cruel, brutal, and inevitably disappointing, and, on the other hand, as the ideal and indeed only solution to social and individual ills. Finally in Austen, despite the myriad examples of failed and brutal marriages, what is emphasized is only its private and personal side, not its institutional or public or ideological nature, and each marriage portrayed remains, not a prototypical one, but a personal, individual one, and so its larger social, public, and institutional nature is obscured or mystified. We can only understand the particular shape of its individual form here, however, by restoring and understanding its institutional nature.

6
Intimacy

> She imagined how in the chambers of the mind and heart
> of the woman who was, physically, touching her, were
> stood, like the treasures in the tombs of kings, tablets
> bearing sacred inscriptions, which if one could spell them
> out, would teach one everything, but they would never
> be offered openly, never made public. What art was there,
> known to love or cunning, by which one pressed through
> into those secret chambers? What device for becoming,
> like waters poured into one jar, inextricably the same,
> one with the object one adored? Could the body achieve,
> or the mind, subtly mingling in the intricate passages of
> the brain? or the heart? Could loving, as people called it,
> make her and Mrs. Ramsay one? for it was not knowl-
> edge but unity that she desired, not inscriptions on tab-
> lets, nothing that could be written in any language
> known to men, but intimacy itself, which is knowledge.
> —Virginia Woolf, *To the Lighthouse*[1]

At its most elemental level, Jane Austen's narrative presents its major characters as growing or maturing or developing as separate or distinct or different individuals, who pass from lonely solipsism to intimate union with an other.[2] The historicity of this life story, as opposed to the life story evident in novels of the mideighteenth century, for example, is likely to escape readers because it is similar to the life narrative that we envision now. As Philip Slater observes about modern concepts of individuality: "The notion that people begin as separate individuals, who then march out and connect themselves with others, is one of the most dazzling bits of self-mystification in the history of the species."[3] Austen is the first English novelist to portray this myth in a fully fashioned form, and this form is in large part the reason for her continued popularity and appeal. In Austen and now, one is not conceived as being born into immanent or preexisting classes or categories—be these categories natural or divine or social—but instead one is born only into or with or as self or identity.[4]

One consequence of this individualist ideology can be seen clearly in the role of the family in Austen's fiction, in which final separation from the family is not presented as painful, or even as joyful, but finally as imma- terial. Marriage is portrayed as the ultimate or final union, rather than as separation or passage—unlike in other cultures, in which a woman's marriage can involve passage from her original or parental family to the family of her husband, sometimes years before the marriage or consummation itself can take place. In Austen, the man to be married rarely has a family to be reckoned with: In *Northanger Abbey, Pride and Prejudice, Emma,* and *Persuasion,* for example, the hero has no mother living. Where there is another family, as in *Sense and Sensibility,* they are distant or hostile, as is the case with Mrs. Ferrars or Lady Catherine de Bourgh. As the novels progress, even the heroine has an increasingly smaller and less important family to reckon with: Anne Elliot is motherless, as are Emma Woodhouse, Harriet, and Jane Fairfax. With the exceptions of Mrs. Weston and Emma's sister, there are no mothers in *Emma,* for all of Austen's late heroines are orphans.[5] *Mansfield Park,* appropriately the only novel to emphasize the importance of family, is the one in which the newlyweds remain in the bosom of the family, for Sir Thomas is "chiefly anxious to bind by the strongest securities all that remained to him of domestic felicity" (MP 471). But even here the couple must eventually be removed from the park itself, leaving Susan Price to replace Fanny as the surrogate daughter. However much family is to be reckoned with there, none of Austen's novels features a romance plot that turns on the discovery and restoration of parents, as so many earlier eighteenth-century novels had, from *Joseph Andrews* and *Tom Jones* to *Humphrey Clinker* and *Evelina*; indeed, Austen parodies such plots in Emma's grandiose expectations of Harriet's parentage. Along the same lines, Mary Burgan observes that unlike both earlier and later novels that very commonly end by stressing genealogical continuity and female fecundity, Austen never ends her novels with celebrations or even hints of the heroine's future children or a flourishing nursery.[6] Despite Darrel Mansell's observation that the heroine must in the end come to accept her family before she is ready to marry, this acceptance does not involve any form of reintegration with the old family, but rather an abandonment of it at the moment of the new family's creation.[7] Like Cinderella, in *Pride and Prejudice* and *Persuasion,* the worthy heroine is rescued from an abusive family and translated to the prince's palace.

This flight from family in Austen is consistent with the changing shape of the family in the eighteenth century, in the long-term shift toward the nuclear family. Philippe Ariès writes of "a steadily extending zone of private life" in his history of

> the triumph of the modern family over that of other types of
> human relationship which hindered its development. The more
> man lived in the street or in communities dedicated to work,

pleasure or prayer, the more these communities monopolized not only his time but his mind. If, on the other hand, his relations with fellow workers, neighbors and relatives did not weigh so heavily on him, then the concept of family feeling took the place of the other concepts of loyalty and service and became predominant or even exclusive.[8]

The term Randolph Trumbach employs to characterize the emergent eighteenth-century English family structure is *domesticity*: "in the generation after 1720 privacy and discretion were increasingly emphasized. . . . Marriage had become, as far as possible, an intense and private experience between husband and wife. It was no longer a spectacle nor even a family occasion. It was the hidden pearl of domestic happiness."[9]

As we have observed before, this growing zone of the private is a consequence of the objectification of social relations, the split between work and family, and the general withdrawal of individuals from the public sphere. But we should also note that the size of the household or family did not change very much across this period; according to Peter Laslett in *The World We Have Lost*, the family size in preindustrial England was both relatively small (4.75 person per household) and relatively constant up to this century.[10] Along this line, Françoise Lautman concludes that the nuclear family is not a consequence of industrialization: "the extended family was only found among the ruling or wealthy classes," for they alone had the power or wealth to accumulate, defend, and transfer. "The real structure and function of the family have not changed. The change lies in the way society views a certain ideal that the ruling classes once practiced effectively."[11] That is to say, what eighteenth-century novels chronicle is not so much a change in the size or shape of the family as a change in attitude and function, and the Bennets, Dashwoods, Woodhouses, and Elliots reflect these changing attitudes. It has been argued that the whole program of the first great domestic novels is based on "making the private public"; in the light of the history of privacy, we might want to restate this formula to say that the eighteenth-century novel capitalizes on a newly created private zone.[12]

In Austen, the extended family is not seen as a haven in a heartless world, but rather as something suffocating, a mediating stage between the larger public world and the private world of intimacy. The place of privacy in Austen and the narrative pattern that is determined by it can be explored through Austen's use of key terms that represent social and personal relations: *intimacy, reserve, openness*, and *solitude*. Intimacy is the *summum bonum* of Austen's fiction, her highest value, the reward of her heroines' struggle, and the goal of her narratives. An indication of the importance Austen attaches to intimacy, in her life as well as her work, can be seen in her letter to her niece Fanny, which is uncharacteristically demonstrative and emotional; rarely does one witness Austen struggling as she does here to achieve "the language of real feeling" (E 265): "It is very, very gratifying to me to know you so intimately. You can hardly think what a pleasure it is to me, to have such thorough pictures of your Heart.—Oh! what a loss it will be when you are married" (L 478–79). Because the significance of intimacy becomes clearest in her last works, we shall concentrate on *Emma*, with a glance at *Persuasion*. These two novels provide a fruitful comparison because though Emma is so much more social and gregarious than Anne Elliot, nevertheless, Emma eventually finds herself threatened by the same solitude.

With all its variants, *intimacy* is used eighty-four times in Jane Austen's fiction.[13] As with other weighty substantives, she employs the word in a variety of meanings, many of which are often ironically contradictory. That is to say, proper and improper or current and debased uses are implicitly set in opposition to one another. As Howard Babb puts it in his study of Austen's conceptual terms, "in Jane Austen's style such concepts are the real actors."[14] *Intimate* can refer to anyone from a distant acquaintance (in *Sanditon*, the word refers to someone the speaker has never met, MW 408), to a sexual partner (in *Mansfield Park*, the affair of Mrs. Rushworth and Henry Crawford is referred to as "an intimacy which was already exposing her to unpleasant remarks," MP 450). According to the OED, it is not a particularly old word in English, having been adopted in the seventeenth century from the French *intimare*, which in turn comes from the Latin *intimatus*, "inmost, innermost, deepest." The principal meaning given in the OED (quoting *Mansfield Park* to illustrate the sense of social intimacies) is "familiar intercourse" or "close familiarity," retaining the earlier sense of interiority and closeness. Though such arguments are rather tenuous, one might argue that the word was not needed until this period, in view of Stone's reconstruction of personal relations in the early modern period, which are characterized by violence, suspicion, and hostility. This world of personal relations would be more accurately typified, not by the platonic friendship idealized in John Lyly's *Euphues*, but rather by Francis Osborn's infamous misanthropy and suspicion: " 'Tis a natural guard, and within the management of the most ordinary capacities, to keep an Enemy out at the Staves end; But suitable only to a superlative prudence, so wisely to govern your words and actions towards a *Friend*, as may preserve you from danger; Not to be done but by communicating to him no more than Discretion or Necessity shall warrant you to reveal."[15]

Austen stresses the central idea of familiarity, as in Marianne's letter to Willoughby, in which she writes of "the familiarity which our intimacy at Barton appeared to me to justify" (SS 187). Such closeness can have physical or spatial suggestions, as it often does in the novels of Fanny Burney, or in *The Watsons,* when Emma refuses Tom Musgrove's offer of his carriage: "she did not like the proposal—she did not wish to be on terms of intimacy with the Proposer," later explaining, "I could not wish . . . the Intimacy which the use of his Carriage must have created" (MW 339 and 341; the scene of threatening intimacy in a carriage is realized in *Emma* when Mr. Elton seizes Emma's hand and proposes on the trip back from the Westons). But despite this wariness, usually in Austen's novels "intimacy" is associated with friends and friendship, between women, men, families, or neighbors, as can be seen in the commonplace expression "intimate friends" or in *Lady Susan,* in which "intimacy" is glossed as "the most particular friendship" (MW 259). The particularity of such close friendship gives a kind of social license, as when it facilitates Colonel Brandon and Elinor's conversation:

> Colonel Brandon's delicate unobtrusive inquiries [about Marianne's unhappiness] were never unwelcome to Miss Dashwood. He had abundantly earned the privilege of intimate discussion of her sister's disappointment, by the friendly zeal with which he had endeavoured to soften it, and they always conversed with confidence. (SS 216)

Again in *Lady Susan,* "intimacy [is] . . . implied by the discussion of such a [delicate] subject" (MW 266); here the suspension of ordinary propriety or decorum that intimacy affords is viewed with suspicion, for such closeness can always prove dangerous: "It is impossible to see the intimacy between them, so very soon established, without some alarm" (MW 259). At the end of *Mansfield Park,* Tom comes to understand "the dangerous intimacy of his unjustifiable theatre" (MP 462), a danger that Edmund had emphasized even more strongly when he argued against admitting an outsider into their theatricals: "I know no harm of Charles Maddox; but the excessive intimacy which must spring from his being admitted among us in this manner [as an actor], is highly objectionable, the *more* than intimacy—the familiarity" (MP 153–54).

Intimacy, then, is a kind of two-edged sword, which is both attractive and desirable, but also seductive and perilous, because it exposes that private interior space that would otherwise remain hidden and protected from the outside world. Rarely, in fact, does Austen use the term with unqualified approval, in the way that she does at the end of *Pride and*

Prejudice: "With the Gardiners, they were always on the most intimate terms. Darcy, as well as Elizabeth, really loved them" (PP 388); similarly, at the close of *Sense and Sensibility*, Edward and Elinor's "intimate knowledge of each other seemed to make their happiness certain" (SS 369). But by the time of *Persuasion*, every use of the word has pejorative connotations, referring either to the suspicious connection between Miss Elliot and Mrs. Clay, Mr. Elliot and Mrs. Smith's late husband, or the "unnecessary intimacy" between Mr. Elliot and Anne (P 214). Most citations of the word in Austen's fiction have similarly negative implications. Captain Wentworth reflects on his relation to the Musgrove girls, "I had not considered that my excessive intimacy must have its danger of ill consequence in many ways" (P 242). The ill consequences of intimacy turn on its desired end, the suspension of those social decorums and circumlocutions. These formal modes of address are replaced with a private directness, as in the conversation between Willoughby and Marianne that Elinor overhears: "she instantly saw an intimacy so decided, a meaning so direct, as marked a perfect agreement between them" (SS 60; this is the only time that intimacy is overseen in the novels, for ordinarily it remains private, hidden from the viewer's eye). In Marianne's case, as with many of Austen's characters, directness opens up a vast vulnerability when the private heart is exposed to another.

In these novels, just as in classical treatises on friendship, the only protection against the perils of close familiarity (as with courtship) is to contract intimacy slowly, laboriously, and wisely.[16] Over and over again, Austen contrasts intimacy of rapid and of slow growth. Perhaps reflecting on her own unwanted relocation in Bath, Austen writes that Emma Watson's strangeness in the community "increased her sense of the awkwardness of rushing into Intimacy on so slight an acquaintance" with the Edwards (MW 322). Any "very speedy intimacy," such as that of Catherine Morland and Isabella Thorpe in *Northanger Abbey* (NA 56), is viewed with suspicion, and this "sudden intimacy" (NA 33) is plainly contrasted with the more sober kind that grows up between Catherine and Miss Tilney, who, even by the end of the novel, are referred to as "improving in intimacy" (NA 222). Austen parodies instantaneous intimacy in *Love and Freindship*: "We flew into each other's arms & after having exchanged vows of mutual Friendship for the rest of our Lives, instantly unfolded to each other the most inward Secrets of our Hearts" (MW 85). Marianne Dashwood argues that "It is not time or opportunity that is to determine intimacy;—it is disposition alone," yet everything in Austen's fiction argues that this view is mistaken (SS 59). Characters who contract sudden intimacies are either poor judges of character such as Catherine Morland or are opportunists: Two characters who "seek" intimacies are Mrs. Norris, who pursues Mrs. Rushworth in order to promote an aggrandizing but disastrous marriage, and John Dashwood, who seeks intimacy with Colonel Brandon because he anticipates the wealthy Colonel Brandon's marriage to his half-sister Elinor (MP 39, SS 228).

Sought intimacy and speedy intimacy are inevitably ruptured. After the Crawfords and the Bertrams first meet, the narrator ominously reports that "their acquaintance soon promised as early an intimacy as good manners would warrant" (MP 44). Conversely, in *Emma,* Mrs. Weston generously observes of Jane Fairfax, "Miss Bates may . . . have . . . hurried her [Jane] into a greater appearance of intimacy than her own good sense would have dictated" (E 286). Austen suggests that this sort of familiarity is of forced, rather than of natural growth, just as when Henry speaks of "continuing, improving, and *perfecting* that friendship and intimacy with the Mansfield Park family" (MP 246). As they find to their cost, friendship, intimacy, and personal relations of all sorts are not houses or estates that can be toyed with or improved. Implicit in Austen's use of *intimacy* is an organic metaphor of growth or development as opposed to mechanics, manipulation, or force. What grows up between two individuals slowly and naturally is set against something synthetically created and enforced, such as "that kind of intimacy [which] must be submitted to" between the Dashwood sisters and the Steeles, a false and manipulative relationship that Sir John Middleton forces upon them (SS 124). Just as patently false is the one-sided familiarity that springs up between Fanny and Mary Crawford, after Fanny is trapped at the parsonage by rain: "Such was the origin of the sort of intimacy which took place between them within the first fortnight after the Miss Bertrams' going away, an intimacy resulting principally from Miss Crawford's desire of something new, and which had little reality in Fanny's feelings" (MP 207–8).

But it is not just improperly formed or hastily contracted intimacies that are ruptured in Austen's novels. At the opening of *Pride and Prejudice,* Charlotte Lucas is introduced as "Elizabeth's intimate friend" (PP 18), yet this long-standing friendship is disrupted by Charlotte's marriage to Mr. Collins, after which "Elizabeth could never address her without feeling that all the comfort of intimacy was over" (PP 146). This pattern of disruption is repeated in Jane's broken intimacy with Miss Bingley and in the suspension of the intimacy that had subsisted between the two sisters. Elizabeth is able to communicate to her sister and former confidant nothing of her changing view of Darcy. Throughout the six novels, the heroines pass from incomplete or partial or false friendship with a female to complete or whole intimacy with a male; that is, from female friendship to marriage.

Austen's heroines either start out removed or distanced from others around them, or they become so in the course of the narrative. The distanced heroines (those described previously as idealizing narcissists), Elinor Dashwood, Fanny Price, and Anne Elliot, from the start have no familiar friendships or intimates from whom they later break. The more convivial or outgoing heroines (those described as mirroring narcissists), Catherine Morland, Elizabeth Bennet, and Emma Woodhouse, on the contrary, all depend upon friendships that are inevitably disrupted in the course of the novels. C. S. Lewis calls *Mansfield Park* and *Persuasion* "the novels of the solitary heroines," but all of the heroines eventually become solitary.[17] In the former novels, the protagonists appear separate and solitary from the start; either by disposition or circumstance, they are not intimate with others. In the latter novels, the narrative is organized around a kind of exercise of definition, a definition by way of negation, as failed or impartial or broken intimacy serves to exemplify what intimacy is not. In *Northanger Abbey*, Catherine Morland rapidly enters into a shallow intimacy with the manipulative Isabella, but later she moves toward what is portrayed as true friendship with the more careful and reserved Miss Tilney. Austen contrasts intimacies between men and women as well; in *Sense and Sensibility*, the treacherous intimacy of Marianne and Willoughby is obviously set against the cautious and laboriously established affection between Elinor and Edward. *Pride and Prejudice* contrasts a multitude of these examples: that dangerously rapid sort between Elizabeth and Wickham, that disrupted between Elizabeth and Jane, and that failed between Elizabeth and Charlotte Lucas. In *Mansfield Park*, contrasts are built around the two families of Bertrams and Crawfords, as Austen demonstrates how quickly the Crawfords establish themselves on an intimate footing with the family at the Park. So, too, Fanny is repulsed by the intimacy that Mary assumes between them. Either by circumstance of character or plot, Austen always leads her heroine to a state in which she has no one in whom to confide. Most obviously in *Pride and Prejudice*, Elizabeth Bennet is alienated from those whom she once trusted, but this separation prevails for the others, who are also brought to a relative state of isolation just prior to the dénouement.

The process by which false intimacies are exploded and true intimacies are disrupted is most fully worked out in *Emma*, in which Austen appears to be exploring most consciously and carefully the dangers of false intimacy and the value of true intimacy. Here especially, Austen works with a series of contrasts: Emma's former closeness with Mrs. Weston is set against her friendship with Harriet Smith; this friendship, or more properly, this patronage of Harriet is set in competition with Mrs. Elton's patronage of Jane Fairfax. Through these contrasts, the reader is regularly shown that Emma prefers the insipid company and unequal friendship of Harriet Smith to the more valuable or more equal and thus more challenging friendship expected but spurned between herself and Jane Fairfax. In this particular relationship, the values of intimacy are explicitly contrasted with the repeated accusations of reserve that makes Jane so repulsive in Emma's eyes. Overall, the remarkable sense of community that makes this novel so extraordinary at every point suggests both the values of and the constrictions inherent in a tiny community where everyone of the same class is inevitably and necessarily on familiar footings with the others. In this fashion, Frank Churchill can enter into an already established intimacy between the Woodhouses and the Westons, exploiting what already exists and what is expected. The flirtation into which he entices Emma is presented as an especially debased example of intimacy; as he puts it in the last letter to Mrs. Weston, "In order to assist a concealment so essential to me, I was led on to make more than an allowable use of the sort of intimacy into which we were immediately thrown" (E 438). In obvious contrast, the long-standing friendship between the Woodhouses and Mr. Knightley is offered as an exemplum of proper intimacy in almost every fashion. Nevertheless, although Emma spends most of this novel surrounded and almost strangled by intimate friends and acquaintances, she, like all of the other heroines, finds herself very much alone just before the end of the story. Emma's only intimate relations are with unequals, with her former governess and with Harriet, and it is this isolation that leaves her so vulnerable.

The sense of false intimacy or something else such as self-interest or patronage masquerading as intimacy is much more prevalent in *Emma* than any of the previous novels. The whole first volume of the novel focuses on Emma's taking up of Harriet Smith, which Mr. Knightley prophesies will bring no good to either. Austen has lifted this plot of dangerous intimacy from Fanny Burney's second novel, *Cecilia,* in which the heroine patronizes a woman of a much lower social class, Henrietta Belfield, who turns out to be a rival for Mortimer Delvile, the man Cecilia herself desires; like Emma, Cecilia is able to turn this friend over to another, less threatening lover. In Austen's novel, Harriet plays a similar role to Henrietta Belfield. With her former intimate, Mrs. Weston, removed to Randalls, Emma's possibilities for a friend of equal social class are painfully limited by the small size and rigid class structure of Highbury. Jane Fairfax appears to be the only logical choice, but most of the

time she does not reside in Highbury. As Mrs. Weston points out, Harriet
is the only realistic possibility for a friend to Emma. She argues to Mr.
Knightley,

> "how fortunate it was for Emma, that there should be such a girl
> in Highbury for her to associate with. Mr. Knightley, I shall not
> allow you to be a fair judge in this case. You are so much used to
> live alone, that you do not know the value of a companion; and
> perhaps no man can be a good judge of the comfort a woman feels
> in the society of one of her own sex, after being used to it all her
> life." (E 36)

Meddlesome though Emma's patronage of Harriet is, this passage
highlights Emma's basic need for companionship and friendship with
someone other than her idiot father and his ossified circle of friends:
"Mrs. and Miss Bates and Mrs. Goddard, three ladies almost always at
the service of an invitation from Hartfield" (E 20; Emma herself makes
the automatic fifth, of course, night after night with this lively crew).[18] In
a passage that is unusually sympathetic for this sharp novel, contact with
Mrs. Weston is explained as Emma's greatest pleasure, however ego-
centric Emma's conversation may be:

> there was not a creature in the world to whom she spoke with
> such unreserve as to [Mrs. Weston]; not any one, to whom she
> related with such conviction of being listened to and understood,
> of being always interesting and always intelligible, the little af-
> fairs, arrangements, perplexities and pleasures of her father and
> herself. She could tell nothing of Hartfield, in which Mrs. Weston
> had not a lively concern; and a half an hour's uninterrupted
> communication of all those little matters on which the daily
> happiness of private life depends, was one of the first gratifications
> of each. (E 117)[19]

With Mrs. Weston gone, Emma's needs might be supplied by the
friendship of either Harriet or Jane, but despite the advantages Jane
Fairfax presents, it is the very closeness and constriction of Highbury that
militate against their becoming close. As Emma tells Harriet of Jane, "we
are always forced to be acquainted whenever she comes to Highbury"
(E 86). Later, in another revealing discussion, Frank Churchill draws
Emma out and teases her into making indiscreet remarks about Jane
Fairfax:

"I have known her from a child, undoubtedly; we have been children and women together; and it is natural to suppose that we should be intimate,—that we should have taken to each other whenever she visited her friends. But we never did. I hardly know how it has happened; a little, perhaps, from that wickedness on my side which was prone to take disgust towards a girl so idolized and so cried up as she always was, by her aunt and grandmother, and all their set. And then, her reserve—I never could attach myself to anyone so completely reserved."

"It is a most repulsive quality, indeed," said he. "Oftentimes very convenient, no doubt, but never pleasing. There is safety in reserve, but no attraction. One cannot love a reserved person."

"Not till the reserve ceases towards oneself; and then the attraction may be the greater. But I must be more in want of a friend, or an agreeable companion, than I have yet been, to take the trouble of conquering any body's reserve to procure one. Intimacy between Miss Fairfax and me is quite out of the question. I have no reason to think ill of her—not the least—except that such extreme and perpetual cautiousness of word and manner, such a dread of giving a distinct idea about any body, is apt to suggest suspicions of there being something to conceal." (E 203)

It is inviting and almost too easy to speculate on all the reasons why this friendship never gets off the ground, from the meager clues of Jane's character, to assumptions of her resentment at Emma's patronage, and on to Emma's reluctance to work at anything, much less an acquaintance. But as was suggested previously, this relationship has all of the signs of having been forced, assumed by others, expected to be so, and thus it is never allowed to develop of its own accord. But Emma appears to want to pick her own friend and not have her only choice dictated by the circle of her father's acquaintance. As Janet Todd has persuasively argued, the undeveloped relationship between Emma and Jane Fairfax is perhaps the most interesting in Austen's novels, a tantalizing possibility of what is never allowed to be, a reminder of what Austen never grants.[20] Toward the end of the novel, Emma looks back regretfully at what was never established between them, explicitly comparing her attraction to Harriet and her antipathy to Jane:

She bitterly regretted not having sought a closer acquaintance with her, and blushed for the envious feelings which had certainly been, in some measure, the cause. Had she followed Mr. Knightley's known wishes, in paying that attention to Miss Fairfax, which was every way her due; had she tried to know her better; had she done her part towards intimacy; had she endeavoured to find a friend there instead of in Harriet Smith; she must, in all probability, have been spared from every pain which pressed on her now.—Birth, abilities, and education, had been equally marking one as an associate for her, to be received with gratitude; and the other—what was she? (E 421)

Emma's intimacy with Jane never develops, and that with Harriet is destroyed, like that between Elizabeth Bennet and Charlotte Lucas: "The intimacy between her and Emma must sink; their friendship must change into a calmer sort of goodwill; and fortunately, what ought to be, and must be, seemed already beginning, and in the most gradual, natural manner" (E 482). What was unnaturally forced at the beginning is allowed to decay naturally at the end.

Like Elizabeth, Emma is taken from intimacy to solitude, from companionship to a state of estrangement. In this movement, Emma becomes more like Jane Fairfax, learning something of the reserve that she has found so repulsive. *Reserve* is a word tied to Jane in this novel, as in the phrase "coldness and reserve—such apparent indifference whether she pleased or not" (E 166):

> She was, besides, which was the worst of all, so cold, so cautious! There was no getting at her real opinion. Wrapt up in a cloak of politeness, she seemed determined to hazard nothing. She was disgustingly, was suspiciously reserved. (E 169)

Austen's most suggestive and extended discussion of reserve occurs in *Sense and Sensibility,* when Edward Ferrars is so startled by Marianne's accusation of reserve, which arises in a discussion of general civility. Just as in *Emma,* reserve is invested with all manner of pejorative connotations:

> "I never wish to offend, but I am so foolishly shy, that I often seem negligent, when I am only kept back by my natural awkwardness. I have frequently thought that I must have been intended by nature to be fond of low company, I am so little at my ease among strangers of gentility!"
>
> "Marianne has not shyness to excuse any inattention of hers," said Elinor.
>
> "She knows her own worth too well for false shame," replied Edward. "Shyness is only the effect of a sense of inferiority in

some way or other. If I could persuade myself that my manners
were perfectly easy and graceful, I should not be shy."

"But you would still be reserved," said Marianne, "and that is
worse." (SS 94)

In *Emma*, Mr. Knightley also remarks on Jane Fairfax's reserve: "Her
sensibilities, I suspect, are strong—and her temper excellent in its power
of forbearance, patience, self-controul; but it wants openness. She is
reserved, more reserved, I think, than she used to be—And I love an
open temper" (E 289; in the end, Emma declares, "I love every thing that
is decided and open" [E 460], suggesting that she has begun to adopt Mr.
Knightley's language as well as his values). As is typical in *Emma*, the
distinctions that Mr. Knightley draws are more careful and judicious
than those that Emma draws in a moment of indiscretion with Frank
Churchill. Where Emma's vocabulary is emotional, the words that Mr.
Knightley uses here are moral, and by them he suggests that there is both
a private and a public openness. Similarly, Emma observes, "There is an
openness, a quickness, almost a bluntness in Mr. Weston, which every
body likes in *him* because there is so much good humour with it" (E 34).
Mr. Weston's geniality may be regarded as a species of openness, but this
geniality is not to be confused with the openness possible in private
intimacy—openness as a kind of public intimacy, and intimacy as a kind
of private openness. The two can be collapsed, as in Emma's desire
toward the end of the novel: "Emma grieved that she could not be more
openly just" with Mr. Knightley (E 463). Both public and private forms
of reserve are the opposite of these forms of openness, but as with
intimacy, openness has both negative and positive connotations. Often
Jane Fairfax's reserve contrasts favorably with the indiscretion of Emma,
who lacks the "forbearance, patience, self-controul" that Mr. Knightley
praises. Jane Fairfax's reserve also serves to contrast with the "ease" or
vulgar familiarity of Mrs. Elton, who is said to have "ease, but not elegance" (E 270); she is "pert and familiar" (E 272); and "self-important,
presuming, familiar, ignorant, and ill-bred" (E 281). Just as with Catherine Morland, Marianne Dashwood, and Elizabeth Bennet before her,
Emma has to be taught the necessity of some reserve. The term does not
necessarily mean cold, secretive, and suspicious, as Emma implies to
Frank Churchill of Jane Fairfax, for reserve can also be a sign of prudence
or discretion.

Emma's learning the necessity of some reserve inevitably involves her
learning not to speak, and her becoming more private, more distant, and
more enclosed, in short, more like Jane Fairfax. At one point Emma
concludes, "Plain dealing was always best" (E 341), yet this remark

occurs just after she has committed her most serious interference with Harriet, which suggests that plain dealing is *not* always best. Emma's reserve, which is learned so late, is predicated on her abandonment of the intimacy with Harriet, the disruption of all of her previous intimacies. Emma has none of the confidants at the end whom she had at the beginning, as all her confidences with both Harriet and with Frank Churchill turn into mortifications, or, in the word Austen uses most often, *blunders*. After the secret engagement has been revealed, Emma is constrained from voicing to Mrs. Weston her disapproval of Frank Churchill, limiting for the first time Emma's principal source of confidence and intimacy. And after Mr. Knightley's proposal, Austen again and again underscores Emma's restraint, and the way her reserve on the subject of Harriet Smith stands as a barrier between her and Mr. Knightley, even at the occasion of his proposal, at which point the narrator concludes: "Seldom, very seldom, does complete truth belong to any human disclosure; seldom can it happen that something is not a little disguised, or a little mistaken" (E 431). Later, "Emma grieved that she could not be more openly just to one important service which his better sense would have rendered her, to the advice which would have saved her from the worst of all her womanly follies—her willful intimacy with Harriet Smith; but it was too tender a subject.—She could not enter on it" (E 463). It is only after Harriet is safely reengaged to Robert Martin that Emma can begin to be open with Mr. Knightley:

> High in the rank of her most serious and heartfelt felicities, was the reflection that all necessity of concealment from Mr. Knightley would soon be over. The disguise, equivocation, mystery, so hateful to her practice, might soon be over. She could now look forward to giving him that full and perfect confidence which her disposition was most ready to welcome as a duty. (E 475)

Emma's history is narrated as a series of succeeding intimacies, from Miss Taylor, who stands in the place of a mother; through Harriet Smith, the female friend; to Mr. Knightley, the husband, just as in all of Austen's novels she must separate the heroines from female friendship in preparation for marriage. This path leads the heroine through stages of increasing separation and loneliness, as if she must be made unhappy before she can be removed from her previous state. For the bulk of the novel Emma is presented as the very pattern of self-satisfied sufficiency, yet in the end she is made to feel inadequate and insufficient.[21] At the opening of the novel, Emma feared that "she was now in great danger of suffering from intellectual solitude" (E 7), but what she comes to by the end is real solitude. The chapter that contains Mr. Knightley's proposal starts by evoking, through dreary, rainy weather, a striking sense of angst and ennui from which Emma suffers: "The weather continued much the same all the following morning; and the same loneliness, and the same melancholy, seemed to reign at Hartfield" (E 424). The submerged metaphor in *reign* is particularly suggestive because for four hundred pages Austen has conveyed the impression that it was Emma who "seemed to reign at Hartfield." Mr. Elton's rather apt charade had complimented Emma with the line, "And woman, lovely woman, reigns alone" (E 71); if Emma ever did reign, she did so all by herself, an imaginary monarch. The novel, in fact, is full of rulers, from Mrs. Churchill, who, Mrs. Weston says "rules at Enscome" (E 121); to Frank Churchill, whom Mr. Knightley refers to as "the practised politician" (E 150); to Mrs. Elton, whom Miss Bates calls "the queen of the evening" (E 329).[22] The power of these others is more obviously illusory, but Emma too has far less power than she thinks she has, for quite plainly, she thinks of herself as the queen of Hartfield and Highbury as well. But in the end, it is not Emma but loneliness that reigns.

The solitary nature of Austen's last protagonist, Anne Elliot of *Persuasion*, provides an instructive comparison with Emma. Unlike Emma, Anne is solitary from the start: Abandoned by Captain Wentworth and ignored by her own family, she has only Lady Russell for a companion. In some respects, Anne's younger sister, Mary, conforms more closely to Emma, for Mary, it is said, "had no resources for solitude" (P 37). Anne, in contrast, employs her solitude, in such forms as "a stroll of solitary indulgence" (P 133). She welcomes the sedative effects of solitude; after Captain Wentworth unexpectedly comes to her aid and lifts the troublesome child off her back, "it required a long application of solitude and reflection to recover her" (P 81). Again, after the emotional interchange with Captain Harville over women's loyalty, she assumes that "Half an hour's solitude and reflection might have tranquillized her" (P 238). Most suggestive in this respect are those passages in which Anne is described as feeling alone in company; after overhearing Captain Wentworth's discussion with Louisa on their walk, Anne's "spirits wanted the solitude and silence which only numbers could give" (P 89). Here, solitude is an emotional and internal state that is only incidentally related to one's company: It has less to do with her being alone and more to do with an essential loneliness. This sort of essential loneliness is portrayed most clearly in the scene in which Anne plays music so that the others may dance, on the periphery of the party, present with the others, yet in her own, private unhappiness excluded and alienated from their pleasure:

The evening ended with dancing. On its being proposed, Anne offered her services, as usual, and though her eyes would sometimes fill with tears as she sat at the instrument, she was extremely glad to be employed, and desired nothing in return but to be unobserved. (P 71)

In such scenes, Austen prefigures later concepts of loneliness, a sense of desolation and emptiness quite different from seventeenth-century notions of melancholy as in Robert Burton's *The Anatomy of Melancholy* or Milton's "Il Penseroso" or the eighteenth-century cultivation of melancholy and solitude in the likes of Robert Blair, Edward Young, and Thomas Gray. Even by midcentury and the time of Gray's "Elegy Written in a Country Churchyard," melancholy and isolation are still being courted and exploited for their pleasurable effects. Samuel Johnson's "vile melancholy" or the isolation felt by his hermit and astronomer in *Rasselas* has little relation to any modern sense of the fear of isolation and emptiness. In earlier fiction as well, the reader may imagine Tom Jones's feeling homesick or perhaps feeling a longing for Sophia, but it is impossible to imagine Tom Jones's feeling lonely in our sense of the term. The same is arguably true of Roxana, Clarissa, Evelina, or even of Tristram Shandy. According to the *Oxford English Dictionary*, earlier meanings of *lonely* and *loneliness* are emotionally neutral and refer simply to a state of being alone or solitary, without company, but not necessarily without anything else. Loneliness acquires its emotional connotations of sadness and dejection only in the early nineteenth century, that is to say, under Romanticism: The first examples of these emotional uses are drawn from Byron and from Wordsworth's *Excursion* of 1814: "He grew up / From year to year in loneliness of soul."[23] This loneliness of soul, as with Anne Elliot and Emma Woodhouse, has little relation to physical location and company, more to state of mind and a sense of emotional well-being.

Emma has been deposed and displaced by this later, desolate type of loneliness, an ever-present but repressed danger throughout the novel. Once Miss Taylor departs, and the idle chatter of Harriet Smith is put away, Emma has nothing but her own resources to fall back upon, and they are shown to be inadequate: Like Mary Musgrove of *Persuasion*, Emma has no resources for solitude. Austen suggests that once the distractions are removed, loneliness has always reigned at Hartfield. Realization of loneliness and alienation is another way of describing what has been more commonly described as Emma's "humiliation" or enlightenment or anagnorisis.

Yet more dangerous than loneliness are the implications of solipsism. Much like Elizabeth Bennet, Emma has prided herself on her penetration, and in both cases this understanding is really a form of imagination; Emma is called an "imaginist" (E 335), because she thinks that she can foresee and thus create a match before anyone else, just as she can invent for Jane Fairfax or Harriet life histories, loves, disappointments, rich parentage, all the essentials of a romantic heroine.[24] The impropriety of such inventions is always made clear to us by Mr. Knightley, but the danger they represent is rather a different matter. Harriet prefaces her declaration of love for Mr. Knightley to Emma with a compliment on her insight:

> "You (blushing as she spoke), who can see into everybody's heart; but nobody else—"
> "Upon my word," said Emma, "I begin to doubt my having any such talent." (E 404)

In the ensuing chapters, Emma comes to understand that seeing into others' hearts is not a talent, that it is not possible. As she has admitted earlier in a conversation with Frank Churchill, "Oh! do not imagine that I expect an account of Miss Fairfax's sensations from you, or from any body else. They are known to no human being, I guess, but herself" (E 202). At this point, however, which is early in the novel, Emma assumes that she can guess Jane Fairfax's feelings. By the end, she is forced to see that it is difficult to know one's own feelings, more difficult to express those feelings to another, and impossible, finally, to know the other's sensations.

The twin threats of loneliness and solipsism serve to emphasize the value of true intimacy: If Emma can never know the inside of Jane Fairfax, the novel is constructed so as to lead us up to the expectation that she can, eventually, know Mr. Knightley. Closing the pattern of false, failed, and broken intimacies, the final marriage serves to mark the expectation and the hope that true intimacy can exist. Austen nowhere examines happy marriage within her novels proper, but her novels are constructed so as to lead up to the hope that such happiness is possible, lying just on the other side, as it were, of the last page of the novel. In this sense, Austen's are novels of courtship but not of marriage, for they always end on the threshold of marriage, where intimate happiness is indicated in the future tense, as something about to be experienced, but not experienced and verified quite yet. True intimacy does not exist within the novel proper because Austen indicates that it cannot be portrayed. This failure to portray suggests less that she does not finally believe in it or that she herself does not know how to express it than that she believes it is not expressible. Language begins to falter in the proposal scene and thereafter is replaced by physicality—facial expression, looks, gestures, and touch, hints of sexuality—all extralinguistic forms of communication and union. True intimacy is quintessentially private, and so to represent it is to violate it, to provide just another false or partial intimacy. The last sentence of *Emma* conveys this sense of intimacy as always expressed in futurity, a condition predicated on hope: "the wishes, the hopes, the confidence, the predictions of the small band of true friends who witnessed the ceremony were fully answered in the perfect happiness of the union" (E 484; the fact that the description of the marriage is reported to us by one excluded from the ceremony furthers the sense of an enclosing privacy). In Austen's novels, marital happiness is dependent upon knowledge of the other, and full knowledge of the other is another word for intimacy: As Virginia Woolf expresses Lily Briscoe's need for Mrs. Ramsay, "it was not knowledge but unity that she desired, not inscriptions on tablets, nothing that could be written in any language known to men, but intimacy itself, which is knowledge."

The deepest fear in these novels, as is so common in late eighteenth-century literature from Sterne to Cowper to Blake to Wordsworth, is of solipsism, but true intimacy, Austen suggests, breaks out of the circle of self-enclosure, the epistemological self-referentiality embodied in her quotation from William Cowper, "Myself creating what I saw" (E 344). The narrative of the "romantic" love story is the perfect antidote to solipsistic enclosure, for it mythologizes a perfect and lasting fulfillment, not just a temporary supplement to essential desire.[25] This need is distinctly different from the family structure of Elizabethan romance and from stage comedy; it is significantly narrower, narcissistic vision, which does not culminate in a reconstituted society, but rather involves finding or creating one other who is like the self, a double who understands, a replication of the inner in the outer world, which provides validation by holding off or deferring solipsism, self-enclosure, coldness, reserve, distance, and loneliness, defeating these within intimacy, in which the two are merged into one.[26]

If all this vision of intimacy seems natural and appropriate, history and anthropology show that it is not. According to Alan Macfarlane,

> one of the major lessons to be learnt from the anthropological discussions of marriage is that the Western concept of "companionate" marriage is unusual. Elsewhere marriage is not entered into for the sake of companionship; it is not the marriage of true minds, it is not the joining of two halves, it is not the completion of a search for someone before whom one can reveal one's inner soul, a companion in life, a mirror. Usually the worlds of men and

women are separate, and this is the case after marriage as it was before. A wife will remain much closer to her female kin and neighbours than to her husband; a man will spend his time and share his interests with other men. The couple will often eat apart, walk apart, and even, for most of the time, sleep apart. They may even dislike each other intensely and yet both honestly proclaim that it is a satisfactory marriage because the economic, political and reproductive ends have been satisfied. The blending of two personalities, two psychologies, is not involved. Often the couple did not know each other the day before they were married and see relatively little of each other for years afterwards, perhaps even being embarrassed to be left alone together. This does not mean that the relationships in such societies are shallow and that affection is absent, but merely that love and affection run towards kin by blood.[27]

This is a far cry from the notions of love and marriage that we find implicit in Jane Austen's novels, a notion of romantic love perfectly stated in Olive Schreiner's letters:

The one and only ideal is the perfect mental and physical life-long union of one man with one woman. That is the only thing which for highly developed intellectual natures can consolidate marriage. All short of this is more or less a failure, and no legal marriage can make a relationship other than impure in which there isn't this union.[28]

To read Austen correctly, we need to see the essentially historical nature of this notion of romantic love. Mary Poovey observes very shrewdly of love in Austen:

As we have repeatedly seen, romantic love purports to be completely "outside" ideology. It claims to be an inexplicable, irresistible, and possibly biological attraction that, in choosing its object, flouts the hierarchy, the priorities, and the inequalities of class society. Romantic love seems to defy self-interest and calculation as completely as it ignores income and rank; as a consequence, if it articulates (or can be educated to articulate) an essentially unselfish, generous urge toward another person, it may serve as an agent of moral reform. . . . But it is crucial to recognize that the moral regeneration ideally promised by romantic love is as individual and as private as its agent. In fact, the fundamental assumption of romantic love—and the reason it is so compatible with bourgeois society—is that the personal can be kept separate from the social, that one's "self" can be fulfilled in spite of—and in isolation from—the demands of the marketplace.[29]

That is to say, intimacy, morally corrective union, functions to efface the ideological contradiction between social responsibility and private withdrawal, for intimacy serves as the private "solution" to alienation and the objectification of social relations—romance and reification are two sides to the same coin or two sides of an ideological contradiction. As Lukács writes, "the man [or the woman] who now emerges [under capital] must be the individual, egotistic bourgeois isolated artificially by capitalism and . . . his consciousness, the source of his activity and knowledge, is an individual isolated consciousness à la Robinson Crusoe."[30] In *Emma*, Hartfield is a type of Crusoe's island, and for Emma herself, markets, production, classes, family, community, language, all social structures, relations, and functions, exist outside, removed and objectified from her, whereas feeling is the only authenticity that lies within. Emma's hope for happiness comes to depend upon validating the one authentic sign of her being by investing in the one true other, Mr. Knightley, who will validate her feelings, and thus her authenticity.

In closing, I would like to suggest that a large part of the continuing appeal of Austen's novels may be due to our implicit awareness that hers is the first recognizable formulation of modern personal relations, relations that are still obscure in the novels of Defoe, Richardson, Fielding, and Smollett and are even only partially visible in the novels of Burney and Charlotte Smith and other domestic novels at the century's end. This is not to say that Austen is the first to embody these new social relations in fiction, as if she had some special insight into bourgeois ideology, for obviously these are the consequences of massive social changes that had been brewing for a long time before her birth. There is no need to insist that Austen is the first novelist to recognize or to describe alienation or objectification. John Richetti's subtle analysis of Defoe's novels traces a similar duality between the interiority of character and an external world, focusing on Moll's (but also Crusoe's, Singleton's, Jack's, and Roxana's) "apartness," in "the ongoing dialectic of self and other":

> Her narrative self is a means of enacting for us independence of the "other", that is, of society, history, and circumstance in general. Novels like Defoe's, of course, pretend to begin with the opposite proposition that the self is precisely defined by the "other" and

claim to spend their time showing us just how the self is indeed derived from the other. We have seen, however, that there is a simultaneous push to assert self at the expense of other, that the real movement of Defoe's novels is not simply towards the determinants of character but rather towards the depiction of a dialectic between self and other which has as its end a covert but triumphant assertion of the self. In *Moll Flanders,* that dialectic is at its clearest; the self is visibly apart from the other.[31]

A similar apartness and dialectic operates in Austen's novels, but it is no longer problematic, because Austen has essentially "solved" the problem by integrating the privatization of human relations into the appropriate vehicle, the courtship narrative or domestic love story. As Lukács observes in *The Theory of the Novel,* "the development of a man is still the thread upon which the whole world of the novel is strung and along which it unrolls."[32] In the novel, biographical form has the effect of reversing explanatory models, explaining the social in terms of the individual, working from the inside out. Walter Benjamin underscores this reversal in his Lukácsian essay on narrative, "The Storyteller": "By integrating the social process with the development of a person, it [the novel] bestows the most fragile justification on the order determining it. The legitimacy it proves stands in direct opposition to reality."[33] In Richetti's terms, the biographical form of development disguises a pre-existing self, a self that is constituent of the external world in its dialectic with the other, the self and the world: "Thus the assertion of a pre-existing self is always what is meant by the development of the self. . . . The real task of this kind of narrative seems to be not the development of a new self but the discovery or establishment of an environment where the self can emerge without blame as a response to reality rather than as the creator of it."[34] In Austen, the dialectic of self and other is situated within the reduced compass of a courtship narrative, and so in the domestic tale of morally cleansing love and union, objectification is cured or banished by a process of exclusion: The family is re-created in ever smaller units, building a wall around Pemberley to exclude the vulgar and foolish, the brutal and the stupid, the selfish, the vicious, and the unprincipled: Mrs. Elton, Mrs. Bennet, Mrs. Norris, Lydia and Wickham, Willoughby and Mr. Collins.

By Austen's time, the domestic novel has also been purged of its inheritance of seventeenth-century religious structures, patterns of theodicy and epic, hagiography, spiritual autobiography, and spiritual diary, leaving her characters spiritually naked and secular.[35] In the light of Lukács's famous opposition of the epic and the novel, wherein the epic tells the history of a community while the novel tells the history of a problematic individual, Henry Fielding's *Tom Jones* represents in some ways the last epic, for its story concerns Squire Allworthy's estate more than the titular hero.[36] The ending sentence of *Tom Jones*, with its emphasis on the estate and its dependents, need only be compared with *Persuasion*, in which the paternal estate is all but ruined: "And such is their Condescension, their Indulgence, and their Beneficence to those below them, that there is not a Neighbour, a Tenant, or a Servant, who doth not most gratefully bless the Day when Mr. *Jones* was married to his *Sophia*."[37] If Fielding's novel is a type of backward-looking epic, Austen's innovation in closure is just that, a kind of closing in of the two protagonists into a hidden privacy of true intimacy. It is no accident that in *Pamela* and in *Sir Charles Grandison* Richardson feels obligated to track the newlyweds much longer, bringing them back to the paternal estate, before the family history can be safely and sensibly concluded. At the close of the *Paradiso* (Lukács's idea of the true epic), Dante can envision closure or climactic union as an absorption by ultimate authority of the individual soul, but by Austen's time, and in Austen's form, climactic union has been reconceived within the ideology of the subject; the narrator describes Captain Wentworth and Anne Elliot at their reunion, lost amid the public crowd in Bath, as two individual "souls dancing in private rapture."

Notes

INTRODUCTION

1. Georg Lukács, *The Theory of the Novel*, trans. Anna Bostock (1971, rpt. Cambridge: MIT Press, 1978), p. 34.

2. Austen's fiction is quoted from *The Novels of Jane Austen*, 5 vols., ed. R. W. Chapman (1923, rpt. Oxford: Oxford University Press, 1978), and *Minor Works*, ed. R. W. Chapman (1954, rpt. London: Oxford University Press, 1975); page numbers are included in the text.

3. Austen's letters are quoted from *Jane Austen's Letters*, ed. R. W. Chapman (1932, rpt. Oxford: Oxford University Press, 1979). Numbers in the text refer to page numbers.

4. Austen evidently kept a record of the responses of others to her novels; see, for example, where she notes that "Mrs. Creed's opinion is gone down on my list" (L 422).

5. William Beatty Warner, *Reading Clarissa, The Struggles of Interpretation* (New Haven: Yale University Press, 1979), pp. 123–42.

6. Marvin Mudrick argues that Austen consistently substitutes irony and distance for emotional engagement. *Jane Austen: Irony as Defense and Discovery* (1952, rpt. Princeton: Princeton University Press, 1962); John Halperin similarly writes that Austen was cold and distant, "a woman deficient in feeling." *The Life of Jane Austen* (Baltimore: The Johns Hopkins University Press, 1984), p. 305.

7. Marilyn Butler, *Jane Austen and the War of Ideas* (Oxford: Clarendon Press, 1975), passim.

8. "*Emma* and its Critics, The Value of Tact," in *Jane Austen, New Perspectives*, ed. Janet Todd, *Women & Literature*, NS 3 (New York: Holmes & Meier, 1983), pp.

257–72; Adena Rosmarin makes much the same point in " 'Misreading' *Emma*: The Powers and Perfidies of Interpretive History," *ELH* 51 (1984), pp. 315–42.

9. Fredric Jameson, *Marxism and Form* (Princeton: Princeton University Press, 1971), pp. 357–58; the passage from Wayne Booth referred to is in *The Rhetoric of Fiction* (Chicago: University of Chicago Press, 1961), pp. 264–65.

10. Michael McKeon, *Politics and Poetry in Restoration England, the Case of Dryden's Annus Mirabilis* (Cambridge: Harvard University Press, 1975), pp. 267–81.

11. LeRoy W. Smith, *Jane Austen and the Drama of Woman* (New York: St. Martin's Press, 1983), pp. 19–20.

12. Francis R. Hart's suggestive study, "The Spaces of Privacy: Jane Austen," *Nineteenth-Century Fiction* 30 (1975), pp. 305–33, is a notable exception, as he demonstrates the importance of privacy as well as the sharp division between private and public in Austen's fiction, but even here these issues need to be much more fully historicized.

13. Though I use the term *middle class,* or more commonly, *gentry* to describe Austen's class, David Spring makes a persuasive case for the term *pseudo-gentry,* which includes professionals such as clergy who were dependent upon but still aspired to or emulated the land-owning gentry. "Interpreters of Jane Austen's Social World," in *Jane Austen, New Perspectives,* ed. Todd, pp. 53–72.

14. Butler, *War of Ideas,* p. 101.

15. Butler, *War of Ideas,* p. 97.

16. Butler, *War of Ideas,* p. 164.

17. Marilyn Butler, *Romantics, Rebels and Reactionaries* (Oxford: Oxford University Press, 1981), pp. 97 and 98.

18. Raymond Williams, *The Country and the City* (New York: Oxford University Press, 1973), p. 115.

19. David Monaghan, *Jane Austen Structure and Social Vision* (London: Macmillan, 1980), p. 7.

20. See, for example, Walton Litz, *"Persuasion*: Forms of Estrangement" in *Jane Austen Bicentenary Essays,* ed. John Halperin (Cambridge: Cambridge University Press, 1975), pp. 221–32; Nina Auerbach, "O Brave New World: Evolution and Revolution in *Persuasion,"* *ELH* 39 (1972), pp. 112–28.

21. Julia Prewit Brown, *Jane Austen's Novels: Social Change and Literary Form* (Cambridge: Harvard University Press, 1979), p. 19.

22. Georg Lukács, *History and Class Consciousness,* trans. Rodney Livingstone (1968, rpt. Cambridge: MIT Press, 1972), p. 156.

23. Lee Gordon, *The Young Lukács* (Chapel Hill: University of North Carolina Press, 1983), pp. 98–100.

24. Paul de Man, *Blindness and Insight* (New York: Oxford University Press, 1971), p. 53.

25. Lukács, *Theory,* p. 66.

26. Lukács, *Theory,* p. 56.

27. J. M. Bernstein, *The Philosophy of the Novel: Lukács, Marxism and the Dialectics of Form* (Minneapolis: University of Minnesota Press, 1984), pp. xviii and 215.

28. Bernstein, *Philosophy of the Novel,* p. 197. For a lucid discussion of the historical and political context of Lukács's work, see George Lichtheim, *Lukács* (London: Fontana/Collins, 1970).

29. Bernstein, *Philosophy of the Novel,* pp. 186 and 197. In his 1967 preface to

History and Class Consciousness, Lukács acknowledges his tendency to collapse "reification," "objectification," and "alienation," p. xxiv.

30. Lukács, *History and Class Consciousness,* p. 135.

31. Lukács, *History and Class Consciousness,* p. 85.

32. Lukács, *History and Class Consciousness,* p. 88.

33. Lukács, *History and Class Consciousness,* p. 90.

34. Bernstein, p. xix.

35. Lukács, *History and Class Consciousness,* p. 87.

36. Bernstein, pp. xvii–xviii.

37. Lukács, *History and Class Consciousness,* p. 86, quoting Karl Marx, *Capital,* 3 vols., ed. Frederick Engels, trans. Samuel Moore and Edward Aveling (New York: International Publishers, 1967), I, 72.

38. Lukács, *History and Class Consciousness,* p. 62.

39. Lukács, *The Theory of the Novel,* p. 34.

40. Lukács, *History and Class Consciousness,* p. 59.

41. *Isolation, fragmentation,* and *atomization* are Lukács's terms, *History and Class Consciousness,* p. 91.

42. *Conversations with Lukács,* ed. Theo Pinkus (Cambridge: MIT Press, 1975), p. 37. Lukács's remarks on Balzac from the same interview are relevant to this issue: "As a great historian of the Restoration period, Balzac showed precisely how the aristocracy came to be the leading force in public life. He showed at the same time, however, how this aristocracy became completely capitalized, how the typical representatives of the aristocracy at this time were essential agrarian capitalists, who drew the greatest possible profit from the Restoration. . . . In this respect I find Balzac a quite great historian, who didn't need a single intellectual contact with Marx to see this duality, i.e., how economic development was irresistible even in opposition to the desires, wishes and thought of the men responsible for it" (p. 128).

43. Georg Lukács, *The Historical Novel,* trans. Hannah and Stanley Mitchell (London: Merlin Press, 1962), p. 58. In some ways, *The Historical Novel* can be read as an extreme revision of *The Theory of the Novel,* purged of its idealism.

44. Among previous studies of Austen's language, most notable are K. C. Phillipps, *Jane Austen's English* (London: Andre Deutsch, 1970) and Norman Page, *The Language of Jane Austen* (New York: Barnes & Noble, 1972). For a less descriptive and more conceptual or thematic study of Austen's language, see Howard S. Babb, *Jane Austen's Novels, The Fabric of Dialogue* (1962, rpt. Hamden: Archon Books, 1967).

45. Jerome McGann argues that romanticism and criticism of it are characterized by an assumption of the transcendence of history: "In the Romantic Age these and similar ideas [eg. the creativity of the Imagination, the centrality of the Self, etc.] are represented as trans-historical-eternal truths which wake to perish never. The very belief that transcendental categories can provide a permanent ground for culture becomes, in the Romantic Age, an ideological formation— another illusion raised up to hold back an awareness of the contradictions inherent in contemporary social structures and the relations they support." *The Romantic Ideology* (Chicago: The University of Chicago Press, 1983), p. 134. As helpful as this corrective is, McGann's unwillingness to ground this Romantic ideology in particular history and politics undermines his effort.

46. See Lennard David, *Resisting Novels, Ideology and Fiction* (New York: Methuen, 1987), for a very suggestive and thorough discussion of these matters.

47. Louis Althusser, *Lenin and Philosophy and Other Essays*, trans. Ben Brewster (New York: Monthly Review Press, 1971), p. 162.

48. Fredric Jameson, *The Political Unconscious* (Ithaca: Cornell University Press, 1981), p. 102.

49. "Who's Afraid of Jane Austen," in *Jane Austen: New Perspectives*, p. 112.

50. For a more thorough discussion of this trend, see James Thompson, "Jane Austen and History," *Review* 8 (1986), pp. 21–32.

51. *The Political Unconscious*, p. 53.

52. In "Traveling Theory," Edward Said warns against the ahistorical appropriation of theory, using explicitly the example of *History and Class Consciousness*. *The World, the Text and the Critic* (Cambridge: Harvard University Press, 1983), pp. 226–47. For Lukács's own remarks on the moment of *History and Class Consciousness*, see his autobiographical writings, *Georg Lukács, Record of a Life*, ed. István Eörsi, trans. Rodney Livingstone (London: Verso, 1983), pp. 75–78.

53. *The Political Unconscious*, p. 75.

54. *The Political Unconscious*, p. 47.

55. For an insightful review of feminist discussions of marriage in Austen, see Karen Newman, "Can This Marriage Be Saved: Jane Austen Makes Sense of an Ending," *ELH* 50 (1983), pp. 693–710.

CHAPTER 1

1. Virginia Woolf, *Collected Essays* I (New York: Harcourt, Brace & World, 1967), p. 220.

2. Austen was disappointed at the Great Exhibition as well, as she reveals at the end of this letter: "there was nothing like Mrs. D. at either. I can only imagine that Mr. D. prizes any Picture of her too much to like it should be exposed to the public eye.—I can imagine he w^d have that sort of feeling—that mixture of Love, Pride & Delicacy" (L 312): It is clear that Austen shared with Darcy some of this proprietary dislike of displaying her creations.

3. "Jane Austen's Methods," *Times Literary Supplement* (9 February 1922), 82a.

4. Robert Alan Donovan, "The Mind of Jane Austen," in *Jane Austen Today*, ed. Joel Weinsheimer (Athens: University of Georgia Press, 1975), p. 110.

5. The dialectic of interpretation and representation comes from J. M. Bernstein's interpretation of Lukács: "For Lukács the novel is a dialectic of form-giving and mimesis, a dialectic of interpretation and representation. . . . The novel is *premised* by the gap between is and ought; the practice of novel writing both recognizes the gap and through the instrumentality of form attempts to bridge it." *The Philosophy of the Novel*, p. xviii.

6. "Jane Austen's Anthropocentrism," in *Jane Austen Today*, p. 133.

7. Although Miss Steele is clearly presented as foolish and vulgar, we should note that her interest in clothing and its cost is not dissimilar to the interest Austen exhibits throughout her letters. Furthermore, Miss Steele's fascination with detail parallels the imagination of the novelist: Nothing escaped *her* minute observation and general curiosity either.

8. Graham Hough's observation about clothing in Austen represents a typically and traditionally half-true confusion of morality and materiality in these novels: "Concern with clothes, objects, and material details is always the sign of

inferiority in the novels. Anyone in Jane Austen who talks about sprigged muslin or boiled eggs is either bad or in some degree ridiculous. If we need any demonstration that her novels are not mere transcripts of her daily experience, that the narrator in charge of her fiction is an ideal construct different from her daily self, we have only to compare her novels with her letters." "Narrative and Dialogue in Jane Austen," in Graham Hough, *Selected Essays* (Cambridge: Cambridge University Press, 1978), p. 67.

9. For a consideration of these issues in a somewhat later period, see Helene E. Robert, " 'The Exquisite Slave': The Role of Clothes in the Making of the Victorian Woman," *Signs* 2 (1977), 554–69, as well as David Kunzle, "Dress Reform as Antifeminism," *Signs* 2 (1977), pp. 570–79.

10. Maria Edgeworth, *Belinda*, 2 vols. (London: Baldwin & Cradock, 1833), I, 3.

11. Accurate generalizations about the change of fashion are difficult to make, but the period from 1790 to 1820 marks a shift in taste from the relative simplicity of Neoclassicism to more elaborate Romantic styles. Accordingly, evening dress becomes increasingly more expensive through the gradual transition from muslins to silk and the addition of expensive trimmings of lace, pearls, and gold and silver embroidery. The basic gown may have not varied all that much in price, but the expense could be dramatically increased by the trimmings. See Geoffrey Squire, *Dress and Society, 1560–1970* (New York: Viking Press, 1974).

12. See Neil McKendrick, "The Commercialization of Fashion," in Neil McKendrick, John Brewer, and J. H. Plumb, *The Birth of a Consumer Society, The Commercialization of Eighteenth-Century England* (Bloomington: Indiana University Press, 1982), pp. 71–81.

13. Christopher Kent observes that the price of muslin varied so much because of the increasing competition between Indian and domestic producers; further, the price may be mentioned because the higher price of imported muslin added to its exclusivity and exchange value. " 'Real Solemn History' and Social History," in *Jane Austen in a Social Context*, ed. David Monaghan (Totowa, NJ: Barnes & Noble, 1981), pp. 96–98.

14. Neil McKendrick, "The Commercialization of Fashion," pp. 34–99. See also Fernand Braudel, *Capitalism and Material Life 1400–1800*, trans. Miriam Kochan (New York: Harper & Row, 1973), pp. 226–43. Braudel observes, "In fact the sovereign authority of fashion was barely enforced in its full rigour before 1700" (p. 231). McKendrick, in turn, traces the rate of change across the eighteenth century: "The accelerating pace of fashion change can only be accommodated by referring to the styles of George I, George II, the 1760s, the 1770s, the 1780s and 1790s and with many fashion goods even that is insufficient and anyone with scholarship worthy of the name would have to refer to individual years" (p. 42).

15. McKendrick describes in detail the ways in which these patterns of fashion were disseminated to the provinces: "By the end of the eighteenth century the competitive, socially emulative aspect of fashion was being consciously manipulated by commerce in pursuit of increased consumption. This new fashion world was one in which entrepreneurs were trying deliberately to induce fashionable change, to make it rapidly available to as many as possible and yet to keep it so firmly under their control that the consuming public could be sufficiently influenced to buy at the dictate of *their* fashion decisions, at the convenience of *their* production lines. Those fashion decisions were increasingly based on economic

grounds rather than aesthetic ones, on the basis of what the factories could produce and what the salesman could sell rather than on what the French court dictated. Commerce was now pulling the strings in control of the fashion doll. They still needed the co-operation of the exclusive world of the fashionable aristocracy. The fashionable few remained what Wedgewood called 'the legislators of taste', but they were no longer the sole beneficiaries of its pleasures, and the fashionable lead they provided was increasingly under the manipulative control of entrepreneurs seeking a quicker access to a mass market" (p. 43).

16. *British Dramatists from Dryden to Sheridan,* ed. George H. Nettleton, Arthur E. Case, and George Winchester Stone, Jr. (1939, rpt. Carbondale: Southern Illinois University Press, 1978), p. 769.

17. McKendrick, "Commercialization of Fashion," p. 51.

18. Sandra Gilbert and Susan Gubar, *The Madwoman in the Attic* (New Haven: Yale University Press, 1979), pp. 128–45.

19. Barbara Hardy's description of the tone of the letters seems just right: they "show a constant but constantly self-amused preoccupation with dress." "Properties and Possessions in Jane Austen's Novels," in *Jane Austen's Achievement,* ed. Juliet McMaster (New York: Harper & Row, 1976), p. 89.

20. Lloyd W. Brown explores Austen's habitual practice of undercutting obvious morals in "The Comic Conclusion in Jane Austen's Novels," *PMLA* 84 (1969), pp. 1582–88.

21. For a suggestive discussion of the role of personal beauty in Jane Austen and contemporary novelists, see Jan Fergus, "Sex and Social Life in Jane Austen's Novels," in *Jane Austen in a Social Context,* ed. Monaghan, pp. 66–85.

22. Alistair Duckworth is among the few who approve of Charlotte Lucas. *The Improvement of the Estate* (Baltimore: Johns Hopkins University Press, 1971), pp. 119–20, n. 3. More typical is Stuart Tave's vehement condemnation. *Some Words of Jane Austen* (Chicago: University of Chicago Press, 1973), p. 136.

23. Darrel Mansell, who explores just how little Austen's heroines know about the world, expresses astonishment that Austen should be declared a realist. *The Novels of Jane Austen* (New York: Barnes & Noble, 1973), pp. 7–12.

24. *The Improvement of the Estate,* pp. 85ff.

25. *The Language of Jane Austen,* p. 56.

26. Ian Watt, *The Rise of the Novel* (Berkeley: University of California Press, 1957), pp. 296–98.

27. "Jane Austen's Anthropocentrism," p. 131.

28. *Studies in European Realism* (New York: Grosset & Dunlap, 1964), pp. 147–54.

29. R. F. Brissenden notes that this section is Austen's most concrete, and he compares the physical sordidness of Portsmouth with the moral sordidness of London. *"Mansfield Park*: Freedom and the Family," in *Jane Austen Bicentenary Essays,* ed. John Halperin (Cambridge: Cambridge University Press, 1975), pp. 157–59.

30. Terry Eagleton, *Criticism and Ideology* (1976, rpt. London: Verso Editions, 1978), p. 71.

31. Randolph Trumbach, in *The Rise of the Egalitarian Family, Aristocratic Kinship and Domestic Relations in Eighteenth-Century England* (New York: Academic Press, 1978), observes that as the nuclear family grows stronger the "patriarch ceases to be father to his servants but becomes their employer and father to his children alone," p. 121. Margaret Kirkham extends the issue of dependency

further, to include not only children and wife, but also the slaves who work Sir Thomas's Antigua plantation. Kirkham observes that Fanny's question to Sir Thomas about the slave trade (MP 198) is never answered; she also notes that the Mansfield decision, to which the title of the novel might allude, concerns the freedom of slaves in England. *Jane Austen, Feminism and Fiction* (Totowa, N.J.: Barnes & Noble, 1983), pp. 116–19.

32. Karl Marx, *Capital,* 3 vols., ed. Frederick Engels, trans. Samuel Moore and Edward Aveling (New York: International Publishers, 1967), I, 72.

33. For a thorough survey of eighteenth-century attitudes toward luxury, see John Sekora, *Luxury, The Concept in Western Thought, Eden to Smollett* (Baltimore: Johns Hopkins University Press, 1977), pp. 63–131.

34. The most thorough discussion of the theme of improvement is found in Duckworth, *The Improvement of the Estate.* See also David Spring, "Austen's Social World," for the connection between the theme of improvement and agrarian capitalism.

35. In "Games in Jane Austen's Life and Fiction," Duckworth convincingly argues that Austen accepts the economic base of her culture; in effect, Duckworth validates Williams's view of Austen in *The Country and the City: Jane Austen Bicentenary Essays,* pp. 279–97.

36. *The Country and the City,* p. 116.

37. *The Country and the City,* p. 117. As suggestive and as perceptive as Williams's remarks always are, this particular statement must be qualified. If Austen does not consciously acknowledge the laboring classes within her novels, she most certainly acknowledges the infinite gradations within or around her own class, bourgeois or pseudogentry who affect or have achieved the look and air of the gentry or the aristocracy. It may be argued, as well, that the splintering of the middle classes into various factions suggests an overall awareness of class division, a division that Austen is only willing or able to see in the immediate terms of her own class and is reluctant to extend, in her fiction at least, to the lower orders.

38. *Marxism and Form,* p. 380; at the opening of *The Making of the English Working Class,* E. P. Thompson is particularly forceful about this relational conception of class: "I do not see class as a 'structure', or even as a 'category', but as something which in fact happens (and can be shown to have happened) in human relationships. More than this, the notion of class entails the notion of historical relationship" (1963, rpt. New York: Vintage Books, 1966), p. 9.

39. Referring to Nietzsche's *Genealogy of Morals,* Jameson writes, "what is really meant by 'the good' is simply my own position as an unassailable power center, in terms of which the position of the Other, or of the weak, is repudiated and marginalized in practices which are then ultimately themselves formalized in the concept of evil." *The Political Unconscious* (Ithaca: Cornell University Press, 1981), p. 117. Such a strategy aptly describes Fanny's, or more properly, the narrator's presentation of Mary Crawford, who, as the dangerous and seductive Other, must be repudiated and expelled, after which she is officially declared an evil influence, of which the Park and the Bertram family, especially Edmund, are well rid.

40. Harold Perkin, *Origin of Modern English Society* (1969, rpt. London: Routledge & Kegan Paul, 1985), p. 209. Perkin (pp. 183–84) quotes a passage from *Blackwood's,* 1820, VII. 90–102: "Everywhere, in every walk of life, it is too evident that the upper orders of Society have been tending, more and more, to a separation of themselves from those whom nature, providence, and law have

placed beneath them. . . . Men have come to deride and despise a thousand of those means of communication that in former days knit all orders of the people together."

41. In this respect, we can employ Jameson's suggestive description of ideology as utopian: The task of Marxist analysis is not only "to unmask and to demonstrate the ways in which a cultural artifact fulfills a specific ideological mission, in legitimating a given power structure, in perpetuating and reproducing the latter, and in generating specific forms of false consciousness (or ideology in the narrower sense). It must not cease to practice this essentially negative hermeneutic function (which Marxism is virtually the only current critical method to assume today) but must also seek, through and beyond this demonstration of the instrumental function of a given cultural object, to project its simultaneously Utopian power as the symbolic affirmation of a specific historical and class form of collective unity." He goes on to specify this "dual perspective—ideology and Utopia," which brings together the instrumental or functional reading with the communal or anticipatory one. *The Political Unconscious*, pp. 291 and 296.

42. Marx and Engels observe, "The division of labour, which we already saw above as one of the chief forces of history up till now, manifests itself also in the ruling class as the division of mental and material labour, so that inside this [hegemonic] class one part appears as the thinkers of the class (its active, conceptive ideologists, who make the perfecting of the illusion of the class about itself their chief source of livelihood)." *The German Ideology*, ed. C. J. Arthur (1947, rpt. New York: International Publishers, 1973), p. 65.

43. Anne D. Hall suggests that characters such as Mrs. Norris may serve Austen as both identification and exorcism for her resentment and envy over dependence on the gentry.

44. The best discussion of class in Austen is Terry Lovell, "Jane Austen and Gentry Society," in *Literature, Society and the Sociology of Literature*, ed. Francis Barker (University of Essex, 1976), pp. 118–32. As with Raymond Williams, however, Lovell tends to assume that Austen's view is of one class only, without giving sufficient weight to the energy Austen puts into repressing the absent, laboring class. For the current debate concerning the degree to which the upper classes were capitalized at this time, see E. P. Thompson, "The Peculiarities of the English," in *The Poverty of Theory and Other Essays* (New York: Monthly Review Press, 1978), pp. 245–301, and Perry Anderson, *Arguments Within English Marxism* (London: New Left Books, 1980).

45. In the *Political Unconscious*, Jameson offers a brief but very suggestive reading of Emily Brontë's *Wuthering Heights* in terms of A. J. Greimas's theory of "actants," in which Heathcliff is both a "donor," injecting capital into the ruined finances of the family, and the agent of history:

"The aging of Heathcliff then constitutes the narrative mechanism whereby the alien dynamism of capitalism is reconciled with the immemorial (and cyclical) time of the agricultural life of a country squiredom; and the salvational and wish-fulfilling Utopian conclusion is brought about at the price of transforming such an alien dynamism into a benign force which, eclipsing itself, permits the vision of some revitalization of the ever more marginalized countryside" (p. 128).

46. Mary Poovey, *The Proper Lady and the Woman Writer* (Chicago: University of Chicago Press, 1984), p. 194. Of this conflict in *Pride and Prejudice*, Poovey observes, "In essence, in awarding Elizabeth this handsome husband with ten

thousand pounds a year, Austen is gratifying the reader's fantasy that such outspoken liveliness *will* be successful in material terms, but she earns the right to do so precisely because Elizabeth's first fantasy of personal power is *not* rewarded. *Pride and Prejudice*, in other words, legitimizes the reader's romantic wishes by humbling the heroine's vanity. At the level of the plot, power is taken from egotism and given to love; at the level of the reading experience, power seems miraculously both to emanate from and to reward individualistic desire" (p. 201).

CHAPTER 2

1. Laurence Sterne, *The Life and Opinions of Tristram Shandy, Gentleman*, ed. James A. Work (Indianapolis: Odyssey Press, 1940), p. 75.

2. "E Pluribus Unum, the Parts and Whole of *Pride and Prejudice*," in Halperin, *Bicentenary Essays*, p. 126.

3. Ian Watt, "On Sense and Sensibility," in *Jane Austen, A Collection of Critical Essays*, ed. Ian Watt (Englewood Cliffs, NJ: Prentice-Hall, 1963), p. 49.

4. April 1850, quoted from *Jane Austen, The Critical Heritage*, ed. B. C. Southam (London: Routledge & Kegan Paul, 1968), p. 128.

5. Jean H. Hagstrum, however, argues that there is considerable passion in Austen. *Sex and Sensibility, Ideal and Erotic Love from Milton to Mozart* (Chicago: University of Chicago Press, 1980).

6. *Distance* is used in a similarly pejorative sense in Marvin Mudrick's description of Austen; her irony consistently distances the object of attack. *Jane Austen—Irony as Defense and Discovery*, passim.

7. See Francis Hart, "The Spaces of Privacy: Jane Austen," *NCF*, 39 (1975), pp. 305–33; Stone, *Family, Sex, and Marriage*, pp. 253–57. Philippe Ariès writes, "In the eighteenth century, the family began to hold society at a distance, to push back beyond a steadily extending zone of private life." Additionally, changing domestic architecture and the development of the corridor in large private houses enabled personal privacy: "This specialization of the rooms in the middle class and nobility to begin with, was certainly one of the greatest changes in everyday life. It satisfied a new desire for isolation." *Centuries of Childhood*, trans. Robert Baldick (New York: Vintage Books, 1962), pp. 398–400.

8. Michael McKeon, *The Origins of the English Novel 1600–1740* (Baltimore: Johns Hopkins University Press, 1987), pp. 25–128. The whole of the section "Questions of Truth," dealing with the debates of the accuracy and verisimilitude of late seventeenth- and early eighteenth-century narrative is relevant here.

9. *The Political Unconscious*, p. 221.

10. In an interesting essay on this subject, Mary Alice Burgan traces Austen's use of proposal scenes, noting, as others have before, that Austen relinquishes direct dialogue in these scenes. Burgan argues, however, that Austen exteriorizes such scenes, that she becomes "aware of the dramatic power of time and place brought together to express the transcendence of the single, intensely felt moment." Why Austen must externalize these moments, Burgan does not say. "Feeling and Control: A Study of the Proposal Scenes in Jane Austen's Major Novels," in *The English Novel in the Nineteenth Century*, ed. George Goodin (Urbana: University of Illinois Press, 1972), pp. 25–51.

11. J. L. Austin observes that a marriage proposal involves one of the most

formulaic uses of language. *How to Do Things with Words* (Cambridge: Harvard University Press, 1962), pp. 5–11.

12. Of this and the other novels, John Halperin objects vociferously, complaining that again and again, Austen "botched" her endings by not narrating them in full. Of *Pride and Prejudice*'s proposal scene, he writes, "It is an anticlimax of awful proportions, and it is a mistake Jane Austen makes in all of her books." "Why did Jane Austen, we may well ask, consistently shy away from detailed treatment of the fulfillment of romantic expectations at the ends of her novels? Is it because 'life isn't like that'—her ongoing emphasis on the importance of correct vision, the destruction of romance? That she provided happy endings at all suggests that she was aware of her readers' (and publishers') expectations." *Life of Jane Austen*, pp. 78 and 108. Objections to her endings would seem to reveal more about readers' expectations than about Jane Austen's personal view of romance.

13. Sterne prefaces his blank page with the following: "To conceive this right,—call for pen and ink—here's paper ready to your hand.—Sit down, Sir, paint her to your own mind—as like your mistress as you can—as unlike your wife as your conscience will let you—'tis all one to me—please put your own fancy in it." *Tristram Shandy*, p. 470.

14. "'The Pen of the Contriver': The Four Fictions of *Northanger Abbey*," in Halperin, *Bicentenary Essays*, p. 104. Norman Page writes, "More generally, it may be suggested that Jane Austen tends to renounce dialogue when events seem about to precipitate a scene with considerable emotional potential." *The Language of Jane Austen*, p. 137.

15. Patricia Meyer Spacks captures Austen's attitude toward and use of Catherine Morland quite nicely: "As naive observer and participant, she both provides satiric focus ('the emperor isn't wearing any clothes') and serves as satiric target." *The Adolescent Ideal, Myths of Youth and the Adult Imagination* (New York: Basic Books, 1981), p. 164.

16. *The Novels of Jane Austen*, pp. 28–29.

17. Mary Poovey explores at length the central paradox of eighteenth-century female stereotypes, which insists that women must both embody and efface sexuality at one and the same time. *The Proper Lady*, pp. 15–30.

18. Stuart Tave observes that Austen is far more likely to use the word *affection* than *love*. *Some Words*, pp. 131–32.

19. On this point, compare Elizabeth Inchbald's *A Simple Story*:

"'It is impossible, my dear Miss Milner,' he gently whispered, 'to say, the joy I feel that your disorder has subsided.'

But though it was impossible to say, it was possible to *look* what he felt, and his looks expressed his feelings." *A Simple Story*, ed. J. M. S. Tompkins (London: Oxford University Press, 1967), p. 98.

20. Although their marriage is expected, there is something slightly subversive about it. In a page, Austen covers an almost incestuous transition from fraternal to connubial love, a violation of exogamy that the narrator glosses over with a glib phrase, "I purposely abstain from dates on this occasion" (MP 470). If Fanny is not Edmund's sister, she is his child/creation: "Loving, guiding, protecting her, as he had been doing ever since her being ten years old, her mind in so great a degree [was] formed by his care" (MP 470). Joseph Wiesenfarth connects this act of creation with the Pygmalion myth. "Austen and Apollo," in *Jane Austen Today*, pp. 46–63. In the same collection of essays, Juliet McMaster discusses Fanny and

Edmund in connection with falling in love with one's teacher. "Love and Pedagogy," pp. 64–91.

21. *Theory of the Novel,* p. 41.

22. In both versions, by apparent happenstance Austen gives Anne Elliot an equal share in initiating the reconciliation, for only in contrived circumstances such as this can the woman have the fullest speech.

23. Marvin Mudrick makes the point that Anne Elliot could not address these ideas to Captain Wentworth directly. *Jane Austen—Irony as Defense and Discovery,* p. 232.

24. It is as if here Austen has brilliantly achieved the desire of fiction: At this point of reversal, as the reader is excluded from the life of the fiction, momentarily the lives of the characters seem most genuine. Darrel Mansell writes of the protagonists here: "Their 'spirits' are 'dancing in private rapture'. For that, no outward show is adequate, on their part or Jane Austen's. What matters is within, and no fiction can quite embody it," p. 207.

25. Daniel Defoe, *Moll Flanders,* ed. Edward Kelly (New York: W. W. Norton & Co., 1973), p. 46.

26. Samuel Richardson, *Pamela,* ed. T. C. Duncan Eaves and Ben K. Kimpel (Boston: Houghton Mifflin Co., 1971), p. 232. See also, E. E. Duncan-Jones, "Proposals of Marriage in *Pride and Prejudice* and *Pamela,*" *Notes and Queries* NS 4 (1957), p. 76.

27. On this subject, see James Fortuna, *"The Unsearchable Wisdom of God," A Study of Providence in Richardson's Pamela* (Gainesville: University of Florida Press, 1980).

28. William Warner discusses the proposal scenes of *Clarissa* in *Reading Clarissa,* pp. 82–85 and 201–5.

29. Samuel Richardson, *Clarissa,* 4 vols. (London: John Dent, 1932), II, 141.

30. Samuel Richardson, *Sir Charles Grandison,* 3 vols., ed. Jocelyn Harris (London: Oxford University Press, 1972), III, 99.

31. Frances Burney, *Evelina,* ed. Edward A. Bloom (London: Oxford University Press, 1970), pp. 351–52.

32. "Patrician hero" is Kenneth Moler's phrase in *Jane Austen's Art of Allusion* (Lincoln: University of Nebraska Press, 1968), pp. 75–108.

33. Frances Burney, *Camilla,* ed. Edward A. Bloom and Lillian D. Bloom (London: Oxford University Press, 1972), p. 545.

34. *Camilla,* pp. 546–47.

35. *Camilla,* p. 900.

36. Henry Mackenzie, *The Man of Feeling,* ed. Brian Vickers (London: Oxford University Press, 1967), p. 105.

37. Henry Brooke, *The Fool of Quality* (London: George Routledge & Sons, Ltd., 1909), pp. 83, 191.

38. *Fool of Quality,* pp. 190–91.

39. Ann Radcliffe, *The Mysteries of Udolpho,* ed. Bonamy Dobrée (London: Oxford University Press, 1970), p. 668.

40. Juliet McMaster argues that the original source for Austen's language of love is Robert Burton, though she gives little weight to the mediation of a century of fiction. *Jane Austen on Love* (Victoria: University of Victoria, 1978).

41. *Jane Austen's Novels,* p. 1.

42. Maria Edgeworth, *Belinda,* 2 vols. (London: Baldwin & Cradock, 1833), II, 345.

43. Inchbald, *A Simple Story*, 337.

44. *Waverley: or 'Tis Sixty Years Since*, ed. Claire Lamont (Oxford: Clarendon Press, 1981), p. 317.

45. The importance of free indirect speech for Jane Austen has most recently been demonstrated by the work of John Dussinger, forthcoming, from which the following discussion derives.

46. For a history of free indirect speech, see Roy Pascal, *The Dual Voice, Free Indirect Speech and Its Functioning in the Nineteenth-Century European Novel* (Manchester: Manchester University Press/Totowa, N.J.: Rowman and Littlefield, 1977). Pascal concludes his discussion of Austen by commenting that "It is astonishing that so rich and sure a use of free indirect speech is to be found in Jane Austen's novels, when she had so slight a tradition to build on" (p. 59). For a substantially more theoretical discussion of free indirect discourse within a typology of methods of presenting consciousness, see Dorrit Cohn, *Transparent Minds, Narrative Modes for Presenting Consciousness in Fiction* (Princeton: Princeton University Press, 1978). Cohn classifies free indirect speech under the mode of narrated monologue, of which "the first extensive practitioner of the form" was Jane Austen, p. 108. Cohn goes on to argue, "The pattern set by Jane Austen thus unfolds throughout the nineteenth century: precisely those authors who, in their major works, most decisively abandoned first-person narration (Flaubert, Zola, James), instituting instead the norms of the dramatic novel, objective narration, and unobtrusive narrators, were the ones who re-introduced the subjectivity of private experience into the novel: this time not in terms of direct self-narration, but by imperceptibly integrating mental reactions into the neutral-objective report of actions, scenes, and spoken words" (p. 115).

47. Graham Hough writes of free indirect speech in terms of "coloured narrative" in "Narrative and Dialogue in Jane Austen," in *Selected Essays* (Cambridge: Cambridge University Press, 1978), pp. 46–82; Norman Page also discusses the technique in *The Language of Jane Austen*: "the supreme virtue of free indirect speech [is]: that it offers the possibility of achieving something of the vividness of speech without the appearance for a moment of a total silencing of the authorial voice" (p. 134).

48. Pascal, *Dual Voice*, pp. 51–52.

49. Butler, *War of Ideas*, pp. 273–74.

50. Kirkham, *Jane Austen, Feminism and Fiction*, pp. 171–72.

51. Pascal, *Dual Voice*, p. 59.

CHAPTER 3

1. *The Notebooks of Samuel Taylor Coleridge*, vol. 2, ed. Katheleen Coburn (New York: Bollingen, 1961), 2998–99. For a discussion of Coleridge and the limits of language see Rainmonda Mondiano, "Words and 'Languageless' Meanings: Limits of Expression in *The Rime of the Ancient Mariner*," *MLQ* 38 (1977), pp. 40–61.

2. Mary Lascelles, *Jane Austen and Her Art* (Oxford: Oxford University Press, 1939), p. 107.

3. Johnson's elegiac *Preface to a Dictionary* tells of his learning that "our language is yet living, and variable by the caprice of every one that speaks it": "Those who have been persuaded to think well of my design, will require that it

should fix our language, and put a stop to those alterations which time and chance have hitherto been suffered to make in it without opposition. With this consequence I will confess that I flattered myself for a while; but now begin to fear that I have indulged expectation which neither reason nor experience can justify. When we see men grow old and die at a certain time one after another, from century to century, we laugh at the elixir that promises to prolong life a thousand years; and with equal justice may the lexicographer be derided, who being able to produce no example of a nation that has preserved their words and phrases from mutability, shall imagine that his dictionary can embalm his language, and secure it from corruption and decay, that it is in his power to change sublunary nature, and clear the world at once from folly, vanity, and affectation." Samuel Johnson, *Rasselas, Poems, and Selected Prose,* ed. Bertrand H. Bronson (New York: Holt, Rinehart and Winston, 1971), pp. 245 and 255.

    4. Stuart M. Tave, *Some Words of Jane Austen,* pp. 25 and 28.

    5. William Wordsworth, *Poetical Works,* ed. Thomas Hutchinson, rev. Ernest de Selincourt (1904, rpt. London: Oxford University Press, 1971), p. 701. The serious examination of Austen's relation to Wordsworth begins with Stuart Tave's important essay "Jane Austen and One of Her Contemporaries," in *Jane Austen Bicentenary Essays,* ed. Halperin, pp. 61–74. Further exploration of the subject can be found in the *Wordsworth Circle* issue on Austen and Romanticism, vol. 7, no. 4 (1976); Susan Morgan's study *In the Meantime, Character and Perception in Jane Austen's Fiction* (Chicago: University of Chicago Press, 1980) takes as its subject "perceiving in time" (p. 8) in Austen and the poets. Finally, see Nina Auerbach, "Jane Austen and Romantic Imprisonment," in *Jane Austen in a Social Context,* ed. Monaghan, pp. 9–27.

    6. M. H. Abrams's *The Mirror and the Lamp* (Oxford: Oxford University Press, 1953) can serve as a model for tracing intellectual currents by way of changes in dominant metaphors; although a transformation in metaphors for language does not necessarily signify a change in practice, at the least it suggests a change in the perception of language.

    7. *Sensible Words, Linguistic Practice in England, 1640–1785* (Baltimore: Johns Hopkins University Press, 1977), p. 81. This sense of concern should be connected with Fredrick Bogel's insightful discussion of the central role of insubstantiality in later eighteenth-century literature. Fredrick V. Bogel, *Literature and Insubstantiality in Later Eighteenth-Century England* (Princeton: Princeton University Press, 1984).

    8. On the limits of language in German Romanticism, see Elizabeth M. Wilkinson, "The Inexpressible and the Unspeakable, Some Romantic Attitudes to Art and Language," *German Life and Letters* NS 16 (1963), pp. 1308–20. Although I do wish to emphasize the discontinuity between Neoclassicism and Romanticism on this subject, it would be foolish to imply that ineffability is at any time new; see, for example, Ann Chalmers Watts, "*Pearl,* Inexpressibility, and Poems of Human Loss," *PMLA* 99 (1984), 26–40. See also *Ineffability, Naming the Unnamable from Dante to Beckett,* ed. Peter S. Hawkins and Anne Howland Schotter (New York: AMS Press, 1984), particularly William Shallenberger, " 'Something' in Wordsworth," pp. 109–21.

    9. Lord Monboddo is given to this sort of comparison, for much of his last three volumes is devoted to comparisons between English and Greek languages. James Burnet, Lord Monboddo, *Of the Origin and Progress of Language,* 6 vols., Edinburgh, 1773–1792.

10. Demonstrating the correlation of poverty of thought and of language, James Beattie relates a remarkable anecdote of a deaf laborer he knew, whose language was limited to the compass of his class: "As he had little knowledge but what belonged to the business of a labourer, his ideas were few, and his language very defective." *The Theory of Language* (1788, rpt. New York: AMS Press, 1974), p. 8.

11. *The Study of Language in England, 1780–1850* (Princeton: Princeton University Press, 1967), and "The Tradition of Condillac: The Problem of the Origin of Language in the Eighteenth Century and the Debate in the Berlin Academy before Herder," in *From Locke to Saussure* (Minneapolis: University of Minnesota Press, 1982), pp. 146–209.

12. Monboddo, *Of the Origin,* IV, 166 and 167.

13. Depending upon one's assumptions, original language was either rude, rough, and crude, as in Monboddo, Warburton, Tooke, Blair, and Johnson, or passionate, powerful, and expressive, as in Herder and Rousseau.

14. William Wordsworth, *The Prelude,* ed. J. C. Maxwell (1971, rpt. New Haven: Yale University Press, 1981), p. 110; III, 184–85 (1805). All references to the *Prelude* are to this edition.

15. See, for example, Gerald Bruns, *Modern Poetry and the Idea of Language* (New Haven: Yale University Press, 1974), pp. 42–44.

16. *The Prose Works of William Wordsworth,* ed. W. J. B. Owen and Jane Worthington Smyser, 3 vols. (Oxford: Clarendon Press, 1974), III, 81. All further references are to this edition.

17. John Dryden, *Of Dramatic Poesy and Other Essays,* ed. George Watson, 2 vols. (London: John Dent, 1962), I, 145 and 176.

18. Dryden, *Of Dramatic Poesy,* II, 276.

19. *The Poems of Alexander Pope,* Gen. Ed. John Butt, 11 vols. (New Haven: Yale University Press, 1939–69), IV, 177; Epistle II, ii, ll. 171–73. Further references to Pope are to this edition.

20. *Spectator Papers,* ed. Donald Bond, 5 vols. (Oxford: Clarendon Press, 1965), III, 560; no. 416.

21. William Wordsworth, *The Poems,* ed. John O. Hayden, 2 vols. (1977, rpt. New Haven: Yale University Press, 1981), I, 359; "Tintern Abbey," ll. 75–76. Further references to Wordsworth's poetry are to this edition. *The Complete Poetical Works of Sir Walter Scott* (Boston: Houghton Mifflin Co., 1900), p. 141; *Marmion,* Canto 6, ll. 148–49. In Romanticism, such expressions are interchangeable in prose and in poetry. Scott uses the same phrases in his fiction; in *Waverley,* for example, Flora Mac-Ivor says of her Jacobite principles, "It is impossible to express to you the devotion of my feelings on this single subject." Of Waverley's fears for Flora, the narrator writes, "The pang attending this reflection was inexpressible." *Waverley,* pp. 141 and 135.

22. Lord Byron, *The Complete Poetical Works,* ed. Jerome J. McGann, vol. III (Oxford: Clarendon Press, 1981), pp. 113 and 226; "The Bride of Abydos," ll. 170–71 and "Lara," ll. 365–66.

23. Schlegel, *Lucinde,* quoted from Philip Rieff, *Freud: The Mind of a Moralist* (1959, rpt. Chicago: University of Chicago Press, 1979), p. 34. Coleridge, *Poetical Works,* ed. Ernest Hartley Coleridge (1912, rpt. Oxford: Oxford University Press, 1980), p. 404; "To William Wordsworth," l. 11. Jerome J. McGann writes of the "Immortality Ode," "From Wordsworth's vantage, an ideology is born out of things which (literally) *cannot* be spoken of. So the "Immortality Ode" is crucial

for us because it speaks about ideology from the point of view and in the context of its origins. If Wordsworth's poetry elides history, we observe in this 'escapist' or 'reactionary' move its own self-revelation. It is a rare, original, and comprehensive record of the birth and character of a particular ideology—in this case, one that has been incorporated into our academic programs." *The Romantic Ideology,* p. 91.

24. Percy Bysshe Shelley, *Complete Poetical Works,* ed. Thomas Hutchinson (1943, rpt. London: Oxford University Press, 1960), p. 19; "Alastor," l. 168. On the importance of silence in Wordsworth, see Stephen Land's valuable essay, "The Silent Poet: An Aspect of Wordsworth's Semantic Theory," *UTO* 42 (1973), pp. 157–69. Gene Ruoff discusses the idea of speech in Wordsworth in "Wordsworth on Language: Toward a Radical Poetics for English Romanticism," *Wordsworth Circle* 3 (1972), pp. 204–11. See also David Sampson, "Wordsworth and 'the Deficiencies of Language,'" *ELH* 51 (1984), pp. 53–68.

25. In this connection, Mary Jacobus writes of Wordsworth, "The episode of the Winander Boy, then, bears obliquely on what one might call the oral fallacy of Romantic theories of language—the pervasive notion that 'the voice / Of mountain torrents' (V, 408–9) speaks a language more profound than that of books and is carried farther into the heart. Wordsworth's naturalization of 'voice' here serves to avert the threat of anarchy that voices bring with them." "The Art of Managing Books: Romantic Prose and the Writing of the Past," in *Romanticism and Language,* ed. Arden Reed (Ithaca: Cornell University Press, 1984), p. 217.

26. See Terry Castle on sexuality and language in the earlier eighteenth century, "Matters Not Fit to Be Mentioned: Fielding's *The Female Husband,*" *ELH* 49 (1982), pp. 602–22, and Maximillian E. Novak, "The Unmentionable and the Ineffable in Defoe's Fiction," *SLI* 15 (1982), pp. 85–102. As one might expect, in John Cleland's *Fanny Hill,* sexual pleasures are regularly said to be inexpressible: "a touching warmth, a tender finishing, beyond the expression of words or even the paint of thought." *Fanny Hill,* ed. Peter Wagner (Harmondsworth: Penguin Books, 1985), p. 153.

27. Johnson, *Rasselas, Poems, and Selected Prose,* pp. 73 and 680.

28. Eric Rothstein explores the function of the unfinished in "'Ideal Presence' and the 'Non Finito' in Eighteenth-Century Aesthetics," *ECS* 9 (1976), pp. 307–32.

29. For a thorough discussion of this notion of imaginative reciprocity, see Kurt Heinzelman, *The Economics of the Imagination* (Amherst: University of Massachusetts Press, 1980), pp. 196–233.

30. Thomas Sheridan, *A Course of Lectures on Elocution* (1762, rpt. New York: Benjamin Blom, 1968), p. 100.

31. Hugh Blair, *Lectures on Rhetoric and Belles Lettres,* ed. Harold F. Harding, 2 vols. (1783, rpt. Carbondale: Southern Illinois University Press, 1965), I, 50 and 66; further references are to this edition.

Burke writes in his treatise on the sublime, "clearness . . . is in some sort an enemy to all enthusiasms," and further, "A clear idea is therefore another name for a little idea." *A Philosophical Enquiry into the Origin of Our Ideas of the Sublime and Beautiful,* ed. James T. Boulton (1958, rpt. Notre Dame: University of Notre Dame Press, 1968), pp. 60 and 63. Though they are not synonymous, obscurity has affinities with the inexpressible, and Burke goes on to recommend a "judicious obscurity": "It may be observed that very polished languages, and such as are praised for their superior clearness and perspicuity, are generally deficient in strength" (pp. 62 and 176). Already in 1757, the polarity of weak and strong, rich and poor has been reversed. Thomas Weiskel writes of Burke, the sublime, and Romanticism, "the failure to understand sometimes has the very highest meaning." *The Romantic Sublime* (Baltimore: The Johns Hopkins University Press, 1976), p. 35.

32. Isolated examples can be found: In "An Abstract of A Treatise of Human Nature," Hume writes "it is impossible by words to describe this feeling," but this is an isolated figure of speech rather than a central argument. *On Human Nature and the Understanding*, ed. Antony Flew (New York: Collier Books, 1962), p. 296. When Beattie uses the word *incommunicable*, it is in a pejorative sense of mystical and meaningless (p. 372).

33. Adam Smith, *Lectures on Rhetoric and Belles Lettres*, ed. John M. Lothian (London: Thomas Nelson, 1963), p. 142.

34. This idea is expanded later: "The signification of our sentiments, made by tones and gestures, has this advantage above that made by words, that it is the Language of nature. It is that method of interpreting our mind, which nature has dictated to all, and which is understood by all; whereas, words are only arbitrary, conventional symbols of our ideas; and, by consequence, must make a more feeble impression" (II, 204).

35. For Sheridan's influence, see Wilbur Samuel Howell, *Eighteenth-Century British Logic and Rhetoric* (Princeton: Princeton University Press, 1971), pp. 214–43.

36. Thomas Sheridan, *A Discourse Being Introductory to His Course of Lectures on Elocution and the English Language* (1759, rpt. Los Angeles: William Andrews Clark Memorial Library, 1969), p. 15; Sheridan, *A Course of Lectures*, p. x.

37. *Course of Lectures*, pp. 43 and 98–99.

38. *Course of Lectures*, p. 100.

39. *Course of Lectures*, p. 111. In such passages, Sheridan seems to parody the hostility to writing that Derrida analyzes in *Of Grammatology*, trans. Gayatri Spivak (Baltimore: The Johns Hopkins University Press, 1974).

40. Johann Gottfried Herder, *Essay on the Origin of Language*, in *On the Origin of Language*, trans. John H. Moran and Alexander Gode (New York: Frederick Ungar, 1966), pp. 151–52.

41. Herder, *Essay*, p. 164.

42. Herder, *Essay*, pp. 153–54.

43. Jean Jacques Rousseau, *Essay on the Origin of Languages*, in *On the Origin of Language*, pp. 21 and 68.

44. For further examples of the metaphor from this period, see Norman Holland, *The First Modern Comedies* (1959, rpt. Bloomington: Indiana University Press, 1967), pp. 51–52; Wilbur Samuel Howell includes several in passing, *Eighteenth-Century British Logic*, pp. 108, 138 note, and 472.

45. Dryden, *Poesy*, II, 207.

46. *Spectator*, III, 561. That similar associations of fashion are found in Quintilian shows how little changed is the use of this comparison between classical and neoclassical times: "Again, a tasteful and magnificent dress, as the Greek poet tells us, lends added dignity to its wearer: but effeminate and luxurious apparel fails to adorn the body and merely reveals the foulness of the mind. Similarly, a translucent and iridescent style merely serves to emasculate the subject which it arrays with such pomp of words." *Institutio Oratoria*, trans. H. E. Butler, 4 vols. (Cambridge: Harvard University Press, 1935), III, 189.

47. George Berkeley, *Treatise Concerning the Principles of Human Knowledge,* in *Principles, Dialogues, and Philosophical Correspondence,* ed. Colin Murray Turbayne (Indianapolis: Bobbs-Merrill, 1965), pp. 20—21.

48. Rosemond Tuve, *Elizabethan and Metaphysical Imagery* (Chicago: University of Chicago Press, 1947), p. 61.

49. The only positive use of this figure in Austen that I have found occurs in *Emma,* as Emma muses on Frank Churchill's "recollection of Harriet, and the words which clothed it, the 'beautiful little friend'," though any commendation of Frank Churchill's polished language of compliment must be viewed with suspicion (E 266).

50. Bruns, *Modern Poetry,* p. 4.

51. This is a much discussed passage of late—see Bruns, *Modern Poetry,* pp. 51—52; Frances Ferguson, *Wordsworth: Language as Counter-Spirit* (New Haven: Yale University Press, 1977), pp. 1—34; Land, "The Silent Poet," pp. 157—69. See also Paul de Man, "Autobiography as De-facement," *MLN* 94 (1979), pp. 919—30, and Cynthia Chase, "The Ring of Gyges and the Coat of Darkness: Reading Rousseau with Wordsworth," in Reed, *Romanticism and Language,* pp. 83—84.

52. Bruns, *Modern Poetry,* p. 13.

53. The clothing metaphor is used by Monboddo, *Of the Origin,* only when it has plainly been borrowed from an earlier writer, as when Monboddo quotes Roger Ascham, and even then, it is used in a pejorative fashion, in connection with overly "ornamented" style (III, 389). The only major writer on language I have found who does use the comparison consistently and in its older sense is Hugh Blair, who writes, for example, that "an elegant writer . . . gives us his ideas clothed with all the beauty of expression" (I, 383).

54. On the exteriority of universal language schemes, see James Thompson, *Language in Wycherley's Plays* (University, Alabama: University of Alabama Press, 1984), pp. 6—13.

55. See also such scholars as Walter Ong, *Ramus, Method, and the Decay of Dialogue* (Cambridge: Harvard University Press, 1958); Leo Spitzer, "On the Significance of *Don Quijote," MLN* 77 (1962), pp. 113—29, and Marshall McLuhen, "The Place of Thomas Nash in the Learning of his Time," Diss. Cambridge University, 1943, for the massive consequences the technology of printing had for the culture as a whole. There is a general analogy between the shift from predominantly oral culture to a written culture, and the concomitant shift to private reading experiences, the internalization of reading, its privatization, so very different from the oral, social, and communal experience of drama and ballad. J. Paul Hunter argues that the solitary reading experience is historically unique to the novel in the "Loneliness of the Long-Distance Reader," *Genre* 10 (1977), pp. 455—84.

56. Cohen, *Sensible Words,* p. 64. For a detailed study of the implications of print as packaging, see Roger B. Moss, "Sterne's Punctuation," *ECS* 15 (1981), pp. 179—200.

57. See R. C. Alston, *A Bibliography of the English Language from the Invention of Printing to the Year 1800,* 11 vols., 1965—77. Pope's sale of his translations of Homer by means of a systematic exploitation of the subscription system may be regarded as the first successful commercial venture in commodifying a linguistic object for the mass market.

58. McKendrick writes on emulative spending, "These characteristics—the closely stratified nature of English society, the striving for vertical social mobility,

the emulative spending bred by social emulation, the compulsive power of fashion begotten by social competition—combined with the widespread ability to spend (offered by novel levels of prosperity) to produce an unprecedented propensity to consume: unprecedented in the depth to which it penetrated the lower reaches of society and unprecedented in its impact on the economy." *The Birth of a Consumer Society,* p. 11.

59. On the parallel history of the metaphor likening words to coins, and its gradual transformation from a realist (gold standard) to a nominal (paper currency) conception, see Thompson, *Language in Wycherley's Plays,* pp. 31–32.

60. Compare Mrs. Elton in *Emma:* "I assure you, Jane Fairfax is a very delightful character, and interests me more than I can express" (E 283).

61. Fanny is lost in "speechless admiration" by the sight of her brother William in his naval uniform (MP 384). Catherine Morland is "speechless" when she is expelled from Northanger Abbey (NA 225), as is Anne Elliot when she finds that it is Captain Wentworth who has relieved her of the annoying child (P 80).

62. In a particularly effective use of this device, when Scott has brought Waverley and the reader to the edge of Fergus Mac-Ivor's execution, but excludes them from the brutality of the beheading itself, the narrator writes of the protagonist's horror, "I will not attempt to describe his sensations," *Waverley,* p. 328.

63. Austen usually reserves this and like words for extreme happiness, or conversely, for extreme discomfort: Elizabeth's mother gives her "inexpressible vexation" (PP 99) and Darcy's remembrance of his conduct is "inexpressibly painful" (PP 367); Emma has "indescribable irritation of spirits" (E 132), Mr. Knightley's affection is "inexpressibly important" (E 415), and Emma's wish to be rid of Harriet is "inexpressibly desirable" (E 435). Similarly, after Louisa Musgrove falls in Lyme, her party has "feelings unutterable" (P 111), and Catherine Morland upon being asked to marry Henry is "wrapt in the contemplation of her own unutterable happiness" (NA 243).

64. The same technique of mocking dismissal is found in *Waverley,* in which, in a scene out of *Rasselas,* Scott ridicules his hero's overly vivid imagination: "A distant sound is heard like the rushing of a swoln stream; it comes nearer, and Edward can plainly distingush the galloping of horses, the cries and shouts of men, with straggling pistol-shots between, rolling forwards to the hall. The lady starts up—a terrified menial rushes in—But why pursue such a description." *Waverley,* p. 17.

65. In the first flush of his infatuation Henry Crawford says of Fanny: "She is exactly the woman to do away every prejudice of such a man as the Admiral, for she is exactly such a woman as he thinks does not exist in the world. She is the very impossibility he would describe—if indeed he has now delicacy of language enough to embody his own ideas" (MP 293). The object of this effusion, of course, is to signify that the speaker himself does have this very delicacy of language.

66. For an exploration of the role of silence in *Sense and Sensibility* as the suppression of Marianne's suffering, see Angela Leighton, "Sense and Silences," in *Jane Austen, New Perspectives,* ed. Todd, pp. 128–41.

67. Fanny's hostility toward the Crawfords may in part be understood as an instance of Nietzschean *ressentiment,* in which the servant, through meekness and passivity, revenges herself upon the master: "the weak and oppressed of every sort . . . practice the sublime sleight of hand which gives weakness the appearance

of free choice and one's natural disposition the distinction of merit." Fredrich Nietzsche, *The Birth of Tragedy and the Genealogy of Morals*, trans. Francis Golffing (Garden City, NY: Doubleday & Company, 1956), p. 180. Fredric Jameson comments, "The Christian reversal of this situation, the revolt of the weak and the slaves against the strong, and the 'production' of the secretly castrating ideals of charity, resignation, and abnegation, are according to the Nietzschean theory of *ressentiment*, no less locked into the initial power relationship than the aristocratic system of which they are the inversion." *The Political Unconscious*, p. 117.

68. Avrom Fleishman, *A Reading of Mansfield Park* (Minneapolis: University of Minnesota Press, 1967), p. 45.

69. Compare the interaction of Marianne and Elinor Dashwood, in *Sense and Sensibility*, who have a similar familiarity with one another and so can read each other's looks: "At these words, Marianne's eyes expressed the astonishment, which her lips could not utter" (SS 262).

CHAPTER 4

1. *Shelley's Prose*, ed. David Lee Clark (1954, rpt. Albuquerque: University of New Mexico Press, 1966), p. 172.

2. Reuben Brower, *Fields of Light* (Cambridge: Harvard University Press, 1951), pp. 172 and 174.

3. Gerald Bruns, *Inventions, Writing, Textuality, and Understanding in Literary History* (New Haven: Yale University Press, 1982), pp. 112 and 115.

4. Darrel Mansell, *The Novels of Jane Austen*, pp. 7–12; Susan Morgan, *In the Meantime, Character and Perception in Jane Austen's Fiction*, p. 4.

5. These issues arise in the poststructural climate of " 'decentering' of the consciousness of the individual subject," as Fredric Jameson puts it. See also Jameson's remarks on Deleuze and Guattari, whose *Anti-Oedipus* exemplifies "this experience of the decentering of the subject and the theories, essentially psychoanalytic, which have been devised to map it are to be seen as the signs of the dissolution of an essentially bourgeois ideology of the subject and of psychic unity or identity (what used to be called bourgeois 'individualism')" (*The Political Unconscious*, pp. 283 and 124–25).

6. For a discussion of these matters and Austen, see Joel Weinsheimer, "Theory of Character: *Emma*," *Poetics Today* 1 (1979), pp. 185–211.

7. Jameson offers a brief but suggestive attempt at situating Freud, *The Political Unconscious*, pp. 62–64.

8. Joel Kovel supplies a Marxist critique of psychoanalysis, historicizing concepts of personality and the self: "psychology and psychoanalysis are part of bourgeois ideology; i.e., they profess to show the bourgeois world as timeless and perfect, where as in fact it is historical and dominated by a concept of time bound by an equation with money and unfree labor." *The Age of Desire* (New York: Pantheon Books, 1981), p. 61.

9. Roy Schafer, *A New Language for Psychoanalysis* (New Haven: Yale University Press, 1976), pp. 188–89. Schafer adds that "Self and identity themselves are changeable. This changeability consists, however, not of alteration of an empirically encountered entity; rather it consists of the observer's changeable purposes in using these terms. It is the kind of changeability that derives from the fact that self and identity are not names of identifiable homogeneous or monolithic

entities; they are classes of self-representations that exist only in the vocabulary of the observer" (p. 189).

10. For the correlation between Freud and Romanticism, see Philip Rieff, *Freud: The Mind of the Moralist* (1959, rpt. Chicago: University of Chicago Press, 1979), p. 34.

11. Leo Bersani, *A Future for Astyanax, Character and Desire in Literature* (Boston: Little, Brown and Co., 1976), pp. 62–63 and 69.

12. Lukács, *Theory of the Novel*, p. 127.

13. *The Philosophy of the Novel*, pp. xviii and xvii.

14. Robert Langbaum, *Mysteries of Identity* (1977, rpt. Chicago: University of Chicago Press, 1982), pp. 25–47.

15. Watt, *The Rise of the Novel*, p. 297.

16. Patricia Meyer Spacks, *Imagining a Self* (Cambridge: Harvard University Press, 1976), p. 7.

17. John O. Lyons, *The Invention of the Self* (Carbondale and Edwardsville: Southern Illinois University Press, 1978), is the fullest (and most unreliable) discussion of eighteenth-century notions of identity; for the first half of the century, see Christopher Fox, "Locke and the Scriblerians: The Discussion of Identity in Early Eighteenth Century England," *ECS* 16 (1982), pp. 1–25, and for the second half of the century, see Stephen D. Cox, *'The Stranger Within Thee' Concepts of the Self in Late Eighteenth-Century Literature* (Pittsburgh: University of Pittsburgh Press, 1980).

18. Fox, "Locke and the Scriblerians," pp. 1–25.

19. David Hume, *A Treatise of Human Nature*, ed. L. A. Selby-Bigge (1888, rpt. Oxford: Oxford University Press, 1973), p. 255.

20. For the most acute recent discussion of Hume on identity, see John J. Richetti, *Philosophical Writing: Locke, Berkeley, Hume* (Cambridge: Harvard University Press, 1983), pp. 218–26.

21. Hume, *Treatise*, pp. 259–60.

22. Hume, *Treatise*, p. 252.

23. Hume, *Treatise*, p. 259.

24. In "A Formal Development: Austen, the Novel, and Romanticism," *Centennial Review* 39 (1984), pp. 1–28, Clifford Siskin argues that development is not so much a theme peculiar to Austen as it is "a formal strategy originating in late eighteenth- and early nineteenth-century discourse for naturalizing the changing interrelations of social and literary forms."

25. In *Mansfield Park*, changeability is presented as significantly more threatening. Following Tony Tanner's introduction to the Penguin edition, Bersani argues that the Crawfords are threatening because of their fluidity, their instability, their very capacity for performance, theatricality, and change. *A Future for Astyanax*, pp. 75–77.

26. *The Proper Lady*, p. 190.

27. *The Prelude, 1799, 1805, 1850,* ed. Jonathan Wordsworth, M. H. Abrams, and Stephen Gill (New York: W. W. Norton, 1975), ms. X, 617–20, p. 260, n. 7.

28. This passage exhibits a curious dissociation of moral worth from social interest—complexity or intricacy, not simple goodness, is what makes the other interesting. Darcy's moral worthiness is attested to by the housekeeper at Pemberley, but Elizabeth's fascination has been stirred long before by the intricacy of his character and the mystery of his personal history. Characters such as the Gardiners are much less complex than the two protagonists, but they are not

found wanting for this reason alone. Mrs. Gardiner, for example, like her sister-in-law, Mrs. Bennet, is fixed in Austen's typical three-adjective sentence: she "was an amiable, intelligent, elegant woman" (PP 139). Compare Mrs. Gardiner's initial description with the three-word portrait of Sir William Lucas: "By nature inoffensive, friendly and obliging, his presentation at St. James's had made him courteous" (PP 18); it is not very far from here to *Emma*'s opening words, "handsome, clever, and rich" (5). These reductive descriptions may function as some sort of inside joke for Austen, as simple characters remain "inoffensive, friendly and obliging," whereas Emma turns out to be much more than "handsome, clever, and rich."

29. I borrow "hermeneutic code" from Roland Barthes, *S/Z*, trans. Richard Miller (New York: Hill and Wang, 1974), pp. 84–88.

30. Character or personality is not especially visible in Austen's fiction; as with her representation of things, character draws attention to itself only when something is amiss or eccentric, such as with Darcy's hostility at the dance—he is not supposed to stand out in the crowd. As Charlotte Lucas observes of Jane Bennet, the invisibility of character applies particularly to women, who are supposed to be self-effacing, anything but directly readable.

31. In this novel, unlike *Persuasion,* it is assumed that knowledge is equivalent to understanding; that is to say, when Elizabeth exclaims, "till this moment, I never knew myself" (PP 208), knowing is simultaneous with comprehending. Familiarity and understanding are more subtly distinguished with Captain Wentworth and Anne Elliot, for he is shown to know her well, but not to understand her fully. We might say that with Darcy's letter comes knowledge, that is, raw information, and gradually Elizabeth comes to comprehend his character as she assimilates this information.

32. "The impossibility of possessing what one desires," in Jonathan Culler's paraphrase, is the subject of Derrida's investigations. *Structuralism and Since, From Levi-Strauss to Derrida,* ed. John Sturrock (Oxford: Oxford University Press, 1979), p. 168. See, in particular, Derrida's exploration of Rousseau's *Confessions* as a text in which "The play of substitution fills and marks a determined lack": "What we have tried to show by following the guiding line of the 'dangerous supplement,' is that in what one calls the real life of these existences 'of flesh and bone,' beyond and behind what one believes can be circumscribed as Rousseau's text, there has never been anything but writing, there have never been anything but supplements, substitutive significations which could only come forth in a chain of differential references, the 'real' supervening, and being added only while taking on meaning from a trace and from an invocation of the supplement, etc. And thus to infinity, for we have read, *in the text,* that the absolute present, Nature, that which words like 'real mother' name, have always already escaped, have never existed; that what opens meaning and language is writing as the disappearance of natural presence." Jacques Derrida, *Of Grammatology,* trans. Gayatri Spivak (Baltimore: The Johns Hopkins University Press, 1974), pp. 157 and 158–59.

33. Sigmund Freud, *The Standard Edition of the Complete Psychological Works of Sigmund Freud,* trans. James Strachey, 24 vols. (London: Hogarth Press, 1953–1974), XII, 100; all further references are to this edition.

34. Reuben Brower is apparently the source of the complaint that the second half of *Pride and Prejudice* is weak and repetitive: "The Controlling Hand: Jane Austen and *Pride and Prejudice,*" *Scrutiny* 13 (1945), p. 108.

35. For a discussion of this deconstruction of love, see Janet Malcolm, *Psycho-*

analysis: The Impossible Profession (1981, rpt. New York: Vantage Books, 1982), pp. 8–9.

36. Geoffrey Gorer, "Myth in Jane Austen" (1941), rpt. *Five Approaches of Literary Criticism,* ed. Wilbur Scott (New York: Collier Books, 1962), p. 94. Other more recent but traditional psychoanalytic studies of Austen include Avrom Fleishman, *A Reading of Mansfield Park* (Minneapolis: University of Minnesota Press, 1967), pp. 43–56, and Bernard Paris, *Character and Conflict in Jane Austen* (Detroit: Wayne State University Press, 1978).

37. Of contemporary psychoanalytic theorists, Kohut is particularly adaptable to literary studies; see the survey of Kohutian studies in Ernest S. Wolf, "Psychoanalytic Psychology of the Self and Literature," *NLH* 12 (1980), pp. 41–60, and the more extended application in Barbara A. Shapiro, *The Romantic Mother, Narcissistic Patterns in Romantic Poetry* (Baltimore: The Johns Hopkins University Press, 1983). Kohut himself discusses the literary use of psychoanalysis in Response, *Critical Inquiry* 4 (1978), pp. 433–50.

38. Kohut, *The Restoration of the Self* (New York: International Universities Press, 1977), p. 137. Further references are to this edition.

39. Spacks, *The Female Imagination* (New York: Alfred A. Knopf, 1975), p. 116.

40. Spacks, *The Female Imagination,* pp. 123 and 121.

41. Heinz Kohut, *The Analysis of the Self* (New York: International Universities Press, 1971), pp. 150–51. Further references are to this edition.

42. As Kohut puts it in his last book, "the self will be seriously impaired only if, after one of the selfobjects of the child has failed to respond, the attempt to acquire compensatory structures via the adequate responses of another selfobject has also come to grief." *How Does Analysis Cure?* (Chicago: University of Chicago Press, 1984), pp. 205–6. However, despite the lack of differentiation between mother and father here, of the six analyses of narcissistic personality disorders presented in detail in *The Psychology of the Self, A Casebook,* ed. Arnold Goldberg (New York: International Universities Press, 1978), all turn on a severe lack of response from the mother, whereas the father's subsequent failure merely contributes to or does not prevent pathology.

43. For a thorough discussion of the inadequacy of Austen's fictional fathers, see Mary A. Burgan, "Mr. Bennet and the Failures of Fatherhood in Jane Austen's Novels," *JEGP* 74 (1975), pp. 536–52.

44. *A Goodly Heritage, A History of Jane Austen's Family* (Manchester: Carcanet New Press, 1983), p. 72. Halperin concurs on the point of Mrs. Austen's hypochondria (*Life of Jane Austen,* p. 19). Halperin also shows evidence of Jane Austen's pattern of considerable and lasting hostility toward her mother (*Life of Jane Austen,* pp. 63–64, 129, 144–45).

45. E. Austen-Leigh, *A Memoir of Jane Austen,* in *Persuasion,* ed. D. W. Harding (Harmondsworth: Penguin Books, 1965), p. 79.

46. "Biographical Notice of the Author," first published in the posthumous volume containing *Northanger Abbey* and *Persuasion,* p. 3.

47. Kohut, *The Search for the Self,* p. 503.

48. From Freud onward, psychoanalysts have argued that narcissism is the dominant personality pattern associated with artists, writers, and especially theorists, who tend to be self-absorbed in their own creations. See Reuben Fine, *A History of Psychoanalysis* (New York: Columbia University Press, 1979), pp. 263–92. For Kohut's treatment of the connection between narcissism and creativity, see *The Search for the Self: Selected Writings of Heinz Kohut: 1950–1978,* ed. Paul H.

Ornstein, 2 vols. (New York: International Universities Press, 1978), pp. 804–23. See, as well, Charles Kligerman, "Art and the Self of the Artist," in *Advances in Self Psychology*, ed. Arnold Goldberg (New York: International Universities Press, Inc., 1980), pp. 383–96. According to Kligerman, the artist is best seen as a narcissist because of her fantasies of omnipotence, grandiosity, and exhibitionism. The work of art itself is conceived of as an idealized selfobject, connected with "the need to regain perfection by merging with the ideals of the powerful selfobjects" (p. 388). The literary example of an artistic standard of perfection that Kohut refers to most often is the role that Nathaniel Hawthorne appears to have played for Herman Melville.

49. Meredith Anne Skura, *The Literary Use of the Psychoanalytic Process* (New Haven: Yale University Press, 1981), p. 56.

50. Lukács, *Theory of the Novel*, p. 80.

51. One of the aims of Kohut's psychology of the self is to rehabilitate the term *narcissism* from its pejorative connotations by means of a vigorous rejection of more traditional and Freudian "health and maturity-morality," which defines normality in terms of a development from regressive narcissism to mature object love. Kohut, "The Two Analyses of Mr. Z.," *International Journal of Psycho-Analysis* 60 (1979), p. 12. Kohut puts the case most strongly in his last work:

"Self psychology holds that self-selfobject relationships form the essence of psychological life from birth to death, that a move from dependence (symbiosis) to independence (autonomy) in the psychological sphere is no more possible, let alone desirable, than a corresponding move from a life dependent on oxygen to a life independent of it in the biological sphere. The developments that characterize normal psychological life must, in our view, be seen in the changing nature of the relationship between the self and its selfobjects, but not in the self's relinquishment of selfobjects. In particular, developmental advances cannot be understood in terms of the replacement of the selfobjects by love objects or as steps in the move from narcissism to object love" (*How Does Analysis Cure?*, p. 47).

Self-psychology leads to the abandonment of that "erroneous conception—that normal development proceeds from helpless dependence to autonomy and from self-love to the love of others" (*Cure*, p. 208). Kohut's theory is particularly helpful for *Emma*, which consistently elicits the most inappropriately moral response from its critics, who again and again complain that at the end Emma has not been sufficiently cured of her vanity or pride or narcissism. An understanding of the novel's underlying narcissistic structure may even help to explain the sense of possessiveness and identity in Jane Austen's attitude toward *Emma*: "She was very fond of Emma," her nephew reports, "but did not reckon her being a general favorite, for, when commencing that work, she said, 'I am going to take a heroine whom no one but myself will much like'" (*Memoir*, pp. 375–76).

52. Bersani, *A Future for Astyanax*, pp. 55–56.

53. *A New Language*, pp. 115–17. Like Schafer, Kovel criticizes Kohut for the idealizing and humanist tendencies of self-psychology, glorifying an amorphous concept of the self into an eternal, transhistorical object. *Age of Desire*, pp. 265–67.

54. *Lenin and Philosophy and Other Essays*, trans. Ben Brewster (New York: Monthly Review Press, 1971), pp. 171 and 173. Kohut's theory of the narcissist's dependence upon mirroring self-objects sounds oddly like Althusser's explanation of ideology, though Althusser's theory of the speculary nature of ideology derives from Lacan's theory of the mirror stage. See Jacques Lacan, *Écrits*, trans.

Alan Sheridan (New York: W. W. Norton, 1977), pp. 1–7; see also Althusser's essay on Lacan in *Lenin and Philosophy*. From the point of view of the post-structural critique of the ideology of the subject, Kohut upholds a view of the primacy and autonomy of the individual subject which both Althusser and Lacan abhor and attempt to deconstruct. Here is Althusser:

"We observe that the structure of all ideology, interpellating individuals as subjects in the name of a Unique and Absolute Subject is *speculary*, i.e. a mirror-structure, and *doubly* speculary: this mirror duplication is constitutive of ideology and ensures its functioning. Which means that all ideology is *centered*, that the Absolute Subject occupies the unique place of the Centre, and interpellates around it the infinity of individuals into subjects in a double mirror-connection such that it *subjects* the subjects to the Subject, while giving them in the Subject in which each subject can contemplate its own image (present and future) the *guarantee* that this really concerns them and Him, and that since everything takes place in the Family (the Holy Family: the Family is in essence Holy), 'God will *recognize* his own in it', i.e.; those who have recognized God, and have recognized themselves in Him, will be saved" (p. 168).

55. Lacan, *Écrits*, p. 171.

56. Christopher Lasch, *The Culture of Narcissism* (New York: Warner Books, 1979), see particularly chapter 2, pp. 71–103. According to Joel Kovel, "pathological narcissism is a leading candidate for the archetypal emotional disorder of late capitalism" (p. 104). This epidemic of narcissism is produced by the antitheses of bourgeois life, the unbridgeable split between home and work, family and public life (pp. 108–32): "The splitting of public and private spheres produces individuals whose social nature is distorted and artificial. Turned inward by alienation, subjectivity flowers like orchids in a greenhouse" (p. 202). See also "Symposium on Narcissism," *Telos* 44 (1980), pp. 49–126, particularly Paul Piccone, "Narcissism after the Fall," pp. 112–21, for a correlation between current theories of narcissism and the work of the Frankfort School.

57. Langbaum, *Mysteries of Identity*, p. 13.

58. Spacks, *Imagining a Self*, p. 16.

59. Kenneth Moler, *Jane Austen's Art of Allusion* (Lincoln: University of Nebraska Press, 1968), pp. 5–6.

60. *Marxism and Literature* (Oxford: Oxford University Press, 1977), p. 129.

61. *Language and Insight* (New Haven: Yale University Press, 1978), pp. 6 and 18.

CHAPTER 5

1. Samuel Johnson, *Rambler 45*, in *Samuel Johnson: Selected Poetry and Prose*, ed. Frank Brady and W. K. Wimsatt (Berkeley: University of California Press, 1977), p. 177.

2. On marriage used as a device for closure, see Northrop Frye, *Anatomy of Criticism* (Princeton: Princeton University Press, 1957), pp. 163–64; on marriage as an emblem of morality, see Murial Brittain Williams, *Marriage: Fielding's Mirror of Morality* (University: The University of Alabama Press, 1973); on the emblematic nature of Fielding's marriages, see Martin Battestin, *The Providence of Wit* (Oxford: Clarendon Press, 1974), pp. 179–92.

3. Mary Poovey, *The Proper Lady and the Woman Writer*, p. 201.

4. Marriage is, of course, an important subject in Austen, and it has attracted especially excellent commentary from, among others, Lloyd Brown, "The Business of Marrying and Mothering" in *Jane Austen's Achievement*, ed. Juliet McMaster (New York: Harper & Row, 1976), pp. 27–43; Julia Prewit Brown, *Jane Austen's Novels—Social Change and Literary Form*; and, more recently, Karen Newman, "Can This Marriage Be Saved; Jane Austen Makes Sense of an Ending," *ELH* 50 (1983), pp. 693–710.

5. As has been pointed out several times, *Persuasion* contains Austen's only use of the word *romance* in the sense of love: because Anne Elliot "had been forced into prudence in her youth, she learned romance as she grew older" (p. 30).

6. Tony Tanner, *Adultery and the Novel, Contract and Transgression* (Baltimore: Johns Hopkins University Press, 1979), p. 144.

7. Tanner, *Adultery*, p. 4.

8. Tanner, *Adultery*, p. 15.

9. The marriage letters to Fanny Knight are numbered 103, 106, 140, 141, and 142.

10. On Jane Austen's relationship with Cassandra and Fanny, see Janet Todd's insightful discussion in *Women's Friendship in Literature* (New York: Columbia University Press, 1980), pp. 396–402.

11. Lloyd Brown in "The Business of Marrying and Mothering" quite rightly observes some important distinctions between Austen's presentation of marriage in her fiction and her attitude toward marriage in the letters and indicates that the former is obviously more idealized; although this observation is certainly true, here I am trying to show the underlying similarity of financial pressure in both life and fiction.

12. Lest we misinterpret this letter to cover solely emotional matters, its central concern is likely to be complicated by property: For a discussion of how property can be alienated from the patrilineal estate by the widow's remarriage, see Randolph Trumbach, *The Rise of the Egalitarian Family, Aristocratic Kinship and Domestic Relations in Eighteenth-Century England* (New York: Academic Press, 1978), pp. 50–61.

13. Similar qualification is commonly found in other correspondence from the period: Mrs. Delaney writes, "I have no notion of love in a knapsack, but I cannot think riches the only thing that ought to be considered in matrimony." *Delaney* (1861), I, p. 173. Quoted from Trumbach, *Egalitarian Family*, p. 105; see also pp. 93 and 99 for similar statements.

14. Scott, *Waverley*, p. 248.

15. Lawrence Stone, *The Family, Sex and Marriage in England 1500–1800* (New York: Harper & Row, 1977), pp. 271–72.

16. Stone, *The Family, Sex and Marriage*, pp. 270–71.

17. Stone, *The Family, Sex and Marriage*, pp. 257–58. That Austen's heroines can be so scornful of interchangeability suggests that it is a moribund attitude.

18. See Jane Nardin's discussion of the changing role of leisure in Austen, from self-improvement toward the idea of socially useful labor, "Jane Austen and the Problem of Leisure," in *Jane Austen in a Social Context*, ed. Monaghan, pp. 122–42. In yet a different context, Adam Smith writes that "The liberal reward of labour encourages marriage"; this holds true in Austen as well, for leisured idleness will never result in prosperous marriage in her novels. Adam Smith, *An*

Inquiry into the Nature and Causes of the Wealth of Nations, ed. Edwin Cannan (Chicago: University of Chicago Press, 1976), II, 76; see also I, 88).

19. Any generalization about marriage theory or practice must be class-specific. Though Alan Macfarlane accepts Stone's conclusions for the wealthy elite, he argues that in this period, "wealthy parents exert more control over their children's choices than parents without property." Alan Macfarlane, *Marriage and Love in England 1300–1800* (Oxford: Basil Blackwell, 1986), 129–40. That is to say, the lower classes could always marry for love whenever there was not much property with which to be concerned. For the aristocratic classes, on the contrary, Trumbach argues, "For beginning in the generation after 1720, arranged marriages so gave way to romantic marriages that by 1780 it could be estimated that three marriages in four were made for love. But it was still expected, even in the generation after 1750, that aristocrats would marry within their own social class." *Egalitarian Family,* p. 97. Trumbach so habitually makes categorical statements as to make his argument suspicious: "the generation after 1750" was "the first generation in which romantic marriage was clearly the rule," p. 94. For his part, Macfarlane, too, seems to exaggerate the ubiquity of love, arguing that it was considered essential to marriage from the thirteenth century onward, yet he draws no fine distinctions between the meaning or use of the word *love* from the thirteenth to the eighteenth century, pp. 174–208. By comparison, both Trumbach and Macfarlane make Stone seem relatively judicious and restrained in his conclusions. For a vivid picture of marriage and domestic life before the rise of affective individualism or the egalitarian family, see Miriam Slater, *Family Life in the Seventeenth Century, The Verneys of Claydon House* (London: Routledge & Kegan Paul, 1984), pp. 60–107.

20. Stone, *The Family, Sex and Marriage,* p. 228.

21. Susan Moller Okin argues that Stone overestimates the legal powers of women in the later part of the century. "Patriarchy and Married Women's Property in England: Questions on Some Current Views," *ECS* 17 (1983), pp. 121–38.

22. Igor Webb observes that almost all of Austen's families have to contend with financial difficulties: *From Custom to Capital, The English Novel and the Industrial Revolution* (Ithaca: Cornell University Press, 1981).

23. For a clear explanation of portion (what we think of as dowry, what the bride's father pays to the groom's father), jointure (annuity or settlement for the widow usually negotiated at the time of the marriage contract), and dower (the widow's common-law right to a portion of her late husband's estate, a right forfeited by jointure), see Macfarlane, *Marriage and Love,* pp. 263–90.

24. *Family Life,* p. 82; cf. Stone, *The Family, Sex and Marriage,* pp. 392–404.

25. Mary Wollstonecraft, *A Vindication of the Rights of Woman,* ed. Carol H. Poston (New York: W. W. Norton & Co., 1975), p. 183. Austen's relation to Wollstonecraft has been explored by Lloyd Brown, "Jane Austen and the Feminist Tradition," *NCF* 28 (1973), pp. 321–38; Alison Sulloway, "Emma Woodhouse and *A Vindication of the Rights of Woman,*" *Wordsworth Circle* 7 (1976), pp. 320–32; and most fully in Margaret Kirkham, *Jane Austen: Feminism and Fiction.*

26. *Belinda,* p. 1. The aunt here is ridiculed for her obsession with the mercantile tactics of courtship, while the heroine goes off in prudent pursuit of the companionate marriage.

27. This passage should be connected with the relatively late justification of self-interest, and the cultural work involved in transforming or rehabilitating self-

interest, greed, and accumulation from being viewed as a sin to a virtue, from a socially damning to a socially useful activity. See Albert O. Hirschman, *The Passions and the Interests, Political Arguments for Capitalism before Its Triumph* (Princeton: Princeton University Press, 1977), pp. 31–48.

28. Julia Prewit Brown, *Jane Austen's Novels*, pp. 8–9.

29. Wollstonecraft, *Vindication*, p. 60.

30. Wollstonecraft, *Vindication*, p. 187. Slater writes of an earlier period: "marriage was considered to be the most important endeavor in a woman's life. In the society of the upper-gentry there were few career options for younger sons, but there was only one for daughters. The prospect of marriage was in fact and for good reason referred to as a woman's 'preferment,' because it was viewed and assiduously sought after as her only possibility for advancement." *Family Life*, pp. 79–80.

31. Wollstonecraft, *Vindication*, p. 75.

32. Wollstonecraft, *Vindication*, p. 187.

33. Wollstonecraft, *Vindication*, p. 19.

34. Wollstonecraft, *Vindication*, p. 170; Stone, *The Family, Sex and Marriage*, pp. 316–17.

35. Karl Marx, *The Economic and Philosophical Manuscripts of 1844*, ed. Dirk J. Struik (New York: International Publishers, 1964), pp. 106 and 108.

36. See István Mészáros, *Marx's Theory of Alienation* (New York: Harper & Row, 1970), pp. 33–36.

37. *The Letters of William and Dorothy Wordsworth*, 2d ed., ed. Ernest De Selincourt (Oxford: Clarendon Press, 1970), no. 440, April 7, 1817, to Daniel Stuart, III, 375.

38. Clifford Siskin, "High Wages and High Arguments: The Economics of Mixed Form in the Late Eighteenth Century," in *The Historicity of Romantic Discourse*, 1987, Oxford University Press, forthcoming. For an exemplary history of Josiah Wedgwood's central role in the transformation, via mass production, from exclusivity to emulative spending, see Neil McKendrick, "Josiah Wedgwood and the Commercialization of the Potteries," in *The Birth of a Consumer Society*, pp. 100–145.

39. This episode concerns the farmer's cart (and labor) that Mary Crawford is unable to hire at harvest time: In a similar fashion, Marx argues in the *Manuscripts of 1844* that money is "men's estranged, alienating and self-disposing *species nature.* Money is the alienated *ability of mankind.* That which I am unable to do as a *man,* and of which therefore all my individual essential powers are incapable, I am able to do by means of *money,*" p. 168.

40. One wonders what has become of old Gibson; does Austen mention him merely to call up old-style paternalism—agricultural laborers and cottagers as extended family—or to suggest that in his precipitous rapacity John Dashwood has had him evicted? Raymond Williams observes that land in Austen's novels is represented as something to own rather than as something to work. *The Country and the City*, pp. 108–19.

41. Marx, *Manuscripts of 1844*, pp. 101–2.

42. Macfarlane observes that the market analogy to marriage was quite common at this time, with, of course, the exception that marriage allowed for no resale. *Marriage and Love*, pp. 165–66. See also M. Dorothy George, *London Life in the Eighteenth Century* (1925, rpt. Chicago: Academy Chicago, 1984), p. 171.

43. In his *Advice to a Lover* (1837), p. 10, for example, William Cobbett

recommends these desirable qualities in a wife: "1. Chastity. 2. Sobriety. 3. Industry. 4. Frugality. 5. Cleanliness. 6. Knowledge of domestic affairs. 7. Good temper. 8. Beauty." Quoted from Macfarlane, *Marriage and Love*, p. 163.

44. For the conditions of the working class in this period, see E. P. Thompson's magisterial study, *The Making of the English Working Class*.

45. This is not unlike the adolescent longing of Stephen Dedalus, who "wanted to meet in the real world the unsubstantial image which his soul so constantly beheld. . . . They would meet quietly as if they had known each other." James Joyce, *A Portrait of the Artist as a Young Man* (Harmondsworth: Penguin Books, 1982), p. 65. The idea of love as mediated desire comes from René Girard, *Deceit, Desire, and the Novel*, trans. Yvonne Feccero (Baltimore: The Johns Hopkins University Press, 1965).

46. As Joseph Wiesenfarth notes, both sisters are attracted to men with secrets or enigmas that must be solved. *The Errand of Form* (New York: Fordham University Press, 1967), p. 42.

47. Austen's letters everywhere make it clear that what is most distressing about the single life for women is the perpetual state of dependence; as Slater writes of seventeenth-century women, "the unmarried woman became a perennial supplicant who had little possibility of returning favors; this placed her in an untenable position in a society which placed high priority on reciprocation." *Family Life*, p. 85.

48. *A Theory of Literary Production*, trans. Geoffrey Wall (London: Routledge & Kegan Paul, 1978), pp. 130–31.

49. The degree to which Austen recognizes this situation as contradictory remains an open and important question, one to which feminist revision of Austen returns again and again. Karen Newman makes a persuasive but, I think, finally unconvincing argument that Austen leaves the contradictions between love and money in her novels as a kind of tense and unresolved silence, "the true place of women in a materialistic culture in which men control money." "Can This Marriage Be Saved," p. 699.

50. Alison Sulloway pointed out the significance of this scene to me.

51. Lukács, *History and Class Consciousness*, p. 90.

52. Gayle Rubin, "The Traffic in Women: Notes on the 'Political Economy' of Sex," *Towards an Anthropology of Women*, ed. Rayna R. Reiter (New York: Monthly Review Press, 1975), pp. 157–210.

CHAPTER 6

1. Virginia Woolf, *To the Lighthouse* (New York: Harcourt Brace Jovanovich, 1955), p. 79.

2. In psychoanalytic terms, this narrative is essentially a vision of maturation from narcissism to object-love, a "transcendence" or breaking through or out of self-enclosure or self-referentiality to closure with the beloved. See chapter 4, note 51, on the controversy about "outgrowing" narcissism.

3. Philip Slater, *Earthwalk* (Garden City: Anchor Press, 1974), p. 49, quoted from Lawrence Stone, *Family, Sex and Marriage*, p. 683.

4. Althusser argues in "Ideology and the State" that the individual is always a subject: "Thus ideology hails or interpellates individuals as subjects. As ideology is eternal, I must now suppress the temporal form in which I have presented

the functioning of ideology, and say: ideology has always-already interpellated individuals as subjects, which amounts to making it clear that individuals are always-already interpellated by ideology as subjects, which necessarily leads us to one last proposition: *individuals are always-already subjects.*" *Lenin and Philosophy,* pp. 175–76. Marx puts it this way in the *Grundrisse*: "human beings become individuals only through the process of history." *Grundrisse,* trans. Martin Nicolaus (Harmondsworth: Penguin Books, 1973), p. 496.

5. On the subject of motherless heroines, see Susan Peck McDonald, "Jane Austen and the Tradition of the Absent Mother," in *The Lost Tradition: Mothers and Daughters in Literature,* ed. Cathy N. Davidson and E. M. Broner (New York: Ungar, 1980), pp. 58–69. See also Nina Auerbach, "Incarnations of the Orphan," *ELH* 42 (1975), pp. 395–419.

6. "Mr. Bennet and the Failures of Fatherhood in Jane Austen's Novels," *JEGP* 74 (1975), p. 551. The reasons for this omission are many, among which Burgan quite rightly numbers Austen's own hostile and fearful attitude toward children and particularly toward childbearing. However, I want to emphasize that the conspicuous absence of the promise of children is but a further sign of the collapse or the constriction of the family in Austen's narrative. Edward Copeland suggests that, unlike the heroines of earlier novels, Austen's heroines have no homes to return to. Edward Copeland, "The Burden of *Grandison,*" in *Jane Austen: New Perspectives,* ed. Todd, pp. 98–106.

7. Darrel Mansell, *Novels of Jane Austen,* pp. 90–91.

8. Philippe Ariès, *Centuries of Childhood,* pp. 398 and 375.

9. Trumbach, *Egalitarian Family,* pp. 114 and 116.

10. Peter Laslett, *The World We Have Lost: England before the Industrial Age* (1965, rpt. New York: Charles Scribner's Sons, 1973), p. 93.

11. Françoise Lautman, "Differences or Changes in Family Organization," in *Family and Society, Selections from the Annales,* ed. Robert Forster and Orest Ranum, trans. Elborg Forster and Patricia M. Ranum (Baltimore: Johns Hopkins University Press, 1976), p. 253.

12. I borrow the phrase "making the private public" from Lennard Davis, *Factual Fictions, The Origins of the English Novel* (New York: Columbia University Press, 1983), p. 187; see also Ian Watt, *The Rise of the Novel,* chap. 6, "Private Experience and the Novel," pp. 174–207.

13. Peter L. DeRose and S. W. McGuire, *A Concordance to the Works of Jane Austen,* 3 vols. (New York: Garland Publishing, Inc., 1982), III, 1615. As a very rough indication of its frequency, in their (descending) list of the frequency order of all words in Austen's canon, *intimacy* falls on page 2 of 30 pages; the other words used eighty-four times are *comes, consciousness, Emma's, lively, necessity, niece, pay, persuade, prevented, quick, reading, required, stand, standing, stood*—a remarkably suggestive list of the concepts and words with which Austen commonly works.

14. Howard Babb, *The Fabric of Dialogue* (Hamden, Conn.: Archon Books, 1967), p. 9.

15. *Advice to a Son,* in *Works* (London, 1673), pp. 87–88.

16. The locus classicus is Cicero's *de amicitia,* in which he argues that friendship ought to be of slow and laborious growth, for otherwise it will not be trustworthy.

17. C. S. Lewis, "A Note on Jane Austen," in *Jane Austen: Twentieth-Century Views,* ed. Watt, p. 29.

18. *Idiot* is Marvin Mudrick's term, *Jane Austen, Irony as Defense and Discovery*, p. 196.

19. Kenneth Moler observes that much of the criticism of *Emma* centers on the question of how Austen can "make such a wrong headed girl so very engaging." *Art of Allusion*, p. 171. I would suggest that Emma is made engaging by passages such as these that reveal Emma's manipulation to be but cover for some familiar needs and vulnerabilities; after all, it is easy to forget with such a lively character that, at the opening of the novel, Emma has, in effect, just lost her mother for the second time. Austen is obviously much less successful at evoking similar needs and vulnerabilities in a character like Fanny Price, and in consequence, *Mansfield Park* as a whole suffers.

20. Janet Todd, *Women's Friendship in Literature*, pp. 274–301.

21. The rebuke to Emma's sense of independence can be seen as a kind of secularized version of the rebuke Raphael delivers to Adam in *Paradise Lost*, after Adam has ominously admitted his sense of Eve's perfection in herself:

> yet when I approach
> Her loveliness, so absolute she seems
> And in herself complete. (VIII, 546–48)

22. I owe this suggestive observation and its neat formulation to my colleague Charles Edge.

23. Wordsworth, *The Excursion*, VII, 402–3, p. 232.

24. I would like to credit Katrin Burlin's acute observations about Charlotte Heywood's fantasy of Clara as exploitation in *Sanditon*, in her essay, "*Sanditon* and the Art of Advertising," forthcoming. Such points, as Professor Burlin observes, have important implications for the novelist's art and the ways in which Austen invents life histories for others, in her letters as well as in her novels.

25. It is not just Emma's fault or her pride and vanity with which Austen is concerned here, but rather this novel follows a common pattern of socialization, in the form of the feminocentric novel: Women are forced to grow up and leave their childish friends. See Nancy Miller, *The Heroine's Text* (New York: Columbia University Press, 1980), pp. 155–56.

26. This pattern has affinities with the interiorization of the sublime as analyzed by Thomas Weiskel, which works by introjection; novelistic portrayals of romantic love constitute a domesticated, thoroughly secularized, bourgeois form of the sublime. *The Romantic Sublime*, p. 93. We might also note that this form of sublimity, in effect, represents a privileging of idealizing narcissism, with its assumption "You are perfect, but I am part of you."

27. Macfarlane, *Love and Marriage*, p. 154.

28. *The Letters of Olive Schreiner, 1876–1920* (Boston: Little Brown, 1924), pp. 151–52, quoted from LeRoy Smith, *Jane Austen and the Drama of Woman*, p. 43.

29. Mary Poovey, *The Proper Lady*, p. 236.

30. Lukács, *History and Class Consciousness*, p. 135.

31. John J. Richetti, *Defoe's Narratives, Situations and Structures* (Oxford: Clarendon Press, 1975), pp. 128 and 96. Richetti writes of *Roxana*, "The self in Defoe's narratives is supposed to be acquired by the movements of an on going external necessity which generates individual freedom within it," p. 197.

32. Lukács, *Theory of the Novel*, p. 82.

33. "The Storyteller," in *Illuminations*, trans. Harry Zohn (New York: Schocken Books, 1969), p. 88.

34. *Defoe's Narratives,* pp. 30–31.

35. The most thorough discussion of the persistence of religious forms in the eighteenth-century English novel is J. Paul Hunter, *The Reluctant Pilgrim* (Baltimore: The Johns Hopkins University Press, 1966).

36. Lukács, *Theory of the Novel,* pp. 56–69.

37. *Tom Jones,* ed. Martin Battestin (1975, rpt. Middletown, Conn.: Wesleyan University Press, 1983), p. 982. Similarly, Richardson's *Pamela* ends, not with the marriage of Pamela and Mr. B nor with the reconciliation of Mr. B and his sister Lady Davers, but rather the whole narrative is stretched out in order to end with the triumphant return to the paternal estate. So, too, Smollett's *Roderick Random* closes with a return to the estate and a similarly elaborate show of affection, deference, and dependence by the servants. As a measure of what has changed by the end of the century, compare these endings with Sir Walter Scott's *Waverley,* in which the estate returned to at the end is pitifully fragile, only recently recovered, and only partially restored.

Index